THE ASSOCIATION OF AMERICAN UNIVERSITY PRESSES

Directory

1994-1995

The Association of American University Presses, Inc.
584 Broadway, New York, New York 10012
(212) 941-6610   Fax: (212) 941-6618
Exhibits Fax: (212) 941-8187

Published by the Association of American University Presses, Inc.
584 Broadway, New York, N.Y. 10012
© 1994 by the Association of American University Presses, Inc.
All rights reserved.
Printed in the United States of America

International Standard Book Number 0-945103-08-5
International Standard Serial Number 0739-3024
Library of Congress Catalog Number 54-43046

Distributed to the trade by:
The University of Chicago Press
11030 South Langley Avenue
Chicago, Illinois 60628
U.S.A.

Calligraphy by Anita Walker Scott

Table of Contents

THE ASSOCIATION 183

PERSONNEL INDEX 208

Preface

This directory serves as a guide to the publishing programs and personnel of the 114 distinguished scholarly presses that have met the standards of admission to membership in the Association of American University Presses. It belongs on the reference shelf of anyone connected to scholarly publishing: scholars preparing materials for publication, booksellers, librarians, scholarly presses interested in joining the AAUP, and, of course, the AAUP's own members. Updated annually, the directory provides the most comprehensive and timely information on these publishers available from any source.

This directory is organized particularly for the convenience of authors, librarians, and booksellers who require detailed information about AAUP members and their wide-ranging publishing programs. The "Subject Area Grid," for example, provides a quick overview of the many disciplines covered by the presses, indicating those most likely to publish a work in a given area. "On Submitting Manuscripts" gives advice to potential authors on preparing and submitting a scholarly manuscript for publication.

For further detail, the individual listing for each press provides information on editorial programs, number of titles published each year, and complete listings of key staff members. Addresses, ordering information, names and number of journals published, and information on sales representation for Canada, the U.K., and Europe is also included.

The last section of the directory focuses on the Association and its purposes, and includes the by-laws, guidelines for admission to membership, and listings of the AAUP's current Board of Directors, committees, and staff.

General Information for Authors

ON SUBMITTING MANUSCRIPTS

JOURNAL ARTICLES

University presses have always been associated with publishing books of merit and distinction. This remains as true today as in the past, but less well appreciated is the extent to which university presses are active in publishing scholarly journals.

Journals form a major part of the publishing program of many presses, and more than half of the Association's members produce at least one periodical. In all, university presses publish over six hundred scholarly periodicals, including many of the most distinguished in their respective fields.

In this directory, titles of journals are listed under most presses' editorial program, with the publications italicized. This makes it easier to identify presses that are currently active in journal publishing. Those interested may also wish to note the list of journals contact persons in the "Press Personnel by Function" section.

Authors submitting papers to a journal should check a current issue of the journal for information on where to submit manuscripts and for guidelines on length and format. Editors of journals often have very precise requirements for manuscript preparation and may return articles that do not meet their specifications.

BOOK MANUSCRIPTS

Selecting a Publisher
If you are looking for a publisher for a book-length manuscript, it is a good idea to do some research on which publisher may be best for your book. You should consider the reputation in your field of various presses and their editors, the design and production quality of their books, and the range and strength of their marketing efforts. To take advantage of group promotions and past experience, publishers tend to specialize in certain subjects. Occasionally a publisher may take on a title in an unfamiliar area, but you are more likely to be successful in your submission if you choose a

publisher who knows the field. Use the Subject Area Grid to find out which publishers have titles in your field. You can then find more specific information about the interests of those publishers under the listings of individual presses or by consulting their catalogs. If your book has a strong regional interest, consider the lists of the university presses active in your state to determine what types of regional books they publish.

You can also find out more about the lists of each publisher by studying brochures received in the mail, reading book advertisements in journals in your field, and by visiting press exhibits at academic meetings. At these exhibits you can meet acquisitions editors from the presses most active in the discipline and talk with them about your manuscript. Such talks can be very helpful to you and the editor in finding out if your manuscript would be suitable for a particular press. If you have already decided which publisher you would prefer for your book, call the appropriate editor before the meeting to make an appointment.

Preparing a Manuscript Prospectus
If you have selected a publisher but do not know an editor, you can use this directory to find the appropriate editor at that press. If you are not sure which editor to approach, write to the director of the press or to its editor-in-chief. It is best not to send the complete manuscript until you have been invited to do so. Publishers vary in the amount of material they want to receive on a first submission, but some or all of the following materials are usually provided:

> a short, informative cover letter including a clear and concise description of your book and its notable features, your opinion of the audience for the book, information on the current status of the manuscript and expected completion date, and some details on the physical characteristics of the manuscript, such as length, number of illustrations, tables, appendixes

> a table of contents

> a preface, introduction, or other brief sample of your manuscript

> a curriculum vitae or biographical notes

If the press is interested, the editor will invite you to submit the complete manuscript or inform you that he or she can proceed to review the materials you sent.

The Review Process
Although some university presses may give advance (i.e., conditional) contracts to experienced authors on the basis of incomplete or unreviewed manuscripts, most must obtain one or more reviews of a completed manuscript before presenting a project for the approval of the university faculty committee charged with overseeing the imprint of the press. As review procedures differ from press to press, check with the editor when you first submit the manuscript to find out what will be involved. He or she should be able to give you a tentative schedule for the review process. It is difficult to predict exactly how long it will take to reach a decision, since often readers' reports encourage authors to make further revisions to the manuscript and the manuscript is usually reviewed again after the author makes the revisions. If your manuscript is also under review at another publisher, be sure to let the editor know. Some editors will not review manuscripts that are under simultaneous consideration elsewhere; others will not object.

Manuscript Preparation
Publishers vary in their requirements for manuscript preparation. In general, the manuscript you submit for review should be as accurate and complete as possible. If a manuscript is carelessly prepared, reviewers may take offense at typographical errors or careless citations and spend precious review space discussing these problems instead of attending to the substance of your manuscript. If, for good reasons, your manuscript is incomplete, you should indicate what material is missing and provide your schedule for completion.

Although some presses will accept a single-spaced manuscript for review, it is best to double-space your text. A double-spaced manuscript is easier to read and will be required when your manuscript reaches the copyediting stage. For book publication, every element of the text should be double-spaced (including quotations, notes, bibliographies, appendixes, figure legends, and glossaries). Once your manuscript is accepted for publication, your editor will advise you on any special requirements imposed by that press's house style.

Publishers often make use of authors' computer disks to facilitate or to produce camera-ready copy. If you are using a computer to prepare your manuscript, ask your publisher for any special instructions.

FURTHER READING

American Psychological Association. "Publication Manual of the American Psychological Association." (3rd ed.). 1983.

AAUP. "Preparing your Electronic Manuscript." New York: 1989.

Appelbaum, Judith and Nancy Evans. *How to Get Happily Published: A Complete and Candid Guide* (rev. ed.). New York: Nal-Dutton, 1982.

Becker, Howard S. *Writing for Social Scientists: How to Start and Finish Your Thesis, Book, or Article.* Chicago: University of Chicago Press, 1986.

Day, Robert A. *How to Write and Publish a Scientific Paper* (4th ed.). Phoenix: Oryx Press, 1994.

Harman, Eleanor and Ian Montagnes, eds. *The Thesis and the Book.* Toronto: University of Toronto Press, 1976.

Katz, Michael J. *Elements of the Scientific Paper: A Step-by-Step Guide for Students and Professionals.* New Haven: Yale University Press, 1986.

Luey, Beth. *Handbook for Academic Authors* (rev. ed.). Cambridge: Cambridge University Press, 1990.

Maggio, Rosalie. *The Bias-Free Word Finder: A Dictionary of Non-Discriminatory Language.* Boston: Beacon Press, 1992.

Mulvany, Nancy C. *Indexing Books.* Chicago: University of Chicago Press, 1993.

Parsons, Paul. *Getting Published: The Acquisition Process at University Presses.* Knoxville: University of Tennessee Press, 1989.

Powell, Walter W. *Getting into Print: The Decision-Making Process in Scholarly Publishing.* Chicago: University of Chicago Press, 1988.

Smith, Datus C., Jr. *A Guide to Book Publishing* (rev. ed.). Seattle: University of Washington Press, 1988.

Strong, William S. *The Copyright Book: A Practical Guide.* (4th ed.). Cambridge, Mass.: MIT Press, 1992.

Strunk, William J. and E. B. White. *The Elements of Style* (3rd ed.). New York: Macmillan, 1979.

Swain, Dwight V. *Techniques of the Selling Writer.* Norman, Okla.: University of Oklahoma Press, 1981.

Trelease, Sam F. *How to Write Scientific and Technical Papers.* Cambridge, Mass.: MIT Press, 1969.

University of Chicago Press. *Chicago Guide to Preparing Electronic Manuscripts.* Chicago: University of Chicago Press, 1987.

University of Chicago Press. *The Chicago Manual of Style* (14th ed.). Chicago: University of Chicago Press, 1993.

SUBJECT AREA GRID

This eight-page grid lists the subject areas in which the individual presses have a particularly strong interest.

Some presses are prepared to consider manuscripts of outstanding quality in areas other than those listed. For a more complete description, consult the "Editorial Program" listing in the Directory of Members section and contact the presses that interest you. (See also "On Submitting Manuscripts" in this directory.)

Subject	Alabama	Alaska	Alberta	A. Chemical	A. Mathematical	A. Psychiatric	Arizona	Arkansas	Beacon	British Columbia	Brookings	Cairo (American)	Calgary	California	Cambridge
African Studies											●		●	●	●
Agriculture							●						●		●
American Indian Studies	●	●					●		●	●				●	●
American Studies	●						●	●	●					●	●
Anthropology	●	●					●		●	●			●	●	●
Cultural	●						●		●	●				●	●
Physical	●						●			●					●
Archaelogy	●	●					●	●		●			●		●
Architecture	●						●			●				●	●
Art & Art History			●				●			●				●	●
Art Criticism														●	●
Art History			●				●							●	●
Decorative Arts							●								●
Design & Graphics														●	●
Painting & Sculpture								●						●	●
Asian Studies									●	●	●			●	●
Astronomy							●							●	●
Bibliography & Reference		●	●					●			●			●	●
Biography	●	●	●				●	●		●			●	●	●
Biological Sciences		●		●			●	●		●			●	●	●
Botany		●					●			●					●
Genetics															●
Marine Biology		●					●			●					●
Microbiology															●
Physiology															●
Zoology			●				●	●							●
Black Studies	●								●	●				●	●
Business									●		●	●			●
Canadian Studies		●	●							●			●		●
Childd Development													●		●
Classics			●				●						●	●	●
Communications	●	●								●				●	●
Broadcast Media															●
Journalism														●	●
Computer Sciences															●
Demography														●	●
Drama														●	●
Earth Sciences		●	●	●			●			●			●	●	●
Geochemistry		●		●											●
Geology		●	●				●								●
Oceanography		●								●					●
Economics										●	●		●	●	●
History			●											●	●
Theory															●
Education		●	●					●		●			●		●
Counseling															●
History			●												●
Learning Disabilities		●													●
Theory & Method		●													●
Engineering				●									●		●
Environment/Conservation		●	●	●			●	●	●	●	●		●	●	●
ESL															●
Ethnic Studies	●	●	●				●		●					●	●
European Studies											●			●	●
Fiction								●							
Film Studies										●				●	●
Gender Studies							●		●	●				●	●
Geography		●					●	●		●			●	●	●
Gerontology															●
History		●	●				●		●	●			●	●	●
African														●	●
American	●						●	●	●					●	●
Asian										●				●	●
British	●		●											●	●
Canadian		●	●							●			●	●	
European														●	●
Latin American	●						●							●	●
Middle Eastern												●		●	●

Subject	Carnegie Mellon	Catholic	Chicago	Chinese	Colorado	Columbia	Cornell	Duke	Florida	Fordham	Gallaudet	Georgetown	Georgia	Georgia State
African Studies			●		●			●	●					
Agriculture					●		●	●	●					
American Indian Studies			●		●		●		●				●	
American Studies			●		●	●	●	●	●	●			●	
Anthropology			●	●	●	●	●	●	●				●	
Cultural			●	●	●	●	●	●	●				●	●
Physical			●		●	●			●					
Archaelogy			●	●	●	●	●		●	●				
Architecture	●		●		●		●		●				●	
Art & Art History	●		●	●	●	●	●	●	●	●			●	
Art Criticism			●		●	●	●		●					
Art History			●	●	●	●	●		●	●				
Decorative Arts								●					●	
Design & Graphics	●							●						
Painting & Sculpture								●	●	●				
Asian Studies			●	●	●	●	●							
Astronomy			●		●									
Bibliography & Reference			●	●	●	●	●	●		●				●
Biography			●	●	●	●	●	●	●	●	●		●	
Biological Sciences			●	●	●	●	●		●				●	
Botany			●	●	●	●	●		●				●	
Genetics					●	●	●							
Marine Biology					●	●	●		●				●	
Microbiology						●								
Physiology					●	●	●							
Zoology			●		●	●	●		●				●	
Black Studies			●		●		●	●	●				●	
Business			●	●		●		●		●				●
Canadian Studies					●									
Childd Development			●		●	●	●	●				●		
Classics			●				●	●	●	●				
Communications			●	●		●		●	●					
Broadcast Media						●		●						
Journalism			●	●		●		●	●					
Computer Sciences				●				●						●
Demography			●			●		●			●			
Drama	●	●	●					●	●			●	●	
Earth Sciences			●		●	●	●							
Geochemistry							●							
Geology			●		●	●	●							
Oceanography			●			●			●					
Economics			●		●		●	●		●				●
History			●		●		●	●		●				●
Theory			●		●		●		●					●
Education			●				●	●				●	●	
Counseling												●	●	
History			●	●			●					●	●	
Learning Disabilities						●								
Theory & Method			●	●								●	●	
Engineering				●										
Environment/Conservation			●		●	●	●	●	●				●	
ESL												●	●	
Ethnic Studies					●	●	●	●	●				●	
European Studies							●	●	●				●	
Fiction		●			●			●					●	
Film Studies			●		●	●	●	●					●	
Gender Studies			●		●	●	●	●					●	
Geography			●		●		●	●					●	
Gerontology							●				●	●		
History			●	●	●	●	●	●	●				●	
African						●						●	●	
American			●	●	●	●	●	●	●				●	●
Asian				●	●		●							
British			●				●		●				●	
Canadian							●							
European			●	●			●	●	●				●	
Latin American		●		●		●			●				●	
Middle Eastern			●				●	●	●				●	

Columns 1–10

	Alabama	Alaska	Alberta	A. Chemical	A. Mathematical	A. Psychiatric	Arizona	Arkansas	Beacon	British Columbia
History (Cont'd) Ancient										
Classical							●			
Medieval										
Modern	●						●			
History of Science	●	●			●		●			
Law		●							●	●
Language			●				●			
Language Arts										
Linguistics	●						●			
Speech										
Latin American Studies	●						●			
Library Science	●									
Literature			●				●	●		
Literary Criticism	●						●	●		
Literary History	●							●		
Literary Theory							●	●		
African										
American	●						●	●		
Asian										
British	●						●			
Canadian			●							
Classical										
Eastern										
European										
Medieval										
Renaissance								●		
Modern	●							●		
Contemporary							●	●		
Folklore	●	●	●				●	●		
Mythology	●	●	●				●	●		
Translations		●						●		
Maritime Studies										●
Mathematics			●	●						
Medicine		●								
General										
History	●	●								
Medieval Studies										
Middle East Studies										●
Military Studies		●								●
Music							●			
History							●			
Theory										
Near Eastern Studies										
Performing Arts							●			
Dance										
Music										
Theatre							●			
Pacific Studies										●
Philosophy			●					●		
Ethics								●		
History of Philosophy										
Logic										
Metaphysics										
Physical Science			●				●			●
Photography							●			
Poetry								●		
Political Science/Public Affairs	●	●					●	●	●	●
Psychiatry						●				
Psychology						●				
Public Health	●									
Publishing										
Regional Studies	●	●					●	●	●	●
Religion	●						●		●	
Social Work			●							●
Sociology	●						●			●
Urban Studies										●
Veterinary Sciences										
Women's Studies	●						●	●	●	●

Columns 11–20

	Brookings	Cairo (American)	Calgary	California	Cambridge	Carnegie Mellon	Catholic	Chicago	Chinese	Colorado
History (Cont'd) Ancient				●	●		●			
Classical				●	●		●			
Medieval				●	●	●	●			
Modern				●	●	●	●			
History of Science				●			●		●	●
Law	●	●	●	●			●	●	●	●
Language				●	●		●	●		
Language Arts				●						
Linguistics				●			●	●		
Speech				●						●
Latin American Studies	●			●	●		●		●	
Library Science	●			●			●			
Literature				●	●	●	●	●	●	●
Literary Criticism				●	●	●	●	●		●
Literary History				●	●		●	●		●
Literary Theory				●	●		●	●		●
African				●	●					
American				●	●		●	●		●
Asian				●	●		●	●		
British				●	●		●	●		
Canadian				●						
Classical				●	●		●			
Eastern				●	●		●			●
European				●	●	●	●			
Medieval				●	●		●	●		
Renaissance				●	●		●	●		
Modern				●	●		●	●		
Contemporary				●	●		●			
Folklore				●	●		●			
Mythology				●	●		●			
Translations				●	●		●	●		
Maritime Studies				●	●		●			
Mathematics			●		●		●			
Medicine		●	●	●				●		
General					●		●			●
History					●		●			●
Medieval Studies				●	●	●	●			
Middle East Studies	●			●	●		●	●		
Military Studies				●	●					
Music			●	●	●	●	●	●	●	●
History				●	●		●	●	●	●
Theory				●	●		●			●
Near Eastern Studies	●			●	●		●			
Performing Arts				●	●					
Dance				●	●					●
Music				●	●					
Theatre					●		●	●		
Pacific Studies				●	●		●			
Philosophy				●	●	●	●	●		●
Ethics				●	●		●	●	●	●
History of Philosophy				●	●		●			
Logic				●	●		●			
Metaphysics				●	●		●	●		
Physical Science				●	●		●		●	●
Photography				●	●			●		
Poetry						●				
Political Science/Public Affairs				●	●		●	●		●
Psychiatry					●		●			
Psychology					●					●
Public Health					●			●		
Publishing					●		●			
Regional Studies				●	●		●		●	●
Religion				●	●		●	●		●
Social Work	●				●			●		
Sociology				●	●		●	●		●
Urban Studies	●			●	●		●			
Veterinary Sciences									●	
Women's Studies				●	●		●			

Columns 21–29

	Columbia	Cornell	Duke	Florida	Fordham	Gallaudet	Georgetown	Georgia	Georgia State
History (Cont'd) Ancient	●	●			●				
Classical	●	●			●				
Medieval	●	●	●		●			●	
Modern	●	●	●					●	
History of Science	●	●			●				
Law	●	●			●	●		●	●
Language	●	●			●	●	●		
Language Arts	●				●	●	●		
Linguistics	●				●	●	●		
Speech	●							●	
Latin American Studies	●	●	●				●		
Library Science									
Literature	●	●	●	●	●		●	●	
Literary Criticism	●	●	●	●	●			●	
Literary History	●	●	●		●			●	
Literary Theory	●	●	●					●	
African		●	●					●	
American	●	●	●	●	●			●	
Asian	●	●	●					●	
British	●	●	●	●				●	
Canadian								●	
Classical	●	●	●	●				●	
Eastern	●	●						●	
European	●	●	●	●				●	
Medieval	●	●	●					●	
Renaissance	●	●	●	●	●			●	
Modern	●	●	●					●	
Contemporary	●	●	●					●	
Folklore	●	●	●					●	
Mythology		●		●				●	
Translations	●	●	●					●	
Maritime Studies									
Mathematics		●		●		●			
Medicine		●	●						
General									
History		●	●						
Medieval Studies	●	●	●	●				●	
Middle East Studies	●	●	●	●					
Military Studies	●	●	●	●					
Music	●	●	●	●				●	
History	●	●	●	●				●	
Theory	●	●	●	●					
Near Eastern Studies	●	●							
Performing Arts		●	●				●	●	
Dance	●	●	●						
Music								●	
Theatre	●				●		●	●	
Pacific Studies	●	●	●						
Philosophy	●	●	●	●	●			●	
Ethics	●	●	●	●		●	●		
History of Philosophy	●	●	●	●					
Logic	●	●		●					
Metaphysics	●	●		●					
Physical Science	●	●		●					
Photography		●	●					●	
Poetry		●		●				●	
Political Science/Public Affairs	●	●	●	●			●	●	●
Psychiatry	●	●				●			
Psychology		●		●	●				●
Public Health		●							●
Publishing		●		●					
Regional Studies	●	●	●	●			●	●	
Religion	●	●	●	●				●	
Social Work			●	●		●			
Sociology	●	●	●	●	●			●	
Urban Studies	●	●	●	●					●
Veterinary Sciences		●		●				●	
Women's Studies	●	●	●	●	●			●	●

Subject strengths of publishers' lists, part 1 (Getty – Louisiana):

Discipline	Getty	Harvard	Hawaii	Howard	Idaho	Illinois	Indiana	Iowa	Iowa State	Jewish	Johns Hopkins	Kansas	Kent SState	Kentucky	Louisiana
African Studies		●		●			●								
Agriculture					●	●			●			●		●	
American Indian Studies		●			●	●	●	●	●			●		●	
American Studies		●	●	●	●	●	●	●	●		●	●	●	●	●
Anthropology		●	●	●	●	●	●	●				●		●	
Cultural		●	●	●	●	●	●	●		●		●		●	
Physical		●	●					●						●	
Archaelogy	●	●	●		●		●	●			●	●		●	
Architecture	●	●	●		●	●								●	
Art & Art History	●	●	●	●			●	●						●	
Art Criticism	●	●	●	●			●								
Art History	●	●	●	●			●	●						●	
Decorative Arts	●	●	●				●								
Design & Graphics	●	●	●												
Painting & Sculpture	●	●	●			●	●								
Asian Studies		●	●				●								
Astronomy		●	●							●					
Bibliography & Reference	●	●	●	●		●	●	●	●		●				
Biography		●	●	●	●	●	●	●	●		●	●		●	●
Biological Sciences		●	●		●		●	●	●		●	●		●	
Botany		●	●		●		●	●	●		●	●		●	
Genetics		●						●	●		●				
Marine Biology		●	●					●							
Microbiology		●													
Physiology		●													
Zoology		●	●		●			●	●		●				
Black Studies		●		●		●	●	●	●		●			●	●
Business		●		●		●	●							●	
Canadian Studies		●												●	
Chilld Development		●		●		●									
Classics		●			●	●		●	●						
Communications		●		●		●	●								
Broadcast Media		●		●		●									
Journalism		●		●		●	●								
Computer Sciences		●				●	●								
Demography		●	●	●											
Drama		●	●	●		●	●			●					
Earth Sciences		●	●					●			●				
Geochemistry		●									●				
Geology		●	●		●			●			●				
Oceanography		●	●								●				
Economics		●	●	●		●	●	●			●				
History		●	●	●		●	●	●			●				
Theory		●		●		●		●			●				
Education		●	●	●		●					●				
Counseling		●	●	●											
History		●		●		●					●				
Learning Disabilities		●		●		●									
Theory & Method	●	●		●						●					
Engineering								●							
Environment/Conservation	●	●		●	●	●	●	●	●		●	●			●
ESL		●													
Ethnic Studies		●	●	●		●	●			●		●			
European Studies		●				●				●					●
Fiction			●			●		●							
Film Studies	●	●	●	●		●	●			●				●	
Gender Studies		●	●	●		●	●	●	●	●				●	
Geography		●	●											●	
Gerontology		●					●							●	
History		●	●	●		●	●	●		●	●	●	●		
African		●		●		●		●				●			
American		●		●	●	●	●	●	●	●	●	●	●	●	●
Asian		●	●			●		●				●		●	
British		●				●	●	●			●	●			
Canadian		●						●	●					●	
European		●				●	●			●	●			●	●
Latin American		●				●	●	●		●				●	●
Middle Eastern		●					●			●					

Subject strengths of publishers' lists, part 2 (McGill-Queen's – Naval):

Discipline	McGill-Queen's	Massachusetts	MIT	Metropolitan	Mexico	Michigan	Michigan State	Minnesota	Mississippi	Missouri	MLA	National Acad.	National Gallery	Naval
African Studies	●	●					●							
Agriculture							●					●		
American Indian Studies	●						●	●	●		●			
American Studies	●	●			●	●	●	●	●	●	●			
Anthropology	●					●	●	●						
Cultural	●					●	●	●	●					
Physical						●								
Archaelogy	●		●	●	●									●
Architecture	●	●	●	●	●				●					
Art & Art History	●	●	●	●	●				●	●	●		●	●
Art Criticism	●	●	●	●	●				●					
Art History	●	●	●	●	●				●				●	
Decorative Arts	●	●												
Design & Graphics		●	●	●					●					
Painting & Sculpture	●		●	●					●					
Asian Studies														
Astronomy				●		●						●		
Bibliography & Reference	●					●	●		●	●	●			●
Biography	●	●				●	●	●		●	●	●		●
Biological Sciences	●					●		●	●			●		
Botany	●					●		●	●			●		
Genetics	●											●		
Marine Biology	●											●		
Microbiology	●											●		
Physiology												●		
Zoology						●	●	●				●		
Black Studies	●	●				●	●	●	●	●		●		
Business				●		●						●		
Canadian Studies	●					●								
Chilld Development			●	●								●		
Classics	●	●		●		●								
Communications	●					●		●		●				
Broadcast Media	●					●		●	●					
Journalism	●									●				
Computer Sciences			●			●						●		
Demography	●					●								
Drama	●			●							●			
Earth Sciences	●					●						●		
Geochemistry	●											●		
Geology	●					●						●		
Oceanography	●											●		●
Economics	●		●			●	●					●		
History	●		●			●	●	●						
Theory	●		●			●	●							
Education	●					●		●				●		
Counseling	●													
History	●					●	●							
Learning Disabilities	●													
Theory & Method	●					●	●							
Engineering				●		●						●		●
Environment/Conservation			●	●		●	●	●	●			●		
ESL								●						
Ethnic Studies	●	●				●	●	●	●	●	●			
European Studies	●						●		●	●				
Fiction									●	●	●			●
Film Studies	●			●			●	●						
Gender Studies	●	●			●	●	●	●	●			●	●	
Geography	●			●				●	●					
Gerontology	●											●		
History	●			●		●			●	●				●
African	●						●							●
American	●	●				●		●		●	●			●
Asian														●
British	●								●					●
Canadian	●						●							●
European	●							●		●				●
Latin American	●					●		●		●				●
Middle Eastern														●

The table is one logical matrix (subjects × institutions); because it has 29 institution columns it is split here into two parts, with the subject column repeated.

	Getty	Harvard	Hawaii	Howard	Idaho	Illinois	Indiana	Iowa	Iowa State	Jewish	Johns Hopkins	Kansas	Kent SState	Kentucky	Louisiana
History (Cont'd) Ancient		●		●			●			●	●				
Classical		●		●			●			●	●				
Medieval		●		●			●			●					
Modern		●		●			●	●		●		●	●	●	
History of Science		●	●	●		●	●	●		●					
Law		●			●										
Language		●	●	●		●									
Language Arts		●	●	●		●									
Linguistics		●	●	●		●									
Speech		●		●		●									
Latin American Studies		●		●			●	●			●				
Library Science						●									
Literature		●	●	●		●	●	●							●
Literary Criticism		●	●	●	●	●	●	●		●	●				
Literary History		●	●	●		●	●	●		●	●				
Literary Theory		●	●	●		●	●	●		●	●				
African		●		●		●	●								
American		●		●	●	●	●	●			●				
Asian		●	●			●									
British		●				●	●	●			●				
Canadian		●				●									
Classical		●		●		●					●				
Eastern		●	●			●									
European		●				●	●				●	●			●
Medieval		●		●		●	●				●				●
Renaissance		●				●	●				●				●
Modern		●		●		●	●				●			●	●
Contemporary		●				●	●	●			●			●	●
Folklore		●	●	●	●	●	●	●		●					
Mythology		●	●	●		●	●			●	●				
Translations		●	●	●		●				●	●				
Maritime Studies		●	●												
Mathematics											●				
Medicine		●		●		●		●			●				
General		●									●				
History		●		●		●		●			●				
Medieval Studies		●		●		●	●			●					
Middle East Studies		●				●		●							
Military Studies		●		●		●	●					●	●	●	
Music		●				●	●	●							●
History		●				●	●	●							
Theory		●				●									
Near Eastern Studies		●				●					●				
Performing Arts			●	●		●	●	●							
Dance			●	●		●	●								
Music			●	●		●	●								
Theatre		●	●	●		●	●				●				
Pacific Studies		●	●	●											
Philosophy		●	●	●		●	●	●		●				●	
Ethics		●	●	●		●	●	●		●				●	
History of Philosophy		●	●	●		●	●								
Logic		●	●			●	●								
Metaphysics		●	●			●	●								
Physical Science		●						●			●				
Photography	●		●	●		●	●								
Poetry						●		●		●	●				●
Political Science/Public Affairs		●	●	●		●	●			●	●	●		●	●
Psychiatry		●		●							●				
Psychology		●		●		●				●	●				
Public Health		●	●	●		●			●	●	●				
Publishing		●		●											
Regional Studies		●	●		●	●	●	●	●	●	●	●	●	●	●
Religion		●	●	●		●	●			●					
Social Work		●		●		●									
Sociology		●	●	●		●	●			●		●		●	
Urban Studies		●		●		●	●	●	●		●	●	●	●	
Veterinary Sciences								●							
Women's Studies		●	●	●	●	●	●	●			●	●	●		●

	McGill-Queen's	Massachusetts	MIT	Metropolitan	Mexico	Michigan	Michigan State	Minnesota	Mississippi	Missouri	MLA	National Acad.	National Gallery	Naval
History (Cont'd) Ancient	●			●										●
Classical	●			●	●									●
Medieval	●			●	●			●						●
Modern	●	●		●					●					●
History of Science	●	●	●	●				●	●			●		
Law	●			●		●								●
Language	●		●	●							●			
Language Arts				●							●			
Linguistics	●		●	●							●			
Speech			●	●							●			
Latin American Studies	●			●				●		●				
Library Science				●										
Literature	●	●	●	●				●	●	●				
Literary Criticism				●	●			●	●	●	●			
Literary History				●	●			●	●	●	●			
Literary Theory				●	●			●	●		●			
African			●						●		●			
American	●	●	●	●			●	●	●	●	●			●
Asian											●			
British	●	●	●	●				●	●	●	●			●
Canadian	●					●	●	●			●			
Classical	●			●	●						●			
Eastern											●			
European	●			●	●			●		●	●			●
Medieval	●			●	●			●			●			
Renaissance		●	●	●	●					●	●			
Modern	●	●		●	●			●	●	●	●			
Contemporary	●			●	●			●		●	●			
Folklore	●			●					●	●	●			
Mythology	●			●							●			
Translations	●			●	●			●			●			
Maritime Studies	●			●		●						●		●
Mathematics				●								●		
Medicine				●								●		
General				●								●		
History	●			●		●								
Medieval Studies	●						●		●					
Middle East Studies	●													
Military Studies	●											●		●
Music		●	●	●					●	●				
History	●	●	●	●					●					
Theory				●			●	●						
Near Eastern Studies														
Performing Arts										●				
Dance				●						●				
Music				●						●				
Theatre				●	●					●				
Pacific Studies	●													
Philosophy	●	●	●	●					●					
Ethics	●	●	●	●					●					
History of Philosophy	●	●	●	●					●					
Logic	●		●	●										
Metaphysics	●		●	●										
Physical Science			●	●									●	
Photography				●		●					●	●		
Poetry	●	●		●										
Political Science/Public Affairs	●	●		●	●	●	●	●	●	●		●		
Psychiatry	●											●		
Psychology						●				●				●
Public Health	●													●
Publishing				●										
Regional Studies	●			●		●	●	●	●	●				
Religion	●			●					●	●				
Social Work				●										●
Sociology	●	●		●					●	●				●
Urban Studies	●	●		●				●	●	●				●
Veterinary Sciences				●										●
Women's Studies				●	●			●	●	●	●	●	●	●

	Nebraska	Nevada	New England	New Mexico	New York	North Carolina	Northeastern	Northern Illinois	Northwestern	Notre Dame	Ohio	Ohio State	Oklahoma	Oregon State	Oxford	Pennsylvania	Penn State	Pittsburgh	Princeton	Puerto Rico	Purdue	Resources	Rice	Rockefeller	Russell Sage	Rutgers	Scandinavian	Smithsonian	South Carolina
African Studies									●		●				●				●			●			●			●	
Agriculture	●						●	●				●			●				●	●	●	●							
American Indian Studies	●	●	●	●		●		●			●	●	●		●								●		●			●	
American Studies	●	●	●	●	●	●	●	●				●			●	●	●		●		●					●	●	●	●
Anthropology	●	●		●		●		●		●		●			●	●	●	●	●	●						●	●	●	
Cultural	●	●		●		●		●		●		●			●	●	●	●	●	●						●	●	●	
Physical							●					●	●		●	●			●									●	
Archaelogy			●			●						●			●	●			●				●			●	●	●	
Architecture		●	●	●	●				●			●			●	●	●		●	●			●			●	●	●	●
Art & Art History			●	●	●			●				●	●		●	●	●		●				●			●		●	●
Art Criticism			●	●	●							●	●		●	●	●		●	●			●					●	
Art History			●	●	●			●				●	●		●	●	●		●	●			●				●	●	●
Decorative Arts			●			●						●	●		●	●			●							●		●	
Design & Graphics			●									●	●		●	●												●	
Painting & Sculpture			●	●								●	●		●	●	●		●									●	
Asian Studies					●							●	●		●	●			●									●	●
Astronomy												●			●				●	●								●	
Bibliography & Reference		●	●		●						●	●	●	●	●	●		●		●			●					●	
Biography	●	●	●	●	●	●	●	●	●	●	●	●	●	●	●	●		●	●	●	●		●	●				●	●
Biological Sciences	●	●										●	●	●	●				●					●			●	●	●
Botany						●						●	●		●	●			●	●							●	●	●
Genetics												●			●	●			●					●		●			
Marine Biology			●												●				●									●	●
Microbiology															●										●				
Physiology															●	●									●				
Zoology											●	●			●	●			●	●			●			●		●	
Black Studies		●			●	●	●					●		●	●	●	●						●		●	●		●	●
Business		●			●	●				●		●			●	●			●				●				●		●
Canadian Studies	●				●							●			●														
Child Development	●				●							●			●				●								●	●	
Classics	●				●	●				●		●		●	●	●	●		●								●	●	
Communications		●	●		●	●						●	●		●	●			●								●	●	●
Broadcast Media					●							●	●		●												●	●	
Journalism		●			●	●									●				●								●	●	
Computer Sciences															●			●										●	
Demography						●									●			●	●						●				
Drama		●							●			●	●		●	●			●							●			
Earth Sciences														●	●			●										●	
Geochemistry															●			●											
Geology		●													●			●									●		
Oceanography															●			●											
Economics				●					●		●		●		●	●		●	●		●				●		●		
History				●	●		●		●		●		●		●	●		●							●				
Theory				●					●				●		●	●		●	●								●		
Education		●		●							●				●				●						●		●		
Counseling															●													●	
History															●														
Learning Disabilities															●												●		
Theory & Method											●				●				●								●		
Engineering															●						●								
Environment/Conservation	●	●	●	●		●						●		●	●				●	●		●				●	●	●	●
ESL															●														
Ethnic Studies		●	●	●	●	●		●		●		●	●		●					●			●		●	●		●	
European Studies	●	●	●		●	●		●		●						●		●		●									
Fiction			●	●				●			●				●								●						
Film Studies			●	●		●						●			●	●			●				●			●		●	
Gender Studies	●	●	●	●	●	●	●	●	●			●	●		●		●		●		●		●		●	●	●	●	●
Geography			●			●					●	●	●	●	●		●			●						●	●		
Gerontology	●		●									●			●					●						●	●	●	
History	●	●	●	●	●	●	●	●	●			●	●		●	●	●	●	●				●		●	●		●	●
African											●	●			●								●			●		●	
American	●	●	●	●	●	●	●	●			●	●	●	●	●	●	●	●	●		●		●		●	●		●	●
Asian											●				●				●									●	
British			●			●					●	●			●	●	●				●								
Canadian			●									●			●												●		
European	●		●		●	●		●			●	●	●		●	●	●	●	●		●								
Latin American	●			●		●		●		●				●	●	●	●	●	●	●			●					●	
Middle Eastern				●	●					●					●		●		●									●	●

	Nebraska	Nevada	New England	New Mexico	New York	North Carolina	Northeastern	Northern Illinois	Northwestern	Notre Dame	Ohio	Ohio State	Oklahoma	Oregon State	Oxford	Pennsylvania	Penn State	Pittsburgh	Princeton	Puerto Rico	Purdue	Resources	Rice	Rockefeller	Russell Sage	Rutgers	Scandinavian	Smithsonian	South Carolina
History (Cont'd) Ancient						●					●	●		●	●	●			●										
Classical						●				●			●		●	●			●	●									
Medieval	●				●	●		●		●		●			●	●	●		●				●				●		
Modern	●	●	●		●	●	●	●				●			●	●	●	●	●		●		●				●		●
History of Science					●	●				●					●	●	●	●	●		●		●	●			●	●	●
Law	●	●			●	●	●		●	●			●		●	●	●	●	●				●		●	●	●		
Language		●			●						●				●	●			●				●				●		●
Language Arts											●				●														
Linguistics					●						●				●	●			●				●				●		
Speech															●														●
Latin American Studies	●			●	●		●		●				●		●		●	●	●	●			●					●	
Library Science															●														
Literature		●	●		●		●		●		●	●			●	●	●		●	●			●				●	●	●
Literary Criticism	●		●		●	●	●	●	●		●	●	●		●	●	●		●	●	●		●				●	●	
Literary History	●		●		●	●	●				●	●	●		●	●	●		●	●	●		●						
Literary Theory	●		●		●	●	●		●		●	●			●	●	●	●	●	●	●		●				●		
African										●					●		●						●						
American	●	●	●		●	●	●	●	●		●	●	●	●	●	●	●		●		●		●				●		●
Asian															●		●	●											
British	●				●	●	●	●			●	●	●		●	●	●		●	●							●		●
Canadian	●		●												●		●												
Classical	●				●									●	●		●	●											
Eastern															●		●	●											
European	●	●					●	●			●				●	●	●		●		●		●				●		●
Medieval	●						●	●			●				●	●	●		●				●						
Renaissance	●						●	●			●				●	●	●		●										
Modern	●		●		●	●	●	●	●		●	●			●	●	●		●		●		●				●	●	●
Contemporary	●	●	●		●	●	●	●			●	●			●	●	●		●	●	●								
Folklore		●	●	●		●			●				●		●	●			●				●					●	
Mythology			●						●						●		●	●											
Translations	●	●	●				●	●			●	●			●	●	●	●	●				●						
Maritime Studies			●											●	●														●
Mathematics															●			●	●								●		
Medicine											●	●			●	●		●									●	●	
General						●									●	●											●		
History											●	●			●	●			●					●			●		
Medieval Studies	●					●			●	●		●			●	●	●		●					●			●		
Middle East Studies				●						●					●	●	●		●								●	●	●
Military Studies				●										●	●		●		●							●		●	●
Music	●		●		●	●			●						●	●			●								●	●	●
History	●		●						●						●	●			●								●		
Theory	●		●						●						●	●			●										
Near Eastern Studies				●											●	●	●		●									●	●
Performing Arts		●	●						●			●			●	●		●	●										
Dance		●	●						●						●		●										●		
Music		●	●			●			●						●	●			●	●							●		
Theatre		●	●						●	●	●				●	●		●											
Pacific Studies															●												●		
Philosophy	●			●			●	●	●	●					●	●	●	●	●	●	●			●		●		●	
Ethics							●	●	●						●	●	●		●	●				●				●	
History of Philosophy						●	●	●	●						●	●	●		●	●	●							●	
Logic								●	●						●				●										
Metaphysics								●	●						●		●	●	●										
Physical Science															●			●	●										
Photography		●	●	●											●				●					●			●		
Poetry		●	●				●		●		●				●		●	●	●	●									
Political Science/Public Affairs	●	●	●		●	●		●		●			●	●	●	●	●	●	●	●	●	●		●			●	●	●
Psychiatry				●					●						●													●	
Psychology	●			●					●						●						●					●		●	
Public Health						●					●				●											●	●	●	
Publishing		●	●		●	●					●				●	●													
Regional Studies	●	●	●	●	●	●	●	●		●	●	●	●	●	●		●	●	●	●			●		●	●		●	●
Religion			●		●	●		●		●					●	●	●		●	●						●	●	●	●
Social Work				●											●											●	●	●	●
Sociology			●		●	●				●		●			●	●	●		●	●						●	●	●	
Urban Studies					●	●						●			●	●	●		●				●		●	●		●	
Veterinary Sciences															●	●					●								
Women's Studies	●	●	●	●	●	●	●	●				●	●		●	●	●		●	●	●		●		●	●		●	●

	Southern Illinois	Southern Meth.	Stanford	SUNY	Syracuse	Teachers	Temple	Tennessee	Texas	Texas A&M	Texas Christian	Texas Tech	Texas Western	Tokyo
African Studies				●	●									●
Agriculture										●				●
American Indian Studies			●	●	●		●	●	●	●	●		●	
American Studies	●		●		●		●	●	●	●	●			●
Anthropology	●		●	●	●		●	●	●	●				●
Cultural	●		●	●	●		●	●	●					●
Physical	●		●	●				●	●					●
Archaelogy	●		●		●			●	●	●				●
Architecture	●				●			●	●	●	●			●
Art & Art History	●				●			●	●	●	●			●
Art Criticism	●							●						
Art History	●		●					●						●
Decorative Arts	●							●	●	●	●			
Design & Graphics	●							●						
Painting & Sculpture	●							●	●					●
Asian Studies			●	●	●									●
Astronomy							●					●		
Bibliography & Reference	●													●
Biography	●		●	●	●		●	●	●	●	●		●	●
Biological Sciences			●	●	●			●	●					●
Botany	●		●		●			●	●		●			●
Genetics			●								●			●
Marine Biology			●					●	●		●			●
Microbiology			●											●
Physiology			●								●			●
Zoology			●		●			●	●		●			●
Black Studies			●	●			●	●	●	●		●		
Business														●
Canadian Studies				●										●
Chilld Development	●		●	●	●	●								●
Classics	●		●	●				●			●			●
Communications	●		●	●			●	●						●
Broadcast Media	●			●			●	●						●
Journalism	●			●			●							●
Computer Sciences														●
Demography			●		●							●		●
Drama	●	●	●		●			●						●
Earth Sciences			●					●	●			●	●	●
Geochemistry			●											●
Geology			●					●	●			●	●	●
Oceanography			●					●	●					●
Economics	●		●						●			●	●	●
History	●		●						●				●	●
Theory	●		●						●				●	●
Education	●		●	●	●									●
Counseling	●		●	●	●									●
History	●		●	●	●									●
Learning Disabilities	●		●	●	●									●
Theory & Method	●		●	●										●
Engineering										●				●
Environment/Conservation	●		●	●			●	●	●	●		●	●	●
ESL					●									
Ethnic Studies			●	●			●	●	●	●			●	●
European Studies	●		●		●				●					●
Fiction		●							●	●	●			
Film Studies	●	●	●	●	●		●		●					
Gender Studies	●		●	●	●	●	●	●	●					●
Geography			●		●			●	●			●		●
Gerontology			●	●										●
History	●		●	●										●
African				●										●
American	●		●	●	●		●	●	●	●	●	●		●
Asian			●	●	●									●
British	●		●		●						●			●
Canadian	●		●		●									●
European	●		●		●						●			●
Latin American			●	●			●		●			●	●	●
Middle Eastern	●			●	●			●						●

	Toronto	U.S. Inst. Peace	Utah	Utah State	Vanderbilt	Virginia	Washington	Washington State	Wayne State	Wilfrid Laurier	Wisconsin	Woodrow Wilson	Yale
African Studies		●				●	●				●	●	●
Agriculture													
American Indian Studies	●		●	●	●		●	●			●	●	
American Studies			●	●	●	●	●	●	●		●	●	●
Anthropology	●		●	●	●	●	●				●	●	●
Cultural	●		●	●	●	●	●				●	●	●
Physical					●		●				●		●
Archaelogy	●		●		●	●	●	●	●		●		●
Architecture	●				●	●	●	●	●		●	●	●
Art & Art History	●				●		●	●	●		●	●	●
Art Criticism					●		●				●		●
Art History	●				●		●		●	●	●		●
Decorative Arts					●	●	●				●		●
Design & Graphics					●						●		●
Painting & Sculpture	●				●		●		●		●		●
Asian Studies	●					●	●				●	●	●
Astronomy													
Bibliography & Reference	●				●						●	●	●
Biography	●		●	●	●	●	●	●	●	●	●		
Biological Sciences					●						●		
Botany			●	●	●						●		
Genetics											●		
Marine Biology						●							
Microbiology													●
Physiology													
Zoology			●	●	●						●		●
Black Studies				●	●	●	●	●			●		●
Business											●		
Canadian Studies	●					●				●			
Chilld Development													●
Classics	●				●				●	●	●		●
Communications	●									●	●	●	
Broadcast Media	●										●	●	
Journalism											●	●	
Computer Sciences													
Demography			●								●		
Drama	●								●		●		
Earth Sciences						●					●		●
Geochemistry													
Geology			●								●		●
Oceanography											●		●
Economics									●		●	●	●
History	●		●									●	●
Theory	●										●		●
Education	●				●						●		●
Counseling													
History	●				●				●		●		●
Learning Disabilities													
Theory & Method	●										●		●
Engineering													
Environment/Conservation	●				●	●		●	●		●	●	●
ESL													
Ethnic Studies	●		●	●		●	●	●	●	●	●	●	
European Studies	●		●		●		●		●		●	●	●
Fiction											●	●	
Film Studies									●	●	●		
Gender Studies					●	●			●		●		●
Geography	●		●	●		●					●		●
Gerontology										●	●		
History	●												●
African		●					●	●			●	●	●
American			●	●	●	●	●	●	●	●	●	●	●
Asian	●						●				●	●	●
British	●		●			●				●	●	●	●
Canadian	●							●	●		●	●	●
European	●					●	●		●	●	●	●	●
Latin American	●		●		●	●					●	●	●
Middle Eastern			●	●			●		●				●

	Southern Illinois	Southern Meth.	Stanford	SUNY	Syracuse	Teachers	Temple	Tennessee	Texas	Texas A&M	Texas Christian	Texas Tech	Texas Western	Tokyo	Toronto	U.S. Inst. Peace	Utah	Utah State	Vanderbilt	Virginia	Washington	Washington State	Wayne State	Wilfrid Laurier	Wisconsin	Woodrow Wilson	Yale
History (Cont'd) Ancient	●		●						●					●	●								●	●	●		●
Classical	●		●						●			●		●	●				●				●	●	●		●
Medieval	●		●	●										●	●	●			●				●	●	●	●	●
Modern	●		●		●		●	●		●		●		●	●			●	●	●			●	●	●	●	●
History of Science			●		●									●	●			●		●				●	●		●
Law	●		●		●		●							●	●						●			●	●		●
Language	●		●	●					●					●	●		●						●		●		●
Language Arts						●			●						●								●		●		
Linguistics	●		●	●		●								●	●		●						●		●		
Speech	●			●																					●		
Latin American Studies			●		●		●		●				●	●		●	●	●	●				●	●	●	●	
Library Science														●													
Literature	●	●	●	●	●			●		●	●	●		●	●				●	●	●		●	●	●	●	●
Literary Criticism	●		●	●	●		●	●	●		●	●			●				●	●	●		●	●	●	●	●
Literary History	●		●		●			●	●		●	●		●	●				●	●	●		●		●		●
Literary Theory	●		●	●	●			●	●			●		●	●				●	●			●	●	●		●
African				●																●					●		●
American	●	●	●		●		●	●	●	●	●								●	●	●		●	●	●		●
Asian			●	●	●									●						●					●		
British	●		●		●			●	●					●					●	●	●		●	●	●		●
Canadian	●		●												●					●					●		
Classical	●		●						●			●		●	●		●		●				●		●		●
Eastern			●	●																●							
European	●		●		●							●			●				●	●	●		●	●	●	●	●
Medieval	●		●	●	●			●							●				●	●			●		●		●
Renaissance	●		●		●			●				●			●				●				●	●	●		●
Modern	●		●		●			●	●						●				●	●	●		●	●	●		●
Contemporary	●				●		●	●	●		●				●				●		●		●		●		●
Folklore	●				●			●	●	●	●	●			●		●	●	●	●	●		●		●		●
Mythology	●							●				●			●			●	●						●		●
Translations	●		●		●		●					●		●					●	●	●		●		●		●
Maritime Studies										●				●							●				●		
Mathematics														●													
Medicine	●	●	●					●						●					●						●		●
General		●	●											●					●								●
History	●			●				●				●		●				●						●	●	●	●
Medieval Studies	●		●	●	●			●						●	●				●				●	●	●		●
Middle East Studies	●			●	●				●					●			●	●					●	●	●		●
Military Studies			●					●		●	●		●	●									●	●	●		●
Music	●		●		●										●				●		●				●		●
History	●		●		●			●			●				●				●		●				●		●
Theory	●							●							●										●		●
Near Eastern Studies	●			●	●									●	●	●					●		●		●	●	●
Performing Arts	●	●	●																						●		
Dance	●																								●		
Music	●		●																						●		●
Theatre	●	●	●																						●		
Pacific Studies			●											●		●			●		●	●			●	●	●
Philosophy	●	●	●	●	●	●	●				●			●	●		●		●					●	●	●	●
Ethics	●	●	●	●			●	●						●	●		●		●					●	●	●	●
History of Philosophy	●		●	●			●					●		●	●				●						●		●
Logic	●		●	●								●		●	●				●						●		●
Metaphysics	●		●	●										●	●				●						●		●
Physical Science			●											●							●						●
Photography	●			●			●		●			●						●	●		●		●				●
Poetry												●		●									●		●		●
Political Science/Public Affairs	●		●	●	●		●		●		●			●	●	●			●	●	●	●	●	●	●	●	●
Psychiatry				●	●																					●	●
Psychology				●	●	●	●	●						●					●	●			●		●		●
Public Health			●		●		●							●							●						
Publishing	●						●							●							●	●	●				
Regional Studies	●	●	●		●			●	●	●	●	●	●	●	●		●		●	●	●	●	●	●	●	●	●
Religion	●	●	●	●	●			●						●	●				●	●	●			●	●	●	●
Social Work														●	●										●		
Sociology	●		●	●	●		●	●						●	●				●	●			●		●		●
Urban Studies	●		●	●		●	●	●	●	●				●	●								●		●	●	●
Veterinary Sciences											●			●													
Women's Studies	●		●	●	●	●	●	●	●	●	●	●		●	●				●		●	●	●	●	●	●	●

PRESSES PUBLISHING JOURNALS

University presses have always been associated with publishing books of merit and distinction. This remains as true today as in the past, but less well appreciated is the extent to which university presses are active in publishing scholarly journals.

Journals form a major part of the publishing program of many presses, and more than half of the Association's members produce at least one periodical. In all, university presses publish more than 700 scholarly periodicals, including many of the most distinguished in their respective fields. The following is a list of those presses that publish journals.

Each individual press listing also gives the number of journals, if any, that a press publishes and usually lists the titles of journals under the press's editorial program. For information concerning a specific periodical, readers are advised to consult a copy of the publication before communicating with the press concerned.

The University of Alabama Press
American Chemical Society
American Mathematical Society
American University in Cairo Press
The University of Arizona Press
The University of Arkansas Press
The Brookings Institution
University of Calgary Press
The University of California Press
Cambridge University Press
Carnegie Mellon University Press
The Catholic University of America Press
The University of Chicago Press
The Chinese University Press
University Press of Colorado
Duke University Press
Fordham University Press
Georgetown University Press
Georgia State University Business Press
J. Paul Getty Trust Publications
The University of Hawaii Press
Howard University Press
University of Idaho Press
The University of Illinois Press

Indiana University Press
The Johns Hopkins University Press
The Kent State University Press
The University Press of Kentucky
Louisiana State University Press
The MIT Press
The Metropolitan Museum of Art
The Michigan State University Press
Modern Language Association of America
National Gallery of Art
Naval Institute Press
The University of Nebraska Press
The University of Nevada Press
University Press of New England
The University of North Carolina Press
Northwestern University Press
University of Notre Dame Press
Ohio State University Press
Oxford University Press
The University of Pennsylvania Press
The Pennsylvania State University Press
Princeton University Press
The University of Puerto Rico Press
The Rockefeller University Press
Scandinavian University Press
State University of New York Press
University of Texas Press
Texas Tech University Press
University of Toronto Press, Inc.
Universidad Nacional Autónoma de México
Washington State University Press
Wayne State University Press
Wilfrid Laurier University Press
The University of Wisconsin Press
Yale University Press

Directory of Members

This "Directory of Members" includes a wealth of information on the AAUP's 114 member presses, including current addresses, phone and fax numbers, and electronic mail addresses. Most presses also list their sales representatives/distributors for Canada, the U.K., and Europe. (Addresses for these representatives are included at the end of the press listing, beginning with page 172.)

Each entry also contains important information describing that press's editorial program. This includes a list of disciplines published, special series, joint imprints, and copublishing programs, and the names of journals published, if any.

Press staff are listed, wherever possible, by the following departments/order: Director/administrative, acquisitions editorial, manuscript editorial, marketing, design and production, journals, and business. In most cases the first person listed within a department is its head. Readers should note that this method of organization is intended to promote ease of use, and is not always indicative of the lines of authority within an individual press.

Information on each press's membership status follows the staff listing. This includes date of press founding, type of membership (full, affiliate, international, or associate), year admitted to membership, title output for 1992 and 1993, and the total number of titles currently in print.

The University of Alabama Press

Street Address:
315 University Boulevard East
Tuscaloosa, AL 35401
(205) 348-5180
Fax: (205) 348-9201
Orders: (800) 825-9980
Cable Address: UNIPRESS, TUSCALOOSA

Mailing Address:
Box 870380
Tuscaloosa, AL 35487-0380

U.K. Representative:
Eurospan Group of Publishers

Director: Malcolm M. MacDonald (348-5180)
    Assistant Director for Business: Linda J. Sandford (348-1567)
    Assistant Director for Marketing and Editor: Judith Knight (348-1568)
    Secretary to the Director: Sandra P. Wilson (348-9703)
Acquisitions Editorial: Nicole Mitchell, Acquisitions Editor (348-1560; E-mail: nmitchel@ualvm.ua.edu)
Manuscript Editorial: Elizabeth May, Managing Editor (348-1563)
    Project Editors: Suzette Griffith (348-9708); TBA (348-1565)
    Editorial and Production Secretary: Sonya F. Foster
Marketing: Judith Knight, Assistant Director for Marketing and Editor (348-1568)
    Marketing Assistants: Rubye F. Taylor (348-1566); Shana Foster (348-9534); Kristi Wheeler-Griffin (348-9665)
Design and Production: John F. Zeigler, Production Manager (348-1571)
    Production Assistant: Paula Dennis (348-1570)
Business: Linda J. Sandford, Assistant Director for Business (and Rights & Permissions) (348-1567)
    Bookkeeper: Jambu Sadasivan (348-1564)
    Assistant Bookkeeper: Mary E. Caine (348-5182)
    Order Processing: Margaret Horne (348-5336)
    Business Secretary: Ann Nichols (348-5180)
    Order Fulfillment: Robert L. Waldrop, Marty E. Colburn (348-5488)

Full Member

Established: 1945

Admitted to AAUP: 1964

Title output 1992: 41

Title output 1993: 45

Titles currently in print: 450

Journals published: 3

Editorial Program
History; political science; public administration; speech
communication; Latin American studies; Judaic studies;
linguistics; southern regional studies; literary criticism; history of
American science and technology; anthropology; archaeology. The
press publishes the journals *The Alabama Review*, *American
Speech*, and *Theatre Symposium*.

Special series, joint imprints and/or copublishing
programs: Judaic Studies Series; Publications of the American
Dialect Society; History of American Science and Technology
Series; Studies in Rhetoric and Communication; Library of
Alabama Classics.

University of Alaska Press

1st Floor Gruening Building
P.O. Box 756240
University of Alaska Fairbanks
Fairbanks, AK 99775-6240
(907) 474-6389
Fax: (907) 474-5502

Director: Claus-M. Naske (474-6389)
Manager: Debbie Van Stone (474-6389)
Acquisitions Editor: Pamela Odom (474-5832)
Managing Editor: Carla Helfferich (474-6389)
Marketing, Design & Production: Debbie Van Stone; Pamela
   Odom

Affiliate Member

Established: 1967   Admitted to AAUP: 1992
Title output 1992: 5   Title output 1993: 7
Titles currently in print: 57

Editorial Program
Scholarly books and informal nonfiction relating to Alaska, with
special emphasis on the circumpolar regions.

Special series: The Rasmuson Library Historical Translation
Series; Classic Reprint Series; Oral Biography Series; Monograph
Series; and LanternLight Library.

The press distributes publications for Limestone Press,

Spirit Mountain Press, White Mammoth, Alaska Division of
Geologic and Geophysical Surveys, Anthropological Papers of the
University of Alaska, KUAC-TV, the Geophysical Institute, and
the University Foundation.

The University of Alberta Press

141 Athabasca Hall
Edmonton, AB
Canada T6G 2E8
(403) 492-3662
Fax: (403) 492-0719
Internet: (user I.D.)@gpu.
    srv.ualberta.ca

<u>European Representative:</u>
Lavis Marketing

<u>Distributor:</u>
University of British Columbia
Press

Director: Norma Gutteridge (492-0717; E-mail: ngutteri)
Editorial: Mary Mahoney-Robson (492-0718; E-mail: mmahoney)
Marketing: Philippa Cole (492-3662; E-mail: pcole)

Full Member
Established: 1969
Title output 1992: 9
Titles currently in print: 136

Admitted to AAUP: 1983
Title output 1993: 8

Editorial Program
Western Canadian history, Canadian literary criticism, northern
ecology, classics, and general nonfiction. The press does not
publish juvenilia, festschriften, plays, or unrevised theses.
    Special imprints: The Pica Pica Press (for textbooks).

American Chemical Society

Publications Division
1155 Sixteenth Street, N.W.
Washington, DC 20036
(202) 872-4600
Fax: (202) 872-4615

Orders: (800) 227-5558
Telex: 440159 ACSP UI
Cable: JIECHEM
Bitnet: pubs@cas
Internet: pubs@acs. org

Director of Publications: Robert H. Marks (872-6215)
Head of the Books & Software Department: M. Joan Comstock
     (872-4564)
          Production Manager: Cheryl Wurzbacher (872-4330)
          Manager of Book Acquisitions: Cheryl Shanks (872-4566)
          Software Editor: Nannette Butterworth (872-4378)
Head of the Journals Department: Charles R. Bertsch (872-4614)
          Manager of Editorial Office: Mary E. Scanlan (614/447-3669)
          Manager of Manuscripts Office: Yvonne D. Curry (872-6032)
Head of Publications Marketing: David Schulbaum (872-4606)
Head of Special Publications: Anthony Durniak (872-8064)
Manager of Distribution Office: Norm Favin (872-4532)
Manager of National and International Sales: William C.
     Hitchcock (872-4366)
Administrator, Copyright & Special Projects: Barbara F. Polansky
     (872-4367)

Associate Member

Established: 1876	Admitted to AAUP: 1990
Title output 1992: 51	Title output 1993: 58
Titles currently in print: 640	Journals published: 25

Editorial Program

Areas of concentration: chemistry; chemical engineering; materials science; biotechnology; environmental science and technology; history of science; and teaching aids for science teachers.

Special book series and imprints: ACS Monographs; Advances in Chemistry Series; ACS Symposium Series; ACS Professional Reference Books; Conference Proceedings Series; History of Modern Chemical Sciences Series; Profiles, Pathways, and Dreams Series; and Chemistry for the Future. The press also publishes directories relating to chemistry research projects, college faculties, laboratory facilities, etc.

Journals: *Accounts of Chemical Research; Biochemistry; Biconjugate Chemistry; Chemical Research in Toxicology; Chemistry of Materials; Chemical Reviews; Energy and Fuels; Environmental Science & Technology; Industrial & Engineering Chemistry Product Research & Development; Industrial & Engineering Chemistry Process Design & Development; Industrial & Engineering Chemistry Fundamentals; Industrial & Engineering Chemistry Research; Inorganic Chemistry; Journal of Agricultural and Food Chemistry; Journal of the American Chemical Society; Journal of Chemical and Engineering Data; Journal of Chemical Information and Computer Sciences; Journal of Medicinal Chemistry; Journal of Organic Chemistry; Journal of*

Physical Chemistry; Langmuir; Macromolecules; Organometallics; and *Chemical Health and Safety.*

Magazines published: *Chemical & Engineering News* (weekly); *CHEMTECH;* and *Today's Chemist at Work.*

The Society also distributes and publishes software of specific interest to those in chemistry and related sciences. It conducts short courses and publishes audio and video courses. In addition, the Society, through its Chemical Abstracts Division, publishes *Chemical Abstracts* in both hardcopy and on-line format; this product consists of abstracts of the world's technical chemical literature.

American Mathematical Society

Street Address:
201 Charles Street
Providence, RI 02940
(401) 455-4000
Fax: (401) 331-3842
Internet: pub@math.ams.org

Mailing Address:
P.O. Box 6248
Providence, RI 02940

Washington Office:
1527 Eighteenth Street, N.W.
Washington, DC 20036
(202) 588-1100
Fax: (202) 588-1853
Internet: msdc@math.ams.org

Mathematical Reviews Office:
416 Fourth Street
P.O. Box 8604
Ann Arbor, MI 48107-8604
(313) 996-5250
Fax: (313) 996-2916
Internet: mathrev@math.ams.
org

Executive Director: William H. Jaco
Publisher: Donald G. Babbitt
Math Reviews Executive Director: TBA
Math Reviews Associate Executive Director: Jane E. Kister
Associate Executive Director: James W. Maxwell
Associate Executive Director: Samuel M. Rankin, III
Associate Executive Director & Director of Computer Services:
     William Woolf
Director of Finance & Administration: Gary G. Brownell
Director of Marketing/Promotions: TBA
Director of Electronic Products & Services: TBA
Director of Production: TBA
Manager of Composition Services: Regina M. Girouard

Manager of Editorial Services: Antoinette Schleyer
Manager of Membership & Customer Services: Carol Ann
    Blackwood
Manager of Printing: Thomas Benedetti
Manager of Russian Translations & Acquisitions Editor: Sergei
    Gelfand
Manager of Technical Support: Ralph Youngen
Production Coordinator: Michelle M. Ogilvie

Associate Member

Established: 1888   Admitted to AAUP: 1989
Title output 1992: 67   Title output 1993: 77
Titles currently in print 1,551   Journals published: 19

Editorial Program
The Society is generally devoted to furthering and disseminating research-level mathematics.

Journals: *Abstracts of Papers Presented to the AMS; Bulletin of the AMS; Current Mathematical Publications; Employment Information in the Mathematical Sciences; Journal of the AMS; Mathematical Reviews; Mathematics of Computation; Memoirs of the AMS; Notices of the AMS; Proceedings of the AMS; Transactions of the AMS; Russian Academy of Sciences: Izvestiya Mathematics; Russian Academy of Sciences: Sbornik Mathematics; Russian Academy of Sciences: Doklady Mathematics; Proceedings of the Steklov Institute of Mathematics; St. Petersburg Mathematical Journal; Theory of Probability and Mathematical Statistics; Sugaku Expositions;* and *Transactions of the Moscow Mathematical Society,* the last eight of these being translations from Russian or Japanese.

Book series: *CBMS Issues in Mathematics Education; CBMS Regional Conference Series; Collected Works: Colloquium Publications; Conference Proceedings of the Canadian Mathematical Society; Contemporary Mathematics; CRM Monograph Series; CRM Proceedings Series; DIMACS Series in Discrete Mathematics and Theoretical Computer Science; Fields Institute Communications; Fields Institute Monographs; Graduate Studies in Mathematics; History of Mathematics Series; Israel Mathematical Conference Proceedings; Lectures in Applied Mathematics; Lectures on Mathematics in the Life Sciences; Park City/IAS Mathematics Series; Mathematical Surveys and Monographs; Mathematical World Series; Proceedings of Symposia in Applied Mathematics; Proceedings of Symposia in Pure Mathematics; Reprints from the Bulletin of the American Mathematical Society; Selected Tables in Mathematical Statistics; SIAM-AMS Proceedings;* and *University Lecture Series;* as well as the translation series *Advances in Soviet Mathematics; AMS Translations - Series I; AMS Translations - Series 2; Proceedings of the Steklov Institute of Mathematics; Selected Translations in Mathematical Statistics and Probability; Transactions of the Moscow Mathematical Society;* and *Translations of Mathematical Monographs.*

The Society also publishes an on-line database and a CD-ROM subscription based on it, provides composition, printing and distribution services for a number of mathematical journals published by other publishers, and publishes videotapes of lectures given at its meetings.

American Psychiatric Press, Inc.

1400 K Street, N.W.
Washington, DC 20005
(202) 682-6268
Fax: (202) 682-6341
Orders: (800) 368-5777
        (202) 789-2648 (Fax)

London Office:
3 Henrietta Street
Covent Garden
London, England WC2E 8LU
(071) 240-0856

Canadian Representative:
Mosby-Yearbook, Ltd.

Director and General Manager: Ronald E. McMillen
      Assistant to the Publisher: Rachel L. Platt
Editor-in-Chief: Carol C. Nadelson
      Editorial Director: Clair Reinburg
      Editorial Administrator: Stacy Jobb
      Managing Editor, Books: Pamela Harley
Journals Managing Editor: John McDuffie
      Editor, *Academic Psychiatry*: Phillip Slaney
      Editor, *American Journal of Geriatric Psychiatry*: Gene D. Cohen
      Editor, *Journal of Psychotherapy: Practice and Research:* Jerald Kay
      Editor, *American Journal on Addictions*: Sheldon I. Miller
      Editor, *Psychosomatics:* Thomas N. Wise
      Editor, *Journal of Neuropsychiatry and Clinical Neurosciences:* Stuart C. Yudofsky
Director of Marketing: TBA
      Marketing Manager: Mark Bloom
Director of Electronic Pre-Press: Jane Davenport

Business Manager: Richard E. Bardes
Operations Manager: Beth Prester
        Fulfillment Manager: Lee Adams
Customer Service Supervisor: Gregory Gilliam
Collector, Accounts Receivable: Nelia Millando

Associate Member

Established: 1981   Admitted to AAUP: 1993
Title output 1992: 36   Title output 1993: 43
Titles currently in print: 578

Editorial Program

Clinical books and monographs in psychiatry and related fields; research monographs; medical textbooks; study guides; nonfiction trade books in mental health; annual review; journals.

Special imprints: American Psychiatric Association; Group for the Advancement of Psychiatry; American Psychopathological Association.

Special series and copublishing programs: Clinical Practice Series; Progress in Psychiatry Series; Concise Guides. The press copublished *The Clinical Interview Using DSM-III-R* with New York University Press and copublishes North American editions of titles by the Royal College of Psychiatrists (UK) and the World Health Organization.

The American University in Cairo Press

113 Kasr El Aini Street   U.S. Representative:
Cairo, Egypt   Columbia University Press
(202) 354-2964
Fax: (202) 355-7565
Bitnet: (user I.D.)@egaucacs.bitnet

Director: Arnold C. Tovell (357-6888; E-mail: atovell)
        Assistant Director for Administration/Permissions
        Manager: Aleya Serour (357-6398; E-mail: aleyas)
Editorial: Neil Hewison, Managing Editor (357-6892; E-mail: rnh)
        Assistant Editor: Simon O'Rourke (357-6892; E-mail: simon)
Marketing: Atef Hoteiby, Sales Manager (357-6891)
        Distribution Coordinator: Tahany Shammaa (357-6895)
        Publicity Assistant: Nabila Akl (357-6896; E-mail: akl)
Production: Nadia Dessouki, Production Manager (357-6893)

Journals: Nabila Akl, Manager (357-6896)
Business: Laila Ghali, Assistant Director for Finance and
        Operations (357-6890; E-mail: lailag)

International Member

Established: 1960   Admitted to AAUP: 1986
Title output 1992: 16   Title output 1993: 25
Titles currently in print: 139   Journals published: 1

Editorial Program
Egyptology, Middle East studies, Islamic art and architecture, social
anthropology, Arabic literature in translation (Naguib Mahfouz
Fund). The press publishes the journal *Cairo Papers*, a quarterly
monograph series in social studies.

Special series, joint imprints, and/or copublishing
programs: Numerous copublishing programs with U.S. and U.K.
university presses and other U.S. and European publishers.

The University of Arizona Press

1230 N. Park Avenue, Suite 102   Warehouse:
Tucson, AZ 85719-4140   330 S. Toole Avenue
(602) 621-1441   Tucson, AZ 85701-1813
Telex: 187167 AZU TUC UT
Fax: (602) 621-8899
Internet: jet@ccit.arizona.edu

Europe, Africa, and Middle East Representative:
William Gills, John Ramsey Marketing

Director: Stephen F. Cox (621-1441)
        Assistant to the Director: Jan Thompson (621-1441)
        Development Officer: Bonnie Kuykendall (621-1851)
Acquisitions Editorial: Joanne O'Hare, Senior Editor (621-1441)
        Acquiring Editors: Christine R. Szuter (621-1441); Amy
        Chapman Smith (621-1441; E-mail: achaps@ccit.
        arizona.edu)
        Editorial Assistant: Robyn Forkos (621-5919; E-mail:
        forkos@ccit.arizona.edu)
Manuscript Editorial: Judith Wesley Allen, Managing Editor (621-
        1441)
        Associate Editors: Alan M. Schroder (621-5814);

Alexis R. Mills (621-5915)
Marketing: Charlotte Tilson, Manager (621-9109)
      Advertising Manager: Wayne Koch (621-7918)
      Publicity Manager: Marjorie Sherrill (621-3920)
      Marketing Assistant: Ted Ellenberger (621-8656)
Design and Production: TBA (621-7917)
      Assistant Production Manager: Lisa DiDonato (621-7916;
      E-mail: lisadi@ccit.arizona.edu)
      Senior Designer: Carrie Nelson House (621-3537)
      Designer: Dennis Roberts (621-5824)
Business and Warehouse: Beth Swain, Business Manager (621-
      5815; E-mail: emswain@ccit.arizona.edu)
      Order Department Supervisor: Risé Cornelio (621-7923)
      Order Clerk: Mary Cantrall (621-5813)
      Warehouse Supervisor: Howard Lundholm (621-3289)

Full Member

Established: 1959	Admitted to AAUP: 1962
Title output 1992: 48	Title output 1993: 53
Titles currently in print: 549	Journals published: 1

Editorial Program

Specialties strongly identified with the universities in the state and other significant nonfiction of regional and national interest. Especially strong fields include the American West; anthropology and archaeology; Chicano studies; the environment; Latin American studies; Native American studies; space science; women's studies. The press publishes the quarterly *Journal of the Southwest.*

Special series: Anthropological Papers of the University of Arizona; The Anthropology of Form and Meaning; Archaeological Method and Theory; Arid Lands Development; Arizona-Sonora Desert Museum Series in Desert Research; Arizona Studies in Human Ecology; Desert Ecology Series; Documentary Relations of the Southwest; The Modern American West; New Chicano Writing; Society, Environment, and Place; Southwest Center Series; Space Science Series; Sun Tracks: An American Indian Literary Series.

The press also distributes titles from the University of Arizona Mexican American Studies and Research Center, Arizona Highways, the Southwest Mission Research Center, the Phoenix Art Museum, and CAB International.

The University of Arkansas Press

201 Ozark Avenue
Fayetteville, AR 72701-1201
(501) 575-3246
Fax: (501) 575-6044

Director: Miller Williams
    Assistant to the Director: Carolyn Brt
Acquisitions Editorial: Kevin Brock, Editor & Copy Editor
Manuscript Editorial: Debbie Bowen, Manager; Monica Phillips;
    Karen Johnson
Marketing: Elizabeth Garrett, Manager
    Publicity: TBA
    Marketing: Liz Lester
Design and Production: John Coghlan, Manager
    Assistant Production Manager: Ellen Beeler
    Designer: Gail Carter
Business: Elizabeth Hudgens, Manager
    Purchasing & Operations Assistant: Jami Coker
    Orders & Fulfillment Assistant: Tammy Edmond
    Warehouse Supervisor: Stuart Finley
    Warehouse Clerk: James Newell

Full Member

Established: 1980	Admitted to AAUP: 1984
Title output 1992: 24	Title output 1993: 26
Titles currently in print: 219	Journals published: 2

Editorial Program

General humanities: biography; short fiction; poetry; literary criticism; history; regional studies; sociology. Submissions are not invited in textbooks or children's books.

Special series: The University of Arkansas Press Reprint Series; Arkansas Poetry Award. The press also publishes the journals *Philosophical Topics* and *The Journal for Disability Policy Studies*.

Beacon Press

25 Beacon Street
Boston, MA 02108-2892
(617) 742-2110
Fax: (617) 723-3097
   (617) 742-2290
Internet: (user I.D.)@world.
   std.com

<u>Canadian Representative:</u>
Oxford University Press

<u>European Representative:</u>
Airlift Book Company

Director: Wendy J. Strothman (E-mail: wstrothm)
   Administrative Assistant to Director and Office Manager:
   Sharon Rice
Acquisitions Editorial:
   Senior Editors: Deanne Urmy (environment, nature
   writing, essays); Deborah Chasman (African American
   studies, Native American studies, gay and lesbian studies)
   Associate Editors: Andrew Hrycyna (policy, current affairs,
   philosophy) (E-mail: ahrycyna); Susan G. Worst (religion,
   regional books) (E-mail: sworst)
   Assistant Editor: Marya Van't Hul (women's studies,
   science)
Managing Editor: Carol Leslie
Marketing: Margaret Klee Lichtenberg, Director
   Publicity Manager: TBA
   Senior Publicist: Todd Berman
   Assistant Marketing Director: Laura Ayr
   Subsidiary Rights Manager: Michele Hanson
   Permissions Coordinator: Victoria Baker
   Special Sales and Exhibits Coordinator: Atissa Banuazizi
Production: Dan Ochsner, Manager
   Art Director: Sara Eisenman
Business: Tom Novak, Chief Financial Officer
   Business Operations Manager: Rebecca Verrill

Associate Member

Established: 1854
Title output 1992: 51
Titles currently in print: 347

Admitted to AAUP: 1988
Title output 1993: 55

Editorial Program
Beacon Press, the nonprofit publisher owned by the ·Unitarian
Universalist Association, publishes scholarly works for the

general reader, specializing in women's studies; religion;
anthropology; African American, Native American, and Asian
American studies; gay and lesbian studies; regional books;
education; philosophy; current affairs; the environment; personal
essays; and nature writing.

Special series and joint publishing programs: Asian Voices;
Barnard New Women Poets (with Barnard College); Black
Women Writers; The Concord Library; Men and Masculinity.

University of British Columbia Press

6344 Memorial Road
University of British Columbia
Vancouver, British Columbia
Canada V6T 1Z2
(604) 822-3259
Fax: (604) 822-6083
Cable Address:
UNIPRESS, VANCOUVER
Internet: milroy@unixg.ubc.ca

Warehouse:
8591 Fraser Street
Vancouver, British Columbia
Canada V5X 3Y1

U.K. Distributor:
Nick Esson
UCL Press

U.S. Repesentative:
Hill/Martın Associates

Director: Peter Milroy (822-3807)
Acquisitions Editorial: Jean Wilson (822-6376); Laura Macleod
    (416/690-6061)
Manuscript Editorial: Holly Keller-Brohman (822-4545)
Marketing:
    Advertising and Promotion: Berit Kraus (822-4546)
    Sales and Agencies: Julie Sedger (822-4547)
Design and Production: George Maddison (822-2053)
Business: Evie Mandel (822-8938)

Full Member
Established: 1971
Title output 1992: 25
Titles currently in print: 243

Admitted to AAUP: 1972
Title output 1993: 28

Editorial Program
Scholarly books and serious nonfiction, with special interest in
archaeology; aquaculture; Northwest Coast art; native studies;
Asian and Pacific studies; business; economics; education;

environment; fisheries; forestry; geography; geomorphology; history; Pacific maritime studies; museology; political science; sociology; urban studies; women's studies.

Special series: International Relations; Northwest Native Studies; Pioneers of British Columbia; Canadian Yearbook of International Law; First Nations Languages.

The Brookings Institution

1775 Massachusetts Avenue, N.W.
Washington, DC 20036-2188
(202) 797-6000, (202) 797-6258
Fax: (202) 797-6195
Cable Address: BROOKINST
Internet: bibooks@brook.edu

U.K. Sales Representative:
University Presses Marketing

Director of Publications: Robert L. Faherty (797-6250)
    Assistant to the Director: Renuka Deonarain (797-6252)
Acquisitions Editor: Nancy D. Davidson (797-6260)
Manuscript Editorial: Caroline Lalire, Managing Editor (797-6253)
    Editors: James R. Schneider (797-6256); Theresa B. Walker (797-6097); Deborah M. Styles (797-6261)
    Editor, *Brookings Review*: Brenda Szittya (797-6257)
Marketing: Jill Bernstein, Manager (797-6254)
    Publicity and Sales Coordinator/Permissions Editor: Beth Benevides (797-6107)
    Direct Mail Coordinator: Gail Sipfle (797-6265)
Design and Production: Norman Turpin, Production Manager (797-6251)
Fulfillment Manager: Terrence Melvin (797-6216)

Full Member

Established: 1916	Admitted to AAUP: 1958
Title output 1992: 31	Title output 1993: 39
Titles currently in print: 463	Journals published: 2

Editorial Program
Economics, government, and foreign policy, with emphasis on the public policy implications of current and emerging issues

confronting American society. The Institution also publishes *Brookings Papers on Economic Activity*, a journal, and *The Brookings Review*, a quarterly public policy magazine. Most of the Institution's books are written by resident and associated staff members employed or commissioned to carry out projects defined by the directors of Brookings research programs. However, the press does publish selected manuscripts acquired from outside authors.

The press has a copublishing program with the Lincoln Institute of Land Policy, and distributes publications of The Twentieth Century Fund Press, the Carnegie Endowment for International Peace, the Royal Institute for International Affairs, the Trilateral Commission, and the Centre for Economic Policy Research.

University of Calgary Press

<u>Street and Mailing Address:</u>
2500 University Drive NW
Calgary, AB T2N 1N4
Canada
(403) 220-7578
Fax: (403) 282-0085
Internet: (user I.D.)@ucdasvm1

<u>Courier Address:</u>
Room 816
MacKimmie Library Tower
404 University Court NW
Calgary, AB T2N 1N4
Canada

Director: Shirley A. Onn (220-2578; E-mail: sonn)
Editorial Secretary: Joan Barton (220-3979; E-mail: jbarton)
Publicity Editor: Sharon Boyle (220-5284; E-mail: sboyle)
Operations Manager: Barb Semple (220-3514; E-mail: bsemple)
Production Editor (Books): John King (220-3511; E-mail: jking)
Fulfillment Coordinator: Leslie Moore (220-7578; E-mail: lmoore)

Affiliate Member

Established: 1981
Title output 1992: 8
Titles currently in print: 95

Admitted to AAUP: 1988
Title output 1993: 16
Journals published: 7

Editorial Program
Scholarly books and journals and serious nonfiction. The publishing program encompasses a wide range of fields including: aesthetics; African studies; agriculture; American studies;

anthropology; archaeology; biology; chemistry; child care; classical studies; drama; economics; education; engineering; environmental studies; fine art; geography; history; interdisciplinary studies; international relations; law; library studies; linguistics; literary criticism; management; musicology; native studies; northern studies; philosophy; politics; psychology; religious studies; resource development; social work; travel; zoology; and the following journals: *Canadian Journal of Program Evaluation; Canadian Journal of Law and Society; Canadian Journal of Philosophy; Classical Views; Journal of Child and Youth Care; Exceptionality Education Canada;* and *The Canadian Review of American Studies.*

Special series, joint imprints and/or copublishing programs: African Occasional Paper Series; The Banff Centre for Management publications; Canadian Archival Inventory Series; Canadian Energy Research Institute publications; Canadian Institute of Resources Law publications; The Industry Canada Research Series; and Place Names of Alberta Series.

University of California Press

<u>Berkeley Office</u>:
2120 Berkeley Way
Berkeley, CA 94720
(510) 642-4247
Fax: (510) 643-7127
(510) 642-1144 (Marketing)
MCI I.D./Telex No. 650 295 9492
Cable Address: UCALPRESS
Internet:
   ucpress@violet.berkeley.edu

<u>Los Angeles Office</u>:
405 Hilgard Avenue
Los Angeles, CA 90024-1373
(310) 825-3018
Fax: (310) 206-8905

<u>New York Office</u>:
50 East 42nd Street, Room #513
New York, NY 10017
(212) 687-8340
Fax: (212) 682-8467

<u>U.K./European Office</u>:
University Presses of
California, Columbia,
and Princeton, Ltd.
1 Oldlands Way, Bognor Reg
West Sussex PO22 9SA
England
Phone: (243) 842165
Fax: (243) 842167

<u>Order Fulfillment</u>:
California/Princeton
   Fulfillment Services, Inc.
1445 Lower Ferry Road
Ewing, NJ 08618-1424
Orders: (800) 822-6657
Fax: (800) 999-1958
Customer Service:
(609) 883-1759, ext. 513

<u>California Warehouse</u>:
1095 Essex Street
Richmond, CA 94801
(510) 642-4240
Fax: (510) 215-0237

Director: James H. Clark (642-4243)
    Assistant to the Director: Valeurie Friedman (642-4244)
    Associate Director: Lynne Withey (642-5393)
    Assistant Director, Los Angeles Office: Stanley Holwitz (310/825-1809)
    Assistant Director, Journals and Electronic Publishing: Sandra Whisler (642-7485)
    Chief Financial Officer: Anna Weidman (642-4388)
Acquisitions Editorial (Berkeley): Sheila Levine, Editorial Director (Asian studies, history) (642-4246)
    Executive Editor for the Humanities: Doris Kretschmer (literary criticism, music) (642-4229)
    Executive Editor for the Social Sciences: Naomi Schneider (social science, women's studies) (642-6715)
    Sponsoring Editors: Douglas Arava (religion) (642-6178); Deborah Kirshman (fine arts) (643-7704); Mary Lamprech (classics) (642-8430); Eileen McWilliam (history, Latin American studies) (642-8244); Monica McCormick (African studies) (643-8331); Lynne Withey (South Asian studies, Middle Eastern studies) (642-5393)
Acquisitions Editorial (Los Angeles):
    Sponsoring Editors: Ed Dimendberg (philosophy, film, cultural studies) (310/825-3522); Stanley Holwitz (anthropology, Jewish studies) (310/825-1809); Elizabeth Knoll (science, history of science) (310/825-7878)
Manuscript Editorial: Marilyn Schwartz, Managing Editor (642-6548)
    Projects Editors: Dore Brown (642-4591); Erika Büky (643-8555); Laura Driussi (643-6858); Stephanie Fay (642-6733); Tony Hicks (643-9513); Betsey Scheiner (643-9792); Rose Vekony (642-6521); Rose Ann White (642-0061)
Marketing: Director, TBA (642-6684)
    Advertising Manager: Marta Gasoi (642-2649)
    Direct Mail Manager: Joan Parsons (642-5054)
    Exhibits and Text Promotion Manager: Julie Christianson (642-6682)
    New York Office Manager: Linda Norton (212/687-8340)
    Paperback & Reprint Editor: Charlene Woodcock (642-1481)

Subsidiary Rights: Dan Dixon (642-4261)
Design and Production: Anthony C. Crouch, Director (642-5394)
    Production Coordinators: Danette Davis (642-5395); Rita
    McDowell (642-9805); Fran Mitchell (642-4245); Lillian
    Robyn (642-0133); Sam Rosenthal (642-9758)
    Art Director: Steven Renick (642-6854)
    Design: Ina Clausen (642-6584); Barbara Jellow (642-0134);
    Nola Burger (643-9167)
Business: Karla Golden, Manager (642-7944)
    California Warehouse: Dave Hataye (642-8744)
    Accountant: Barbara Riley (642-4401)
    Personnel: Doris Floyd (642-5338)
Journals: Sandra Whisler, Director (642-7485)
    Journals Manager: Rebecca Simon (642-5536)
    Journals Advertising: Marge Dean (642-6188)

Full Member

Established: 1893   Admitted to AAUP: 1937
Title output 1992: 180   Title output 1993: 290
Titles currently in print: 3,300   Journals published: 31

Editorial Program

African studies; anthropology; arts and architecture; Asian studies; biological sciences; classical studies; cultural studies; film and drama; folklore and mythology; geography; history; Jewish studies; labor relations; Latin American studies; law; literary criticism and theory; literature; medicine; Middle Eastern studies; music; natural history and ecology; philosophy; physical sciences; political science; religion; Soviet and post-Soviet studies; sociology; urban studies; women's studies.

Journals: *Agricultural History; Asian Survey; Berkeley Women's Law Journal; California Law Review; Classical Antiquity; Computing Systems; East European Politics and Societies; Ecology Law Quarterly; Federal Sentencing Reporter; Film Quarterly; High Technology Law Journal; Historical Studies in the Physical & Biological Sciences; Index to Foreign Legal Periodicals; Industrial Relations Law Journal; International Tax & Business Lawyer; Journal of Musicology; Journal of Palestine Studies; La Raza Law Journal; Mexican Studies/Estudios Mexicanos; Mountain Research & Development; Music Perception; Nineteenth-Century Literature; Nineteenth-Century Music; Pacific Historical Review; The Public Historian; Representations; Rhetorica; Romance Philology; Social Problems;* and *Viator: Medieval and Renaissance Studies.*

Special series, joint imprints and/or copublishing programs: Centennial Books; Philip E. Lilienthal Asian Studies

Imprint and the University of California Publications; paperbound
scientific monographs in the fields of anthropology, botany,
catalogues and bibliographies, classical studies, entomology,
folklore and mythology, geography, geological sciences, modern
philology, Near Eastern studies, oceanography, zoology.
Submissions are not invited in original poetry or fiction.

Cambridge University Press

40 West 20th Street
New York, NY 10011-4211
(212) 924-3900
Fax: (212) 691-3239
Internet: (user I.D.)cam@
acfcluster.nyu.edu
Cable Address: CANTABER

Head Office:
The Edinburgh Building
Shaftesbury Road
Cambridge CB2 2RU
England

<u>West Coast Office:</u>
Press Building
Stanford University
Stanford, CA 94305
(415) 723-0663
Fax: (415) 723-0625

<u>Business Office and Warehouse:</u>
110 Midland Avenue
Port Chester, NY 10573-4930
(914) 937-9600
Fax: (914) 937-4712

<u>Cambridge:</u>
Chief Executive: Anthony K. Wilson
Managing Director, Publishing: R. Jeremy Mynott

<u>New York:</u>
Director: Barbara Colson (ext. 300)
Deputy Director: Richard Ziemacki (ext. 310)
Editorial: Sidney Landau, Director (ext. 400)
Executive Editor: Terry Moore (humanities) (ext. 458)
Executive Editor: Mary Vaughn (ESL) (ext. 406)
Executive Editor: Frank Smith (social sciences) (ext. 412)
Executive Editor: Richard Barling (science, technology,
medicine) (ext. 419)
Editors: Lauren Cowles (mathematics, computer science)
(ext. 438); Deborah Goldblatt (ESL) (ext. 456); Catherine Flack
(physical sciences) (West Coast Office); Alan Harvey
(computer science and mathematics) (West Coast Office);
Alex Holzman (politics, sociology, history of science) (ext.
448); Julia Hough (psychology/cognitive sciences) (ext. 450);

Florence Padgett (physical sciences) (ext. 446); Scott Parris (economics) (ext. 414); Beatrice Rehl (fine arts & media studies) (ext. 410); Robin Smith (life sciences) (ext. 416)
Royalties: Sheaver Woodfaulk (ext. 420)
Marketing: Barbara Colson, Director
Marketing Manager, Social Sciences and Humanities: Catherine Friedl (ext. 343)
Marketing Manager, ESL: Carine Mitchell (ext. 348)
Marketing Manager, Science & Math/Reference: Peter-John Leone (ext. 327)
Marketing Manager, Operations: Elaine Anderson (ext. 314)
Library Promotion: Laraine Karl (ext. 324)
Marketing Systems Analyst: Chris Richter (ext. 318)
Exhibits Manager: James Murphy (ext. 325)
Rights and Permissions Manager: Marc Anderson (ext. 352)
Sales: Joseph G. Bock, Director (ext. 356)
Production: Pauline Ireland, Production and Design Manager (Books) (ext. 460)
Production Editing Manager: Sophia Prybylski (ext. 466)
Journals: James Alexander, Director (ext. 363)
Journals Editor: Chris Fell (ext. 365)
Journals Production Supervisor: Edward Carey (ext. 353)
Journals Marketing Manager: Beverly McGrath (ext. 334)
Journals Advertising Coordinator: Elaine Rowland (ext. 324)
Personnel: Carol D. New, Director (ext. 304)

<u>Port Chester:</u>
Operations Director: Richard Milstein (ext. 124)
MIS Manager: George Ianello (ext. 109)
Acting Controller: Paul McLaughlin (ext. 108)
Order Fulfillment Manager: Janet Alberti (ext. 121)
Journal Fulfillment Manager: Joseph Hranek (ext. 128)
Assistant Inventory Control Manager: Holly Verrill (ext. 144)
Fulfillment and Customer Service Manager: Lynda DiCaprio (ext. 175)
Credit Manager: Randy Zeitlin (ext. 129)
Operations Manager: Don Frederico (ext. 152)

Full Member
Established: 1534
American Branch: 1949   Admitted to AAUP: 1950
Title output 1992: 1,174   Title output 1993: 1,241
Titles currently in print: 11,600   Journals published: 129

Editorial Program

A broad range of academic titles in the humanities; social sciences; biological and physical sciences; mathematics; music; psychology; law; religious studies; reference works; English as a Second Language; and Bibles.

The press also publishes the following journals: *Abstracts of Working Papers in Economics; Acta Numerica; The African Archaeological Review; Ageing and Society; Ancient Mesoamerica; Anglo-Saxon England; Annals of Human Genetics; Annual Review of Applied Linguistics; Applied and Preventive Psychology; Applied Psycholinguistics; Arabic Sciences and Philosophy; AIEDAM: Artificial Intelligence for Engineering Design, Analysis and Manufacturing; Behavioral and Brain Sciences; Biological Reviews of the Cambridge Philosophical Society; Bird Conservation International; The British Journal for the History of Science; British Journal of Music Education; British Journal of Nutrition; British Journal of Political Science; Bulletin of the London Mathematical Society; Cambridge Archaeological Journal; The Cambridge Law Journal; Cambridge Opera Journal; Cambridge Quarterly of Healthcare Ethics; The Cambridge Review; Clinics in Developmental Medicine; Combinatorics, Probability and Computing; Comparative Criticism; Comparative Studies in Society and History; Contemporary European History; Continuity and Change; Current Directions in Psychological Science; Development and Psychopathology; Developmental Medicine and Child Neurology; Early Music History; Econometric Theory; Economics and Philosophy; Edinburgh Journal of Botany; English Today; Epidemiology and Infection; Ergodic Theory and Dynamical Systems; European Journal of Applied Mathematics; European Journal of Phycology; European Journal of Sociology; Experimental Agriculture; Experimental Physiology; Fetal and Maternal Medicine Review; Financial History Review; Genetical Research; Geological Magazine; The Historical Journal; International Affairs; International Journal of Middle East Studies; International Journal of Technology Assessment in Health Care; International Labor and Working-Class History; International Review of Social History; The Journal of African History; The Journal of Agricultural Science; Journal of American Studies; Journal of Anatomy; Journal of Child Language; Journal of Dairy Research; The Journal of Ecclesiastical History; The Journal of Economic History; Journal of Fluid Mechanics; Journal of French Langauge Studies; Journal of Functional Programming; Journal of the International Neuropsychological Society; Journal of Latin American Studies; Journal of Linguistics; Journal of the London Mathematical Society; Journal of the Marine Biological Association; The Journal of Modern African Studies; Journal of Navigation; The Journal of Physiology; Journal of Plasma Physics;*

Journal of Public Policy; Journal of the Royal Asiatic Society; Journal of Social Policy; Journal of Tropical Ecology; The Knowledge Engineering Review; Language in Society; Language Teaching; Language Variation and Change; Laser and Particle Beams; Legal Theory; Mathematical Proceedings of the Cambridge Philosophical Society; Mathematical Structures in Computer Science; Meteorological Applications; Modern Asian Studies; Mycological Research; The Mycologist; Nations and Nationalism; Natural Language Engineering; The New Phytologist; New Testament Studies; New Theatre Quarterly; Nutrition Research Reviews; Parasitology; Personal Relationships; Philosophy; Phonology; Plainsong and Medieval Music; Polar and Glaciological Abstracts; Polar Record; Popular Music; Probability in the Engineering and Informational Sciences; The Proceedings of the Nutrition Society; Prospects; Protein Science; Psychological Medicine; Psychological Science; Psychology of Women Quarterly; Psychophysiology; Quarterly Reviews of Biophysics; Radical History Review; Religious Studies; Res: Anthropology and Aesthetics; Review of International Studies; Robotica; Rural History: Economy, Society, Culture; Science in Context; Social Anthropology; Social Philosophy and Policy; Studies in American Political Development; Studies in Second Language Acquisition; Urban History; Visual Neuroscience; Zygote.

Special imprints: Canto (trade paperbacks).

Special series, joint imprints and/or copublishing programs (partial list): Cambridge Companions to Philosophy; Cambridge Earth Science Series; Cambridge Edition of the Works of F. Scott Fitzgerald; Cambridge Film Classics; Cambridge History of China; Cambridge History of Japan; Cambridge History of Science Series; Cambridge Studies in Medieval Life and Thought; Cambridge Monographs on Mathematical Physics; Cambridge Opera Handbooks; Cambridge Studies in American Literature and Culture; Cambridge Studies in Ecology; Cambridge Studies in Mathematical Biology; Cambridge Studies in Publishing and Printing History; Cambridge Tracts in Mathematics; Cambridge Texts in the History of Political Thought; Developmental and Cell Biology Series; Cambridge Edition of the Works of D. H. Lawrence; Econometric Society Monographs; Cambridge Medical Reviews; Haematological Oncology; Neurobiology and Psychiatry; New Directions in Language Teaching; Studies in Economic History and Policy; the United States in the Twentieth Century; Studies in Natural Language Processing; Woodrow Wilson Center Press Series.

Carnegie Mellon University Press

Carnegie Mellon University
Box 21, Baker Hall
Pittsburgh, PA 15213-3825
(412) 268-6348
Fax: (412) 268-5288

Director: Gerald Costanzo
Acting Managing Editor & Production Manager: Irma Tani
        (E-mail: it12@andrew.cmu.edu)
Account Administrator: Anna M. Matyas
Assistant: Jacqueline Uytenbogaart

Affiliate Member

Established: 1972
Title output 1992: 8
Titles currently in print: 148

Admitted to AAUP: 1991
Title output 1993: Not reported
Journals published: 5

Editorial Program
Particular strength lies in the Carnegie Mellon Poetry Series. The press also publishes in art, fiction, literary criticism, music, the performing arts, and social history.

Journals: *Aris—The Journal of the Carnegie Mellon Department of Architecture; Assays—Critical Approaches to Medieval and Renaissance Texts; Theatre Three; Three Rivers Poetry Journal; Journal of Social History;* and *The Violexchange.*

The Catholic University of America Press

303 Administration Building
620 Michigan Avenue, N.E.
Washington, DC 20064
(202) 319-5052
Fax: (202) 319-5802
Internet: (user I.D.)@cua.edu

<u>Customer Service</u>:
P.O. Box 4852
Hampden Station
Baltimore, MD 21211
(410) 516-6953
Fax: (410) 516-6998
Attn: Deborah Hoerner

<u>Warehouse (Returns only):</u>
2200 Girard Avenue
Baltimore, MD 21211

Director: David J. McGonagle (E-mail: mcgonagle)
    Administrative Assistant: Marguerite Leonard
Acquisitions Editorial: David J. McGonagle (all fields)
    Staff Editors: Susan Needham (E-mail: needham); Edward
    A. Strickland (E-mail: strickland)
Marketing Manager: Val Poletto (E-mail: poletto)
Design and Production: Joyce Kachergis (Kachergis Book Design,
    100 Small Street, North, Pittsboro, NC 27312)
Journals: Gordon A. Conner, Administrative
    Assistant (E-mail: conner)

Full Member

Established: 1939	Admitted to AAUP: 1985
Title output 1992: 18	Title output 1993: 15
Titles currently in print: 289	Journals published: 3

Editorial Program

American and European history (both ecclesiastical and secular);
Irish studies; American and European literature; philosophy;
political theory; theology. Periods covered range from late
antiquity to modern times, with special interest in late antiquity
and patristics and in the medieval period. Submissions are not
invited in fiction, poetry, mathematics, the natural sciences and
related professional fields.

Special series, joint imprints and/or copublishing
programs: Studies in Philosophy and the History of Philosophy;
The Fathers of the Church: A New Translation; Irish Dramatic
Texts; Irish Drama Selections (from Colin Smythe, Ltd.). Journals
managed: *Anthropological Quarterly; The Catholic Historical
Review; The Americas.*

The University of Chicago Press

<u>Books Division:</u>
5801 South Ellis Avenue
Chicago, IL 60637-1496
(312) 702-7700
Fax: (312) 702-9756

<u>Business Office/Warehouse:</u>
11030 South Langley Avenue
Chicago, IL 60628
(312) 568-1550
Fax: (312) 660-2235

Journals Division:
5720 Woodlawn Avenue
Chicago, IL 60637-1603
(312) 702-7600
Fax: (312) 702-0172 (Marketing)
       (312) 702-0694 (Production)

U.K. Representative:
University Presses Marketing

Canadian Representative:
David Stimpson
The University Press Group

Internet Addresses: (first initial)(last name)@press.uchicago.edu

---

Director: Morris Philipson (702-8878)
    Associate Director: Penelope Kaiserlian (702-7906)
    Assistant to the Director: Virginia Allen (702-8879)
Acquisitions Editorial: Susan E. Abrams (historical, philosophical, and social studies of science) (702-7641); T. David Brent (anthropology, philosophy, psychology, psychiatry) (702-7642); Kathleen Hansell (music) (702-0427); Geoffrey Huck (linguistics, economics) (416/693-0905; E-mail: huck@vm.utcs.utoronto.ca); Vicki Jennings (physical sciences, math) (617/232-7206; Fax: 617/734-2182; E-mail: vj@world.std.com); Whitney Linder (NBER) (702-7631); Douglas Mitchell (history, sociology) (702-7639); Christie Rabke (biological sciences) (702-0468); Alan Thomas (literature, religion) (702-7644); John Tryneski (political science, law, criminology, education) (702-7648); Karen Wilson (art, architecture, classics, women's studies) (702-7633)
    Paperback Editor: Margaret Hivnor (702-7649)
    Assistant Paperback Editor: Janet Deckenbach (702-7034)
Manuscript Editorial: Margaret Mahan, Managing Editor (702-7634); Alice Bennett; Jean Eckenfels; Jo Ann Kiser; Kathryn Kraynik; Kathryn Krug; Salena Krug; John McCudden; Lila Weinberg
    Electronic Manuscript Supervisor: Jennie Lightner (702-7499)
    Production Editor: Claudia Rex (702-7495)
Marketing: Robert Oppedisano, Director (702-7717)
    Marketing Assistant: Jim Willis (702-7490)
    Sales Manager: Anna Bullard (702-7248)
    Assistant Sales Manager: Leslie White (702-7723)
    Sales Representatives: Marilyn Abel (New York); Michele Barnard (Midwest); Herbert Mitchell (Midwest); Adena Siegel (East Coast); Duke Hill (West Coast)
    International Sales: Dean Blobaum (702-7706)
    Director of Promotions: Rina Ranalli (702-3714)
    Advertising Manager: Ellen Gibson (702-3233)

Promotions Managers: Craig Gill (702-7898); Mary Jo
    Robling (702-7897)
    Direct Marketing Manager: Carol Kasper (702-7733)
    Assistant Direct Mail Manager: Stuart Kisilinsky (702-
    8924)
    Exhibits Manager: Tracy Uselmann (702-0285)
Design and Production: John Spottiswood, Manager (702-3479)
    Assistant Production Manager: Sylvia Hecimovich (702-
    7924)
    Design Manager: Joseph Alderfer (702-7654)
Journals: Robert Shirrell, Manager (702-7600)
    Marketing Manager and Associate Journals Manager:
    Patricia Scarry (702-7359)
    Assistant Journals Manager: Michele Bettis Freiler (702-
    7362)
    Assistant Marketing Manager: Casimir Psujek (702-7956)
    Advertising Manager: Tim Hill (702-8187)
    Advertising and List Rental: Cheryl Jones (702-7361)
    Production Manager: Everett Conner (702-7632)
    Assistant Production Manager: Teresa Mullen (702-7442)
    Production Manager, *The Astrophysical Journal*: Tulie
    O'Connor (753-3372)
    Special Publications Manager: Jenny K. Philipson (702-7676)
    Chief Manuscript Editor: Mary E. Leas (702-7961)
    Circulation Manager: Florence Dowdell (753-1197)
Business Office and Warehouse: Donald A. Collins, Chief
    Financial Officer (660-2200)
    Press Accountant: Ryan Knight (660-2202)
    Customer Service Manager: Carolyn Shaternick (660-2221)
    Credit and Collections, A/R Manager: Carolyn Shaternick
    (660-2226)
    M. I. S. Manager: Mark Vander Veen (660-2232)
    Distribution Center Manager: Willie Cameron (660-2238)
    Royalty Manager: Cassandra Wisniewski (660-2201)
Contracts and Subsidiary Rights: Estelle Stearn, Manager (702-7907)
    Assistant Manager, Foreign Rights: Elizabeth Davidson
    (702-7741)
    Permissions Editor: Perry Cartwright (702-6096)
    Assistant: Lisa Lucas (702-7636)
Information Systems: Bruce Barton, MIS Manager (702-7651)

Full Member

Established: 1891	Admitted to AAUP: 1937
Title output 1992: 253	Title output 1993: 297
Titles currently in print: 4,065	Journals published: 55

Editorial Program

Sociology; anthropology; political science; business and economics; history; English; American and foreign literatures; literary criticism; biological and physical sciences and mathematics; conceptual studies of science; law; philosophy; linguistics; geography and cartography; art history; classics; architecture; education; psychiatry and psychology; musicology. Submissions are not invited in fiction or poetry or in conventional textbooks.

Journals: *American Journal of Education*; *The American Journal of Human Genetics*; *American Journal of Sociology*; *The American Naturalist*; *The Astrophysical Journal*; *The Astrophysical Journal Supplement Series*; *Child Development*; *Child Development Abstracts and Bibliography*; *Classical Philology*; *Clinical Infectious Diseases*; *Comparative Education Review*; *Critical Inquiry*; *Current Anthropology*; *Economic Development and Cultural Change*; *The Elementary School Journal*; *Ethics*; *History of Religions*; *International Journal of American Linguistics*; *International Journal of Plant Sciences*; *Isis*; *Journal of British Studies*; *The Journal of Business*; *The Journal of Consumer Research*; *The Journal of Geology*; *Journal of the History of Sexuality*; *The Journal of Infectious Diseases*; *Journal of Labor Economics*; *The Journal of Law and Economics*; *The Journal of Legal Studies*; *The Journal of Modern History*; *Journal of Near Eastern Studies*; *Journal of Political Economy*; *The Journal of Religion*; *Law and Social Inquiry*; *The Library Quarterly*; *Modern Philology*; *Molecular Biology and Evolution*; *Monographs of the Society for Research in Child Development*; *Osiris*; *Perspectives in Biology and Medicine*; *Perspectives on Science*; *Physiological Zoology*; *Public Culture*: *Public Opinion Quarterly*; *The Quarterly Review of Biology*; *Signs*; *Social Service Review*; *Technology and Culture*; and *Winterthur Portfolio*; the following annuals: *Adolescent Psychiatry*; *Crime and Justice*; *International Annals of Adolescent Psychiatry*; *Ocean Yearbook*; and *The Supreme Court Review*; and the following distributed title: *Metropolitan Museum Journal*.

Special imprints: Phoenix Books (trade paperbacks), Midway Reprints (short-run paperback reprints), Chicago Original paperbacks.

Special series, joint imprints and/or copublishing programs: Publications of the Newberry Library; National Society of the Study of Education Yearbooks; National Bureau of Economic Research publications; National Museums of Canada; Chicago Historical Society.

The Chinese University Press

The Chinese University of Hong Kong
Shatin, New Territories, Hong Kong
(852) 609-6461
Fax: (852) 603-6692
Telex: 50301 CUHK HX
Cable Address: SINOVERSITY

Director: T. L. Tsim (609-6461)
    Secretary to the Director: Cherry B. B. Mui (609-6461)
    Assistant to the Director/Business Manager: Patrick T. H. Kwong (609-6507)
Managing Editor: William C. C. Ho (609-6454)
Production Manager: Kingsley K. H. Ma (609-6467)
Manager of Audio-Visual Division: Winnie C. Lai (609-6702)
Promotion Associate: Vincent W. S. Kwok (609-6508)
Business Records: W. K. Mak (609-6508)

International Member

Established: 1977	Admitted to AAUP: 1981
Title output 1992: 27	Title ouput 1993: not reported
Titles currently in print: 334	Journals published: 1

Editorial Program

Chinese studies as well as Hong Kong and Southeast Asian studies in literature; history; philosophy; languages and linguistics; art; anthropology; sociology; economics; political science; physical and natural sciences.

Special series, joint imprints and or/copublishing programs: Ch'ien Mu Lecture in History and Culture; Institute of Chinese Studies Monograph Series; Historical Material Series; Bibliography and Index Series; Centre for Chinese Archaeology & Art Publication Series; HKCER Series; Renditions Books.

The Chinese University Press also publishes dictionaries and general books in both the English and Chinese languages as well as audiovisual products.

University Press of Colorado

Street Address:
4699 Nautilus Court South
Suite 307
Boulder, CO 80301
(303) 530-5337
Fax: (303) 530-5306
Orders: (800) 268-6044

Mailing Address:
P.O. Box 849
Niwot, CO 80544-0849

European Sales Agent:
Gazelle Book Services

Director and Editor: Luther Wilson (E-mail: lwilson@
     spot.colorado.edu)
Managing Editor: Jody Berman
Marketing Manager: Peter Hammond
Design & Production Manager: Stephen Adams
Journals Manager: Stephen Adams
Business Manager: Judy Wilson

Affiliate Member

Established: 1965

Admitted to AAUP: 1982

Title output 1992: 28

Title output 1993: 32

Titles currently in print: 138

Journals published: 9

Editorial Program

Physical sciences; natural history; ecology; American history; Western history; anthropology; archaeology; regional titles; and the following journals: *Frontiers: A Journal of Women Studies; American Indian and Alaska Native Mental Health Research; Colorado Journal of International Environmental Law and Policy; Colorado Review: A Journal of Contemporary Literature; Writer's Forum; Nineteenth-Century Prose; The Emily Dickinson Journal; Victorian Periodicals Review; University of Colorado at Denver Historical Studies Journal.* Submissions are not invited in fiction, drama, or poetry.

Special series, joint imprints and/or copublishing programs: World Resources and Environmental Issues; Mesoamerican Worlds; copublishing arrangements with the Denver Museum of Natural History and the Colorado Historical Society.

Columbia University Press

562 West 113th Street
New York, NY 10025
(212) 666-1000
Fax: (212) 316-3100/9422

Business Office & Warehouse:
136 South Broadway
Irvington-on-Hudson, NY   10533
(914) 591-9111
Fax: (914) 591-9201

U.K. Office:
University Presses of
California, Columbia,
and Princeton
1 Oldlands Way, Bognor Regis
West Sussex PO22 9SA
England
Phone: (243) 842165
Fax: (243) 842167

New York City:
President and Director: John D. Moore (ext. 7118; E-mail:
     jm235@columbia.edu)
     Assistant to the Director: Curtis Bertschi (ext. 7117)
Acquisitions Editorial: Kate Wittenberg, Editor-in-Chief (history;
     political science, political economy, international affairs,
     Asian studies in the social sciences) (ext. 7119)
     Assistant Director for Reference Publishing: James Raimes
     (ext. 7142)
     Publisher for the Humanities: Jennifer Crewe (American,
     English, and foreign literature, literary criticism and
     theory, Asian literature and philosophy, film studies,
     feminist theory) (ext. 7145)
     Executive Editor: Edward E. Lugenbeel (life sciences,
     geology, geophysics, astronomy and space sciences,
     evolutionary studies) (ext. 7115)
     Associate Executive Editor: Ann Miller (gay and lesbian
     studies, art history, journalism, American studies) (ext.
     7121)
     Associate Executive Editor: John L. Michel (political science,
     social work, Morningside Books, anthropology) (ext. 7137)
Manuscript Editorial: Anne McCoy, Managing Editor (ext. 7111)
     Copy Chief: Jonathan Director (ext. 7108)
     Assistant to Managing Editor: TBA (ext. 7110)
     Chief Manuscript Editor: Joan McQuary (ext. 7138)
     Senior Manuscript Editor: Ivon Katz (ext. 7149)
     Manuscript Editor: Susan Pensak (ext. 7139)
     Electronic Manuscripts Administrator: Leslie Bialler (ext.
     7109)
Marketing: Hal Dalby, Director of Marketing and Sales (ext. 7132)
     Associate Director of Marketing: Kate Hammon (ext. 7125)

Marketing Associate: Allison Richardson (ext. 7129)
National Sales Manager: Mark Saunders (ext. 7130)
Assistant Sales Manager and West Coast Sales
Representative: Michael McCullough (ext. 7129)
Publicity Manager: Eric Brandt (ext. 7126)
Senior Publicist: Mark Fortier (ext. 7127)
Publicity Assistant: TBA (ext. 7133)
Advertising Manager: Laura Cusack (ext. 7124)
Promotion Coordinator: Seth Messinger (ext. 7113)
Exhibits & Special Sales Manager: Katherine Stebbins
(ext. 7131)
Subsidiary Rights Manager: Bob Mangino (ext. 7128)
Subsidiary Rights Assistant: TBA (ext. 7147)
Copywriter: John Wyeth (ext. 7134)
Midwest Sales Representative: Melissanne Scheld (ext. 7129)
East Coast Sales Representative: Marcus Ratliff (ext. 7129)
Design and Production: Audrey Smith, Director (ext. 7105)
Design Manager: Teresa Bonner (ext. 7140)
Designer: Linda Secondari (ext. 7102)
Macintosh Systems Manager/Desktop Publishing: George
Louis-Jacques (ext. 7106)
Junior Designer: Andrea Ratazzi (ext. 7103)

<u>Irvington</u>:
Business: Veronica F. Quinn, Chief Financial Officer (ext. 6211)
Assistant to the Financial Officer: Phyllis Belliveau (ext.
6231)
Accounting Manager: Dan Ceccarelli (ext. 6227)
Distribution Manager: Carlos Almaguer (ext. 6220)
Computer Manager: Pam Rifenburg (ext. 6233)
Benefits Administrator, Personnel Manager: Grace Dronzek
(ext. 6217)
Accounts Receivable Manager: Margaret Collins (ext. 6216)
Warehouse Manager: Dennis Murphy (ext. 6218)
Royalty Coordinator: Louise Erickson (ext. 6229)

Full Member

Established: 1893   Admitted to AAUP: 1937
Title output 1992: 185   Title output 1993: 192
Titles currently in print: 1,578 cloth; 785 paper

Editorial Program

General encyclopedias; poetry reference; geographical reference;
literary histories; and other reference works in print and electronic
form.

Scholarly works, serious general interest books, and

professional books and upper-level textbooks in the humanities, social sciences, and life sciences. Subjects include history; literary theory and criticism; European and Asian philosophy; Asian studies; American studies; film; feminist theory; journalism; art; gay and lesbian studies; anthropology; social work; political science; political economy; international affairs; geology; geophysics; astronomy and space science; and evolutionary studies. The press publishes poetry, fiction, and drama in translation only.

Special imprints: Morningside Books; King's Crown Paperbacks; King's Crown Music Press; Columbia University Music Press.

Special series; joint imprints and/or copublishing programs: Bampton Lectures in America; Contemporary American History Series; Companions to Asian Studies; European Perspectives; ACLS Lectures on the History of Religions; Neo-Confucian Studies; New Directions in World Politics; George B. Pegram Lecture Series; Radner Lectures; Records of Civilization; South Asian Institute Studies; Studies of the East Asian Institute, Columbia University; Columbia Studies of Social Gerontology and Aging; Complexity in Ecological Systems; Translations of the Asian Classics; Columbia History of Urban Life; Gender and Culture; Wellek Library Lectures; Psychoanalysis and Culture; Between Men–Between Women: Lesbian and Gay Studies; Film and Culture; Social Foundations of Aesthetic Forms.

Columbia University Press is the distributor in the United States and Canada for Free Association Books; in the United States, Canada and Latin America for Edinburgh University Press and University of Tokyo Press; and worldwide for American University in Cairo Press and East European Monographs.

Cornell University Press

Street Address:
Sage House
512 East State Street
Ithaca, NY 14850
(607) 277-2338
Fax: (607) 277-2374

Mailing Address:
P.O. Box 250
Ithaca, NY 14851
(607) 277-2338
Fax: (607) 277-2374

Order Fulfillment:
CUP Services
750 Cascadilla Street
Ithaca, NY 14850
Orders/Customer Service:
(800) 666-2211
Fax: (800) 688-2877

U.K. Representative:
University Presses Marketing

European Representative:
Trevor Brown Associates

Director: John G. Ackerman (ext. 210)
> Assistant Director & Chief Financial Officer: Roger A. Hubbs (277-2696)
> Assistant Director & Marketing Manager: Susan M. Kuc (ext. 255)
> Assistant to the Director: Mary Ellen Blish (ext. 210)

Acquisitions Editorial: Bernhard Kendler, Executive Editor (classics, literature) (ext. 229)
> Acquisitions Editor and Coordinator: Roger Haydon (politics and international relations, philosophy, political theory, history of science, Slavic studies) (ext. 225)
> Editors: Peter Agree (American politics and history, law, agriculture, anthropology) (ext. 233); Robb Reavill (science) (ext. 234); TBA (sexuality studies, Middle Eastern studies, music) (ext. 232)

Manuscript Editorial: Kay Scheuer, Managing Editor (ext. 244)
> Senior Manuscript Editors: Barbara H. Salazar (ext. 250); Carol Betsch (ext. 261); Helene C. Maddux (ext. 236)
> Manuscript Editors: Teresa Jesionowski (ext. 249); TBA (ext. 260)
> Production Editor: Elizabeth Holmes (ext. 246)

Marketing: Susan M. Kuc, Marketing Manager (ext. 255)
> Associate Marketing Manager: Linda Wentworth (ext. 256)
> Subsidiary Rights Manager: TBA (ext. 231)
> Advertising Manager: TBA (ext. 257)
> Direct Mail Manager: Lou Robinson (ext. 262)
> Exhibits Manager: Mary Lash (ext. 259)
> Permissions Coordinator: Tonya Cook (ext. 248)

Sales: Mary T. Mellow, Manager (ext. 251)

Design and Production: Richard Rosenbaum, Director (ext. 243)
> Associate Production Director: George Whipple (ext. 237)
> Production Coordinator: Arnie Olds (ext. 238)
> Designers: Milenda Lee (ext. 241); David DeMello (ext. 263)

Business: Roger A. Hubbs, Chief Financial Officer (277-2696)
> CUP Services Business Manager: Christopher Quinlan (277-2969)
> Client Services, Accounts Receivable, Royalties: Linda Bryan (277-2037)

Customer Service and Order Entry: Rosemary Manley (277-2211)
Warehouse and Shipping: Jon Austin (277-2827)

Full Member
Established: 1869; reestablished in present form: 1930
Admitted to AAUP: 1937
Title output 1992: 154   Title output 1993: 151
Titles currently in print: 2,200

Editorial Program
Serious nonfiction, with particular strengths in anthropology; Asian studies; classics; history; literary criticism and theory; nature study; philosophy; politics and international relations; psychology; veterinary science; women's studies; and Slavic studies. Submissions are not invited in poetry or fiction.

Special imprints: Comstock Publishing Associates.

Special series, joint imprints, and/or copublishing programs: Agora Paperback Editions; Ancient Commentators on Aristotle; The Anthropology of Contemporary Issues; Asia East by South; Aspects of Greek and Roman Life; Contestations: Cornell Publications in the History of Science; The Cornell Concordances; Cornell Studies in Classical Philology; Cornell Studies in the Philosophy of Religion; Cornell Series in Insect Biology; Cornell Studies in Political Economy; Cornell Studies in Security Affairs; The Cornell Wordsworth; The Cornell Yeats; Documents in American Social History; Explorations in Chemical Ecology; Food Systems and Agrarian Change; Islandica; Masters of Latin Literature; Myth and Poetics; The Natural History of Mammals; Politics and International Relations of Southeast Asia; Reading Women Writing; Rhetoric and Society; Townsend Lectures; Williams College Center for the Humanities and Social Sciences; The Wilder House Series in Politics, History, and Culture.

Duke University Press

Street Address:
905 West Main Street
Suite 18-B
Durham, NC 27701
(919) 687-3600
Customer Service: (919) 688-5134
Fax: (919) 688-4574 (Books)
    (919) 688-3524 (Journals)
Internet: tfdpress@acpub.duke.edu
Indiv: (user I.D.)@acpub.duke.edu

Mailing Address:
Box 90660
Durham, NC 27708-0660

Warehouse:
Duke University Press
Shipping Department
West Pettigrew Street
Durham, NC 27705
(919) 684-3874

U.K./European Representative:
Academic & University Publishers Group

Canadian Representative:
Lynn McClory, Cassandra Book Sales

Executive Director: Stanley Fish (687-3623; E-mail: sfish)
    Assistant to the Director: Katie Courtland (687-3657; E-mail: kcourtla)
Director of Publishing Operations: Stephen A. Cohn (687-3606; E-mail: stevec)
    Office Manager: Susan Ryman (687-3633; E-mail: ryman)
Acquisitions Editorial: J. Reynolds Smith, Executive Editor (literary and cultural theory and history: North and South America, Europe, Asia, and Africa) (687-3637; E-mail: jrs3)
    Editor: Rachel Toor (legal studies, women's history, dance history and criticism, classics, medicine) (687-3641; E-mail: rst)
    Editor: Ken Wissoker (anthropology, cultural studies, post-colonial theory, lesbian and gay studies, constructions of race, gender, and national identity, literary criticism, film, popular music) (687-3648; E-mail: kwiss)
Manuscript Editorial: Jean Brady, Managing Editor (687-3603)
    Assistant Managing Editor: Pamela Morrison (687-3630)
Marketing: Emily Young, Associate Director and Marketing Manager (687-3654; E-mail: eyoung)
    Assistant Marketing Manager: H. Lee Willoughby (687-3646; E-mail: hlwillou)
    Publicity Coordinator: Sarah Ball Damberg (687-3650)
    Assistant Sales Manager: Marc Brodsky (687-3604; E-mail:

mbrodsky)
Exhibits Coordinator: Dave Stetson (687-3647)
Subsidiary Rights and Permissions: Valerie Millholland
(687-3628)
Design and Production: Mary Mendell, Assistant Director &
Design/Production Manager (687-3627)
Assistant Production Manager: Deborah Wong (687-3629)
Graphic Designers: Cherie Westmoreland (687-3643); Brian
Luter (687-3622)
Journals: Patricia S. Thomas, Journals Manager (687-3639; E-mail:
patrish)
Journals Production Manager: Michael P. Brondoli (687-
3605; E-mail: mbrondol)
Designer & Special Projects Coordinator: Anne Keyl (687-
3620; E-mail: akeyl)
Managing Editor: Christopher Mazzara (687-3626; E-mail:
cmazzara)
Accounting Specialist: Miriam Morgan (687-3621)
Circulation and Sales Coordinator: TBA
Journals Marketing Assistant: Janet Pursell Schipporeit
(687-3636; E-mail: jschipp)
Journals Fulfillment Supervisor: Cynthia Foltz (687-3613)
Business & Book Fulfillment: Stephen M. Salemson, Assistant
Director & Business Manager (687-3635; E-mail: salemson)
Data Processing Specialist: Thomas Fenske (687-3611; E-
mail: tfdpress)
Book Fulfillment Supervisor: Margie Ferettino (687-3640)
Warehouse Manager: Margie Clayton (684-3874)

Full Member

Established: 1921　　　　　　　　　Admitted to AAUP: 1937
(as Trinity College Press)
Title output 1992: 69　　　　　　　Title output 1993: 67
Titles currently in print: 792　　　Journals published: 24

Editorial Program
Scholarly books in the humanities and social sciences, with lists in
cultural studies; literary theory and history; legal studies; gay and
lesbian studies; American studies; African-American studies;
Asian studies; Latin American history and literature; Soviet and
Post-Soviet/East European studies; cultural anthropology;
minority politics and post–colonial issues; music and dance; film
and TV; environment; resources; political science and political
philosophy; religion; and classics.
　　　Journals: *American Literature; Black Sacred Music;
boundary 2; Duke Mathematical Journal; Ethnohistory; French*

Historical Studies; Hispanic American Historical Review; History of Political Economy; International Mathematics Research Notes; Journal of Health Politics, Policy & Law; Journal of Medieval and Renaissance Studies; Journal of Personality; Mediterranean Quarterly; Modern Language Quarterly; The Opera Quarterly; Poetics Today; Positions; Socialist Review; Social Science Computer Review; Social Science History; Social Text; South Asia Bulletin; South Atlantic Quarterly; and *Southern Cultures.*

Special series, joint imprints and/or copublishing programs: Post–Contemporary Interventions; Bicentennial Reflections on the French Revolution; The Roman Jakobson Series in Linguistics and Poetics; Duke Monographs in Medieval and Renaissance Studies; Duke Studies in Political Psychology; the Collected Letters of Thomas and Jane Welsh Carlyle; Living with the Shore; Central Asia Book Series; Series Q; Constitutional Conflicts; New Americanists; *American Literary Scholarship* (annual); and Sources of Music and Their Interpretation: Duke Studies in Music.

University Press of Florida

---

15 N.W. 15th Street
Gainesville, FL 32611-2079
(904) 392-1351
Fax: (904) 392-7302
Orders: (800) 226-3822
Internet: (user I.D.)
    @nervm.nerdc.ufl.edu

<u>U.K. Representative:</u>
Eurospan Group of Publishers

Director: Kenneth J. Scott (E-mail: kscott)
    Assistant to the Director: Bennie Watson (E-mail: bennie)
Acquisitions Editorial: Walda Metcalf, Associate Director & Editor-in-Chief (E-mail: metcalf)
    Editor: Alexandra Leader
    Assistant to the Editor-in-Chief: Jenny Brown
Manuscript Editorial: Judy Goffman, Assistant Director & Managing Editor
    Editors: Deidre Bryan, Michael Senecal (E-mail: senecal)
Marketing: James Denton, Assistant Director & Marketing Manager (E-mail: denton)
    Marketing Associate: Lisbeth Kent (E-mail: kent)
    Exhibits Manager: Cindy Tomas
Design and Production: Lynn Werts, Assistant Director &

Production Manager (E-mail: werts)
Design Director: Larry Leshan
Production Editor: Nicole Sorenson
Business: Ben Layfield, Associate Director & Business Manager
Warehouse and Shipping Manager: Charles Hall

Full Member

Established: 1945

Admitted to AAUP: 1950

Title output 1992: 47

Title output 1993: 50

Titles currently in print: 631

Editorial Program

Floridiana; Southeastern archaeology; international affairs; contemporary Latin America; the Caribbean; the Middle East; Africa; southern history and culture; Native Americans; folklore; postmodern literary criticism and theory; philosophy; women's studies; ethnicity; natural history; humanities; medieval studies; poetry. Submissions are not invited in prose fiction or physical sciences.

Fordham University Press

Street Address:
2546 Belmont Avenue
Bronx, NY 10458-5172
(718) 817-4795
Fax: (718) 817-4785

Mailing Address:
University Box L
Bronx, NY 10458-5172

U.K. Representative:
Eurospan Group of Publishers

Canadian Representative:
Scholarly Book Services, Inc.

Director: Saverio Procario (817-4790)
Acquisitions Editorial: Mary Beatrice Schulte, Executive Editor
(817-4787)
Marketing Assistant: Margaret Van Cott (817-4782)
Production Editor: Loomis Mayer (817-4788)
Business Office: Margaret M. Noonan, Office Manager (817-4780)

Full Member

Established: 1907

Admitted to AAUP: 1938

Title output 1992: 26

Title output 1993: 22

Titles currently in print: 180   Journals published: 1

Editorial Program
Fordham University Press publishes primarily in the humanities
and the social sciences, with emphasis on the fields of philosophy,
theology, history, classics, economics, sociology, psychology, law,
and literature as well as the fine arts. Additionally, it publishes
books focusing on the metropolitan New York region, as well as
books of interest to the general public. The following journal is
also published: *Traditio: Studies in Ancient and Medieval History,
Thought, and Religion.*
     Special imprints: Rose Hill Books.
     Special series, joint imprints and/or copublishing
programs: Sleepy Hollow Press (distribution and copublication);
Istituto della Enciclopedia Italiana (distribution and
copublication); The Irish in the Civil War Series; The Philosophy
Series; American Philosophy Series; Perspectives in Continental
Philosophy Series; Moral Philosophy and Moral Theology Series;
Creighton University Press (distribution).

Gallaudet University Press

800 Florida Avenue, N.E.
Washington, DC 20002-3695
(202) 651-5488
Toll-free: (800) 451-1073
Fax: (202) 651-5489

Director: Elaine Costello (651-5488)
Editorial: Ivey Pittle Wallace, Managing Editor (651-5662)
Marketing: Dan Wallace, Coordinator (651-5661)
Sales: Barbara Olmert, Direct Marketing Coordinator (651-5380)
     Customer Service Supervisor: Joyce Wagner (651-5488)
     Sales Coordinator: Karen Fisanich (651-5488)
Design and Production: Mary Ellen Carew, Coordinator
     (651-5429, fax only)
Business: Regina Martin, Coordinator (651-5380)

Affiliate Member
Established: 1980   Admitted to AAUP: 1983
Title output 1992: 9   Title output 1993: 6
Titles currently in print: 140

Scholarly books and serious nonfiction in the following areas as they are related to hearing loss and deafness: linguistics, sign language, law, history, education, audiology, speech pathology, gerontology, medicine, and literature. Also, both instructional and fictional children's works.

Special imprints: Kendall Green Publications (children's works) and Clerc Books (instructional materials).

Georgetown University Press

Office Address:
3619 O Street, N.W.
Washington, DC 20007
(202) 687-5889
Fax: (202) 687-6340
Internet: (user I.D.)@guvax.
georgetown.edu

Order Address:
P.O. Box 4866
Hampden Station
Baltimore, MD 21211-4866
(410) 516-6995
Fax: (410) 516-6998

Director: John Samples (687-5912; E-mail: samplesj)
Marketing: Gail Grella, Director (687-5641; E-mail: grellag)
Production Manager: Patricia Rayner (687-6251; E-mail: raynerp)
Office Manager: Christine Quigley (687-5889; E-mail: cquigley)

Full Member

Established: 1964

Admitted to AAUP: 1986

Title output 1992: 12

Title output 1993: 19

Titles currently in print: 116

Journals published: 2

Editorial Program

Languages and linguistics, especially Romance linguistics; applied ethics; international affairs; public policy.

The press also publishes *The Annual of the Society of Christian Ethics* and the annual *Georgetown University Round Table on Languages and Linguistics*.

University of Georgia Press

Office Address:
330 Research Drive
Athens, GA 30602-4901
(706) 369-6130
Internet: ugapress@uga.cc.
    uga.edu
Indiv: (user I.D.)@uga.cc.
    uga.edu

Warehouse Address:
Whitehall Road
Athens, GA 30602-6427

Orders and Customer Service:
(706) 369-6163
Fax: (706) 369-6131

Canadian Representative:
Scholarly Book Services, Inc.

Europe, Middle East, Africa:
Eurospan Group of Publishers

Director: Malcolm L. Call (369-6139; E-mail: mlcall)
    Associate Director: Karen K. Orchard
    Assistant Directors: Charles J. Apostolik (Business); Sandra
    Strother Hudson (Design & Production)
Acquisitions Editorial: Karen K. Orchard, Executive Editor (369-
    6143; E-mail: korchard)
    Paperbacks Editor: Laura Sutton (369-6145; E-mail: lsutton)
    Assistant Acquisitions Editor: Molly Thompson (369-6142;
    E-mail: mthomp)
    Editorial Assistant (permissions, poetry and fiction
    competitions): Jane Kobres (369-6140; E-mail: jkobres)
Manuscript Editorial: Managing Editor: TBA (369-6136)
    Assistant Managing Editor: Matt Brook (369-6135; E-mail:
    mbrook)
    Project Editors: Kelly Caudle (369-6137; E-mail: kcaudle);
    Kim Cretors (369-6138; E-mail: kcretors)
Marketing: David Des Jardines, Manager (369-6158)
    Publicity: Tom Payton (369-6160; E-mail: tpayton)
    Rights and Contracts: Laura Sutton (369-6145; E-mail:
    lsutton)
    Advertising and Awards: Susan Brook (369-6161; E-mail:
    sbrook)
    Designer: Anne Richmond Boston (369-6159; E-mail:
    arboston)
Design and Production: Sandra Strother Hudson, Manager (369-
    6154)
    Assistant Production Manager and Designer: Kathi Dailey
    (369-6152; E-mail: kldailey)
    Electronic Prepress Coordinator and Designer: Walton
    Harris (369-6155; E-mail: wwharris)

Production Coordinators and Designers: Betty P. McDaniel (369-6151; E-mail: bpmcdan); Erin Kirk New (369-6150; E-mail: ekirknew)
Business: Charles J. Apostolik, Manager (369-6134; E-mail: cja)
  Accounts Receivable/Credit & Collections: Phyllis Wells (369-6146)
  Customer Service: Joelyn Heslep (369-6163; E-mail: jheslep)
  Warehouse Manager: Ray Antwine (542-9279)

Full Member

Established: 1938	Admitted to AAUP: 1940
Title output 1992: 82	Title output 1993: 79
Titles currently in print: 686	

Editorial Program

General scholarly nonfiction with particular interests in American and Southern literature; biography and memoir; literary nonfiction; American history; medieval and renaissance studies; eighteenth-century studies; folklore; material culture; American studies; women's studies; civil rights; legal history; African-American studies; Latin American studies; critical theory & film; popular culture and cultural criticism; photography; anthropology; natural history and life sciences; environmental ethics; and regional trade titles.

Special series, joint imprints and/or copublishing programs: Associated Writing Programs Award for Creative Nonfiction; Atlanta Historical Society Series; Brown Thrasher Books; The Chaucer Library; Contemporary Poetry Series; Flannery O'Connor Award for Short Fiction; Georgia Southern University Averitt Lecture Series; Mercer University Lamar Lectures; Proceedings of the J. Lloyd Eaton Conference on Science Fiction and Fantasy Literature; Proceedings of the Southern Anthropological Society; South Atlantic Modern Language Association Award; Southern Voices from the Past: Women's Letters, Diaries, and Writings; The Spirit of the Laws; Studies in the Legal History of the South; United States and the Americas Series; The University of Georgia Humanities Center Series on Science and the Humanities; The Works of Tobias Smollett; Wormsloe Foundation Publication Series.

Distributor for the Georgia Humanities Council, the Morris Museum of Art, and Golden Coast Books.

Georgia State University Business Press

Street Address:
35 Broad Street
Suite 424
Atlanta, GA 30303
(404) 651-4253
Fax: (404) 651-4256
Internet: (user I.D.)@gsusgiz.gsu.edu

Mailing Address:
University Plaza
Atlanta, GA 30303-3093

Director: R. Cary Bynum (651-4258; E-mail: bpurcb)
Acquisitions Editorial: Carolyn P. Neal, Senior Editor (651-4263; E-mail: bpucpn)
Manuscript Editorial: Margaret F. Stanley, Managing Editor (651-4262; E-mail: bpupfs)
    Editorial Assistant: Jennifer W. DeLaune (651-4261; E-mail: bpujwd)
Marketing: Michal N. Yanson, Manager (651-4260; E-mail: bpumny)
    Project Coordinator: Dianne E. Farmer (651-4255; E-mail: bpudef)
Design and Production: James M. Kerr (651-4265; E-mail: bpujmk)
Business: Gerald B. Garrett, Fulfillment Supervisor (651-4252; E-mail: bpugbg)

Affiliate Member

Established: 1975

Title output 1992: 10

Titles currently in print: 145

Admitted to AAUP: 1992

Title ouput 1993: 10

Journals published: 1

Editorial Program

Scholarly and applications-oriented books, research monographs, and software, with special emphasis in the business sciences, e.g., accounting, decision sciences, economics, finance, insurance, management, and marketing, but also including counseling/psychology, healthcare, history, law, reference/information, and urban studies.

Special series, joint imprints and/or copublishing programs: Individual and the Future of Organizations Series; Business Strategy Series; Future of Private Enterprise Series; Center for the Study of Regulated Industry Series; Self-Study Series; and a contractual arrangement with the American Marketing Association for editing of *Marketing Management*.

J. Paul Getty Trust Publications

Street Address:
401 Wilshire Boulevard
Suite 850
Santa Monica, CA 90401-1455
(310) 395-0388
Fax: (310) 395-0461
Internet: (user I.D.)@getty.edu

Orders (U.S. & Canada):
Distribution Center
Box 2112
Santa Monica, CA 90407-2112
Customer Service and
Credit Card Orders: (800) 223-3431
Fax: (310) 453-7966

Project development and editorial functions are managed by the individual Getty programs listed below:

The Getty Art History Information Program
> Publication Projects Manager: Howard Batchelor (395-1025; E-mail: hbatchelor)

The Getty Center for Education in the Arts
> Manager of Publications: Kathy Talley-Jones (451-6505; E-mail: ktalleyjones)

The Getty Center for the History of Art and Humanities
> Assistant Director, Publications: Julia Bloomfield (458-9811; E-mail: jbloomfield)

The Getty Conservation Institute
> Director: Miguel Angel Corzo (822-2299; E-mail: mcorzo)
> Production Coordinator: Dinah Berland (822-2299; E-mail: dberland)

The J. Paul Getty Museum
> Publisher: Chris Hudson (459-7611; E-mail: chudson)
> Managing Editor: Mark Greenberg (459-7611; E-mail: mgreenberg)

Publication Services Department:
> Director: Richard R. Kinney (451-6506; E-mail: dkinney)
> Design Manager: Deenie Yudell (451-6508; E-mail: dyudell)
> Production Manager: Karen Schmidt (451-6504; E-mail: kschmidt)
> Marketing Manager: Patrick Callahan (451-6536; E-mail: pcallahan)

Associate Member

Established: 1983

Title output 1992: 15

Titles currently in print: 153

Admitted to AAUP: 1989

Title output 1993: 17

Journals published: 3

Editorial Program
Scholarly works on the visual arts: architecture, art education, conservation, and history of art and the humanities. The J. Paul Getty Museum publishes in areas related to its collections, specifically: Antiquities, Decorative Arts, Drawings, Manuscripts, Paintings, Photographs and Sculpture.

Journals published: *The J. Paul Getty Museum Journal* (annual); *Art and Archaeology Technical Abstracts; Res: Anthropology and Aesthetics.*

Harvard University Press

79 Garden Street
Cambridge, MA 02138-1499
(617) 495-2600
Customer Service:
(800) 448-2242
(617) 495-2480/2577

London Office:
Harvard University Press
Fitzroy House
11 Chenies Street
London WC1E 7ET, England
(071) 306-0603
Fax: (071) 306-0604

Fax: (617) 495-5898 (General)
(617) 496-4677 (Editorial & Dir. Off.)
(800) 962-4983 (Customer Service, U.S.)
(617) 495-8924 (Customer Service, Intl.)
(617) 496-2667 (Production)
(617) 496-2550 (Marketing)
PUBNET, SAN: 200-2043
Internet: (user I.D.)@harvarda.harvard.edu

Director: William P. Sisler (495-2601; E-mail: wsisler)
Executive Administrator, Office of the Director and Human Resources: Susan J. Seymour (495-2602; E-mail: seymour)
Copyright and Permissions Manager: TBA
Subsidiary Rights Manager: Stephanie Gouse (495-2603)
Acquisitions Editorial: Aïda D. Donald, Assistant Director and Editor-in-Chief (495-4703)
Executive Editors: Lindsay Waters (humanities, esp. literary criticism, philosophy) (495-2835; E-mail: lwaters); Michael G. Fisher (science and medicine) (495-2674; E-mail: mfisher); Joyce Seltzer (history and contemporary affairs) (212/337-0280 Tel.; 212/337-0259 Fax)
Acquisitions Editors: Michael Aronson (social sciences, esp. law and economics) (495-1837; E-mail: aronson); Margaretta L. Fulton (humanities) (495-8122); Angela von der Lippe

(behavioral science and neuroscience) (495-0486)
Manuscript Editorial: Jennifer Snodgrass, Managing Editor
        (495-1846; E-mail: edwing)
Marketing: Paul Adams, Marketing Director (495-4710)
        Advertising Manager: Denise Waddington (495-4712)
        Promotion Manager: Sheila Barrett (495-2618)
        Exhibits and Export Sales Manager: William Beard (495-
        2650)
        Publicity Director: Claire Silvers (495-4713)
        Sales Manager: Chris Palma (495-2606)
Design and Production: John Walsh, Assistant Director for Design
        and Production (495-2623)
        Art Director: Marianne Perlak (495-2667)
Business: William A. Lindsay, Assistant Director & Chief
        Financial Officer (495-2613: E-mail: bill))
        Accountant: Fred Waters (495-4868)
        Credit Manager: William O'Donnell (496-1345)
        Customer Services Manager: Joan O'Donnell (495-2661; E-
        mail: jco)
London Office: Ann Sexsmith, Manager

Full Member

Established: 1913   Admitted to AAUP: 1937
Title output 1992: 124   Title output 1993: 119
Titles currently in print: 2,800

Editorial Program

Scholarly books and serious works of general interest in the
humanities, the social and behavioral sciences, the natural
sciences, and medicine. The press does not normally publish
poetry, fiction, festschriften, memoirs, symposia, or unrevised
doctoral dissertations.

Special imprints: The Belknap Press.

Special series, joint imprints and/or copublishing
programs: The Adams Papers; American Foreign Policy Library;
Ailsa Mellon Bruce Studies in American Art; Cognitive Science
Series; Developing Child Series; W.E.B. DuBois Lectures; Godkin
Lectures; Harvard Armenian Texts and Studies; Harvard Books in
Biology; Harvard Books in Biophysics; Harvard Books on
Astronomy; Harvard Center for International Affairs; Harvard
East Asian Series; Harvard Economic Studies; Harvard English
Studies; Harvard Film Studies; Harvard Historical Monographs;
Harvard Historical Studies; Harvard Judaic Monographs; Harvard
Middle Eastern Studies; Harvard Monographs in the History of
Science; Harvard Oriental Series; Harvard Political Studies;
Harvard Publications in Music; Harvard Slavic Monographs;

Harvard Studies in American-East Asian Relations; Harvard
Studies in Business History; Harvard Studies in Classical
Philology; Harvard Studies in Comparative Literature; Harvard
Studies in Cultural Anthropology; Harvard Studies in Urban
History; Publications of the Harvard-Yenching Institute; Harvard-
Yenching Institute Studies; Oliver Wendell Holmes Lectures;
Interpretations of Asia Series; Carl Newell Jackson Lectures;
William James Lectures; John Harvard Library; Publications of the
Joint Center for Urban Studies; Language and Thought Series;
Loeb Classical Library; Loeb Classical Monographs; Martin Classical
Lectures; Charles Eliot Norton Lectures; Paperbacks in Art History;
Questions of Science; Revealing Antiquity Series; Russian
Research Center Studies; Source Books in the History of the
Sciences; Studies in Cultural History; Twentieth Century Fund
Books/Reports; Wertheim Publications in Industrial Relations;
William E. Massey, Sr. Lectures in the History of American
Civilization.

The press distributes publications of Harvard University's
Center for Middle Eastern Studies, Center for Jewish Studies,
Council on East Asian Studies, Institute for International
Development, Korea Institute, Peabody Museum of Archaeology
and Ethnology, and the Ukrainian Research Institute. It also
distributes for the Jewish Theological Seminary.

University of Hawaii Press

2840 Kolowalu Street
Honolulu, HI 96822-1888
(808) 956-8257
(800) 956-2840
Fax: (808) 988-6052
Fax: (808) 988-7811
Internet: (user I.D.)@uhunix.
    uhcc.hawaii.edu

<u>Warehouse Address:</u>
99-1422 Koaha Place
Aiea, HI 96701

<u>Orders:</u>
(800) 956-2840
(808) 956-8255

Director: William H. Hamilton (956-8257; E-mail: hamilton)
    Secretary to the Director: Agnes Hiramoto
    Computer Operations Manager: Wanda China (956-6227; E-
    mail: wchina)
Acquisitions Editorial: Iris Wiley, Executive Editor (Hawaiiana,
    natural history, children's books) (956-8696)
    Acquisitions Editors: Patricia Crosby (East Asian history,
    social sciences, art history, religion) (956-6209);

Pamela Kelley (Pacific studies, Southeast Asian studies)
(956-6207); Sharon Yamamoto (philosophy, literature, Asian
American studies) (956-6210)
Editorial Assistant: Ann James (956-8694)
Manuscript Editorial:
Managing Editors: Cheri Dunn (956-8695), Sally Serafim
(956-6208)
Marketing: Manager TBA (956-6417)
Exhibits Manager: Nini Dinmore (956-6374)
Publicity and Promotion Manager: Steven Hirashima (956-
8698)
Direct Mail Manager: Stephanie Chun (956-6426)
Design and Production: Janet Heavenridge, Manager (956-8275)
Designers: Kenneth Miyamoto, Paula Newcomb
Production Editors: Paul Herr, Lucille Aono, Santos Barbasa
Typesetting: Cindy Chun, Mary Young
Fiscal Support Specialist: Terri Miyasato
Journals: JoAnn Tenorio, Manager (956-8873; E-mail: tenorio)
Production Editors: Keith Leber, Shirley Samuelson
Advertising/Marketing Manager: Ann Ludeman (956-6790)
Subscriptions: Lori-Lee Kalama (956-8833)
East-West Export Books: Royden Muranaka, International Sales
Manager (956-8830)
Order Processing: Brenda Batt
Business: Kay Kimura, Manager (956-8255; E-mail: kkimura)
Credit Manager: Lorraine Nitta
Order Processing: Doris Shiraishi, Alice Hawes
Warehousemen: David Nishimura, Kyle Nakata, Clifford
Newalu

Full Member

Established: 1947   Admitted to AAUP: 1951
Title output 1992: 60   Title output 1993: 63
Titles currently in print: 738   Journals published: 12

Editorial Program
Asian and Pacific studies in history; art; anthropology;
architecture; economics; sociology; philosophy; languages and
linguistics; literature; political science; physical and natural
sciences; and the following journals: *Asian Perspectives; Asian
Theatre Journal; Biography; Buddhist–Christian Studies; China
Review International; The Contemporary Pacific; Journal of
World History; Korean Studies; Mānoa; Oceanic Linguistics;
Pacific Science;* and *Philosophy East and West.*
Special series, joint imprints and/or copublishing
programs: East–West Center Books; Center for Southeast Asian

Studies (Kyoto University); Kolowalu Books; Korean Studies;
Oceanic Linguistics Special Publications; PALI Language Texts;
Pacific Islands Monographs; Harold L. Lyon Arboretum; Hawaii
Chinese History Center; Society for Asian Comparative
Philosophy Series; Kuroda Institute Studies in East Asian
Buddhism; Hawaiian Historical Society Publications; State
Foundation on Culture and the Arts Publications; Research
Corporation of the University of Hawaii; School of Hawaiian,
Asian and Pacific Studies, South Sea Books.

Howard University Press

1240 Randolph Street, N.E.
Washington, DC 20017
(202) 806-4935
Fax: (202) 806-4946

<u>Warehouse Address:</u>
220 Girard Avenue
Baltimore, MD 21211

Director: Edwin Gordon (806-4939)
    Assistant Director/Business Manager: William S. Mayo
    (806-4940)
Acquisitions and Manuscript Editorial: Edwin Gordon
    Managing Editor: Renee Mayfield (806-4944)
    Senior Editors: Fay Acker; Ruby Essien (806-4945)
Marketing: Edwin Gordon
    Publicity and Promotions Specialist: Dedra Owens (806-4941)
Design and Production: Catherine Cauman, Manager (806-4942)
Business: William S. Mayo, Assistant Director/Business Manager
    (806-4940)
    Accountant: James Smith (806-4934)
    Customer Service Coordinator: Venia Brown (806-4932)
    Computer Operations: Constance McKoy, Administrative
    Assistant (806-4938)
Rights and Permissions: Cynthia L. Lewis (806-4937)
Book Publishing Institute: William S. Mayo

Full Member
Established: 1972
Title output 1992: 8
Titles currently in print: 168

Admitted to AAUP: 1979
Title output 1993: 7
Journals published: 3

Editorial Program
The press welcomes the submission of any serious nonfiction in

virtually every area of scholarship. Particular focus is on African-American and African studies, humanities, communications, history, literature, and the social sciences. The press publishes the *Journal of Religious Thought*, the *Journal of Negro Education*, and the *Howard Journal of Communications*.

Special series, joint imprints and/or copublishing programs: The press publishes a trade paperback series, Howard University Press Library of Contemporary Literature, which was created to preserve works that received critical acclaim when first published but are currently out of print.

University of Idaho Press

16 Brink Hall
University of Idaho
Moscow, ID 83844-1107
(208) 885-6245
Fax: (208) 885-9059
Order Department: (800) UIPRESS
Internet: uipress@raven.csrv.uidaho

Director: Peggy Pace (885-7925)
Marketing Manager: Peg Harvey-Marose (885-5939)
Production Manager: Tamara Shidlauski (885-7564)
Business Manager: Beth Rumpel (885-6245)
Hemingway Review Editor: Susan F. Beegel (508) 325-7157

Full Member

Established: 1972	Admitted to AAUP: 1990
Title output 1992: 8	Title output 1993: 6
Titles currently in print: 75	Journals published: 1

Editorial Program
Western history; American Indian studies; regional studies; Western literature and literary criticism; nature and the natural sciences; resource and policy studies; health and fitness.

Special series, joint imprints and/or copublishing programs: Idaho Yesterdays; Northwest Folklife Series; and Northwest Naturalist Books.

The press distributes publications of the Idaho State Historical Society and the Opal Laurel Holmes editions of the Vardis Fisher Novels. The press also copublishes *The*

University of Illinois Press

1325 S. Oak
Champaign, IL 61820-6903
(217) 333-0950
Fax: (217) 244-8082

<u>Warehouse Address:</u>
P.O. Box 4856
Hampden Post Office
Baltimore, MD 21211

<u>Europe and Middle East Representative:</u>
Trevor Brown Associates

Director: Richard L. Wentworth (244-4680)
> Associate Director: Elizabeth G. Dulany (244-0158)
> Assistant to the Director, Administration: Janice Roney (244-4691)
> Assistant to the Director, Editorial: TBA

Acquisitions Editorial: Richard L. Wentworth, Editor-in-Chief (American history, African-American studies, regional books, communications, sport history) (244-4680)
> Acquisitions Editors: Elizabeth G. Dulany (Western history, religious studies, anthropology, archaeology) (244-0158); Judith M. McCulloh (music, folklore) (244-4681); Richard J. Martin (political science, sociology, law, philosophy, architecture) (244-8085); Karen M. Hewitt (environmental studies, women's studies, communications) (244-4687); Ann Lowry (literature) (244-6856)

Manuscript Editorial: Theresa L. Sears, Managing Editor (244-6494)

Marketing: David M. Perkins, Director of Marketing (244-4931)
> Sales Manager: Katherine Dressel (244-4683)
> Publicity Manager: Stephanie Smith (244-4689)
> Direct Mail Manager: Barbara Horne (244-4686)
> Exhibits Manager: Susie Warren (244-4703)

Design and Production: Raymond L. Slanker, Art Director (244-4705)
> Production Manager: Mary Lou Menches (244-4701)

Journals: Ann Lowry, Manager (244-6856)

Business: William C. Ackermann, Business Manager (244-0091)
> Office Manager: Nancy Barrett (333-3057)

Development: Judith M. McCulloh, Director (244-4681)

Permissions: Cynthia Mitchell (244-6496)

Subsidiary Rights: Susan Verner (244-4690)

Full Member

Established: 1918	Admitted to AAUP: 1937
Title output 1992: 121	Title output 1993: 114
Titles currently in print: 1,500	Journals published: 12

Editorial Program
Scholarly books and serious nonfiction, with special interests in American history; American literature (especially twentieth century); critical theory; American music; African-American history and literature; sport history; religious studies; communications; cinema studies; law and society; regional photography and art; philosophy; architectural history; environmental studies; sociology; western history; women's studies; working-class history. The press also publishes short fiction and poetry and the following journals: *American Journal of Psychology; American Music; The Bulletin of the Center for Children's Books; Ethnomusicology; Illinois Journal of Mathematics; Journal of Symbolic Logic; The Journal of Aesthetic Education; Journal of English and Germanic Philology; Journal of the Abraham Lincoln Association; Law and History Review; Library Trends;* and *Social Politics.*

Special series, joint imprints and/or copublishing programs: Asian-American Experience; Blacks in the New World; Folklore and Society; Illinois Short Fiction; Illinois Studies in Communications; Music in American Life; Sport and Society; Statue of Liberty–Ellis Island Centennial Series; The Working Class in American History; Women in American History; International Nietzsche Studies; Creative Nonfiction; and History of Communication.

Indiana University Press

601 North Morton Street	<u>Warehouse Address:</u>
Bloomington, IN 47404-3797	802 East 13th Street
(812) 855-4203	Bloomington, IN 47408-2101
Fax: (812) 855-7931	(812) 855-4362
Telex: 272279	
Internet: iupress@indiana.edu	<u>U.K. Representative:</u>
Indiv: (user I.D.)@indiana.edu	Open University Press

Director: John Gallman (855-4773; E-mail: jgallman)

Assistant Director/General Manager: Patricia Newforth
(855-6314; E-mail: pnewfort)
Assistant Director & Senior Sponsoring Editor: Joan
Catapano (855-2756; E-mail: jcatapan)
Assistant Director for Sales & Operations: Richard
Granich (855-5366)
Acquisitions Editorial: Senior Sponsoring Editors: Joan Catapano
(women's studies, film, folklore, Black studies,
anthropology, literary theory, regional studies, cultural
history and critical theory) (855-2756; E-mail: jcatapan);
Janet Rabinowitch (Russian and East European studies,
philosophy, African studies, Middle Eastern studies, Jewish
studies, art) (855-5063; E-mail: jrabinow)
Sponsoring Editor: Robert Sloan (religious studies,
semiotics, drama & theatre, criminal justice, medical
ethics, science, history, public affairs) (855-7561; E-mail:
rjsloan)
Editor & Music Sponsor: Natalie Wrubel (music) (855-6468)
Manuscript Editorial: Terry Cagle, Managing Editor (855-5428; E-
mail: caglet)
Assistant Managing Editor: Jeff Ankrom (855-5261; E-mail:
jankrom)
Manuscript Editors: Roberta Diehl (855-2175); Jane Lyle (855-
9686); Nancy Miller (855-5262); Natalie Wrubel (855-6468)
Marketing: Sue Havlish, Marketing Manager (855-6553; E-mail:
shavlish)
Text & Electronic Promotions Manager: Rachel Stewart
(855-9137; E-mail: rastewar)
Promotions Manager & Designer: Deborah Rush (855-4415;
E-mail: drush)
Promotions & Permissions Coordinator: Lucy Palmer
Beavans (855-8287; E-mail: lbeavans)
Exhibits Coordinator: Nancy Jacobus (855-4255; E-mail:
njacobus)
Publicity Assistant: Theresa Halter (855-8054; E-mail: thalter)
Sales: Richard Granich, Assistant Director for Sales & Operations
(855-5366)
Sales Manager: Janice Wood (855-6657)
Sales Rep (Midwest): Darrin Pratt (855-6445)
Design and Production: Harriet Curry, Production Manager (855-
5563)
Assistant Production Manager: Marilla Schwomeyer (855-
6259)
Designers: Pam Albert (855-0264); Sharon Sklar (855-9640);
Matthew Williamson (855-8778)
Business: Joe L. Phillips, Business Manager (855-4901; E-mail:
jlphilli)

Assistant Business Manager for Accounts Receivable &
Customer Service: Kimberly Childers (855-4134; E-mail:
kchilder)
Assistant Business Manager for Network Systems & Order
Processing: Carol Jane Fender (855-1588; E-mail: cjfender)
Warehouse Manager: Sara Hacker-Machacek (855-4362)
Journals: Kathryn Caras, Journals Manager (855-3830; E-mail:
kcaras)
Business Manager/Journals Division: Pam Wilson (855-
9449)

Full Member

Established: 1950   Admitted to AAUP: 1952
Title output 1992: 156   Title output 1993: 166
Titles currently in print: 2,200   Journals published: 12

Editorial Program

African studies; anthropology; archaeology; Asian studies; Arab
and Islamic studies; art; African-American studies; cultural and
critical theory; environment and ecology; film; folklore; history;
Jewish studies; linguistics; literary criticism; medical ethics;
Middle East studies; military studies; music; philanthropy;
philosophy; politics and international relations; public policy;
religious studies; science; semiotics; criminal justice; drama and
theatre; Russian and East European studies; state and regional
studies; translations; Victorian studies; women's studies; and the
following journals: *Camera Obscura: A Journal of Feminism and
Film Theory; Journal of Women's History; Hypatia; Differences: A
Journal of Feminist Cultural Studies; Discourse: Journal for
Theoretical Studies in Media and Culture; Philanthropic Studies
Index; Contention: Debates in Society, Culture and Science;
Victorian Studies; Jewish Social Studies: History, Culture, and
Society; Research in African Literatures; Religion and American
Culture;* and *History and Memory.* Submissions are not invited in
fiction and poetry.
    Special imprints: Midland Books (paperbacks).
    Special series, joint imprints and/or copublishing
programs: Advances in Semiotics; African Systems of Thought;
America Since World War II; American West in the Twentieth
Century; Arts and Politics of the Everyday; Blacks in the Diaspora;
Caribbean and Latin American Studies; Chinese Literature in
Translation; Drama and Performance Studies; Everywoman:
Studies in History, Literature and Culture; Folkloristics; Folklore
Studies in Translation; Folklore Today; Indiana–Michigan Series
in Russian and East European Studies; Indiana Series in the
Philosophy of Technology; Indiana Series in the Philosophy of

Religion; Indiana Series in Arab and Islamic Studies; Indiana Studies in Biblical Literature; Interdisciplinary Studies in History; International African Library; International Women Filmmakers; Jewish Literature and Culture; Jewish Political and Social Studies; The Library of Indiana Classics; Medical Ethics; Midwestern History and Culture; Minorities in Modern America; The Modern Jewish Experience; Music Scholarship and Performance; Peirce Studies; Public Affairs; Race, Gender and Science; Religion in North America; Science, Technology, and Society; Soviet History, Politics, Society, and Thought; Studies in Chinese Literature and Society; Studies in Continental Thought; Theories of Contemporary Culture; Theories of Representation and Difference; Traditional Arts of Africa; Women of Letters; Unnatural Acts: Theorizing the Performative; Visions; British Film Institute, Indiana Historical Society, Indianapolis Museum of Art, and Cleveland Museum of Art Publications.

University of Iowa Press

Editorial Offices:
119 West Park Road
100 Kuhl House
Iowa City, IA 52242-1000
(319) 335-2000
Fax: (319) 335-2055
Internet: (user I.D.)@uiowa.edu

Order Department:
100 Oakdale Campus
M105 OH
Iowa City, IA 52242-5000
(319) 335-4645
Fax: (319) 335-4039

U.K./European Representative:
Academic & University Publishers Group

Director: Paul Zimmer (335-2011; E-mail: paul-zimmer)
    Assistant to the Director: Sharon Rebouche (335-2000)
Editorial: Holly Carver, Assistant Director and Managing Editor
    (335-2013; E-mail: holly-carver)
    Manuscript Editor: Robert Burchfield (335-2022)
Marketing: TBA, Marketing Manager
    Marketing Assistants: Edie Roberts (335-2015); Carol Johnk
    (335-2008)
Design and Production: Karen Copp, Manager (335-2014; E-mail:
    karen-copp)
Business: Phyllis Hicks, Credit Manager (335-4645)

Full Member

Established: 1969 — Admitted to AAUP: 1982
Title output 1992: 33 — Title output 1993: 35
Titles currently in print: 306

Editorial Program
Literary criticism and history; short fiction; American history; regional studies; poetry; early music; jazz studies; archaeology/anthropology; Midwestern natural history; natural sciences; Victorian studies; history of photography; aviation history; biography/autobiography; women's studies.

Special series, joint imprints and/or copublishing programs: Iowa Short Fiction Award Series; Iowa Poetry Series; Bur Oak Books; The Iowa Series in North American Autobiography; The American Land and Life Series; Studies in Theatre History and Culture; The Iowa Száthmary Culinary Arts Series.

The Iowa State University Press

2121 South State Avenue
Ames, IA 50014
(515) 292-0140
Fax: (515) 292-3348

Director: Linda Speth
    Assistant to the Director: Sherry L. Johnson
Acquisitions Editorial: Bill Silag, Editor-in-Chief
    Acquisitions Editor: Gretchen Van Houten
Manuscript Editorial: Carla Tollefson, Managing Editor
    Editors: Lynne Bishop, Jane Zaring
Marketing: Sally Clayton, Sales Manager
    Administrative Assistant/Marketing: Julie Plahn
    Direct Mail: Susan Lucke
    Publicity Coordinator: Beverly Fisher
Design and Production: Robert A. Campbell, Production Manager
    Designer: Kathy Walker
    Composition Supervisor: Robert W. Cook
Business: Brenda O'Neall-Smith, Chief Financial Officer
    Chief Accountant: Sue Johnson
    EDP: Judy Brown

Full Member

Established: 1924
Title output 1992: 44
Titles currently in print: 734

Admitted to AAUP: ca. 1945
Title output 1993: 61

Editorial Program

Aviation; agriculture; journalism; design; engineering; home economics; education; sciences and humanities; veterinary medicine; regional history. Submissions are not invited in poetry or fiction.

The press is also publisher for the Center for Agriculture and Economic Development; North Central Regional Center for Rural Development; and the Center for Agriculture and Rural Development.

The Jewish Publication Society

1930 Chestnut Street
Philadelphia, PA 19103
(215) 564-5925
Fax: (215) 564-6640

<u>Israeli Address:</u>
2 Yavetz Street
Jerusalem, Israel
Phone/Fax: (02) 248 237

<u>Orders:</u>
JPS
O'Neill Highway
Dunmore, PA 18512
(800) 355-1165
Fax: (717) 348-9297

<u>Warehouse Address:</u>
JPS
600 Sanders Street
Scranton, PA 18506

<u>European Representative:</u>
Kuperard Ltd., London

President, Board of Trustees: D. Walter Cohen
Executive Vice President: Rabbi Michael A. Monson
Editor-in-Chief: Ellen Frankel
Editorial and Publication Committee: Chaim Potok, Chair
Editor of Children's Books: Bruce Black
Managing Editor: Diane Zuckerman
Production Manager: David Murphy
Director of Publishing Operations: Jean Sue Libkind
Telemarketing and Exhibits Coordinator: Dolores Verbit
Director of Marketing: Donna Shear Weber
Director of Membership Services: Delores Kaplan
Bookkeeper: Melveeta Grooms
Publisher's Representative, Israel: Shimon Lipsky

Sales Representative, Israel: Uri Rucham, Sefer ve Sefel

Associate Member

Established: 1888 — Admitted to AAUP: 1993
Title output 1992: 14 — Title output 1993: 7
Titles currently in print: 175

Editorial Program

Scholarly and trade books of special interst to the American Jewish community: history, Holocaust, Israel and Zionism; fiction, poetry, belles lettres; Jewish thought, practice, Bible studies; art and photography. JPS also has a century-old commitment to quality children's books. *TANAKH, The New JPS Translation of the Holy Scriptures According to the Traditional Hebrew Text* is the standard English translation of the Jewish Bible.

JPS was founded by its membership to provide books in the English language to further the traditions and religion of the Jewish people. The Society continues to offer its own books and those of other publishers to its membership as well as distributing JPS titles through the normal channels.

The Johns Hopkins University Press

2715 N. Charles Street
Baltimore, MD 21218-4319
(410) 516-6900
Fax: (410) 516-6998/6968

<u>U.K. Representative</u>:
University Presses Marketing

<u>Distribution Center</u>:
2200 Girard Avenue
Baltimore, MD 21211

Director: J. G. Goellner (516-6971)
>   Administrative Assistant: Regina Bolduc (516-6971)
>   Assistant to the Director: Arlene W. Sullivan (Rights & Permissions) (516-6972)
>   Associate Director and Journals Manager: Marie R. Hansen (516-6981)
>   Assistant Director and Marketing Manager: Douglas Armato (516-6931)
> Acquisitions Editorial: Eric Halpern, Editor-in-Chief (literary and cultural studies, ancient studies) (516-6906)

Executive Editor: Henry Y. K. Tom (history, political
science, economics) (516-6908)
Editors: Wendy Harris (medicine and public health) (516-
6907); Jacqueline C. Wehmueller (consumer health,
pediatric medicine, history of medicine, higher education)
(516-6904); Robert J. Brugger (American history, history of
science and technology, documentary editions, regional
books) (516-6909); George F. Thompson (environmental
studies, geography) (703/433-6841); Robert Harington
(life sciences, earth and space sciences, mathematical
sciences) (516-6919); Douglas Armato (American culture,
cinema studies) (516-6931)
Acquisitions E-mail: acquire@jhuvms.hcf.edu
Manuscript Editorial: Barbara B. Lamb, Managing Editor (516-6905)
Assistant Managing Editor: Lee C. Sioles (516-6910)
Staff Editors: Carol Ehrlich, Kimberly F. Johnson,
Jane Warth, Anne M. Whitmore, Carol L. Zimmerman
Marketing: Douglas M. Armato, Marketing Manager (516-
6931)
Promotion Manager: Robert T. Oeste (516-6933)
Sales Manager: Michael Donatelli (516-6936)
Medical/Scientific Promotion Coordinator: Judy Adkinson
(516-6935)
Export Sales and Promotion Manager: Mary Katherine
Callaway
Advertising/Publicity Coordinator: Karen Willmes (516-
6932)
Publicist/Promotions Coordinator: Inger M. Forland (516-
6939)
Direct Mail Promotion Coordinator: John M. Holmes (516-
6928)
Senior Graphic Artist: Susan J. Ventura (516-6940)
Design and Production: Anita Walker Scott, Manager (516-6921)
Assistant Design and Production Manager: Sandy W.
Adams (516-6922)
Designers: Glen Burris (516-6924); Martha Farlow (516-6926);
Ann Walston (516-6925)
Business: Robert Dircks, Jr., Chief Financial Officer (516-6992)
Manager, Information Systems: Stacey L. Armstead (516-
6979)
Manager, Fulfillment Operations: William F. Bishop (516-
6961)
Journals: Marie R. Hansen, Associate Director & Journals Manager
(516-6981)
Journals Online Projects Manager: Susan E. Lewis (516-
3875)
Journals Marketing Manager: Barbara Berlin Caplan (516-

6983)
Journals Production Supervisor: Judy Lerner (516-6985)
Journals Production Coordinators: Carol Hamblen (516-6986); Rosanna Demps (516-6929)
Journals Circulation Supervisor: Alta Anthony (516-6938)
Journals Marketing Coordinator: Sandy Fleming (516-6984)
Journals Advertising Coordinator: Tara Dorai-Berry (516-6982)

Full Member

Established: 1878 — Admitted to AAUP: 1937
Title output 1992: 173 — Title output 1993: 186
Titles currently in print: 2,212 — Journals published: 43

Editorial Program

American and European history; ancient studies; biological, Earth, and space sciences; conceptual studies of science; Latin American studies; economics and economic development; environmental studies and human geography; higher education; history of science, technology, and medicine; international relations and comparative politics; literary studies; mathematical sciences; medicine and consumer health; natural history; clinical psychology and psychiatry; public health and health policy; reference books; regional books of general interest; theater and cinema studies; U. S. government; and the following journals: *American Imago; American Journal of Philology; American Journal of Mathematics; American Quarterly; Arethusa; Bulletin of the History of Medicine; Callaloo; Configurations; Diacritics; ELH; Eighteenth-Century Life; Eighteenth-Century Studies; Griffithiana; Human Rights Quarterly; Imagine; Journal of Democracy; Journal of Early Christian Studies; Journal of the History of Ideas; Journal of Modern Greek Studies; Kennedy Institute of Ethics Journal; Late Imperial China; The Lion and the Unicorn; Literature and Medicine; MLN; Modern Judaism; Modernism/Modernity; New Literary History; Performing Arts Journal; Philosophy, Psychiatry, and Psychology; Prooftexts; Reviews in American History; Theatre Journal; Theatre Topics;* and *World Politics.* The press distributes *The Henry James Review; ICSID Review; Philosophy and Literature;* and *Wide Angle.* The press also handles subscription fulfillment for publications of EBRI (Employee Benefit Research Institute), *EBRI Issue Brief* and *Employee Benefit Notes;* for the United Nations, *Development Business;* and for Princeton University Press, *Annals of Mathematics* and *Philosophy & Public Affairs.*

Submissions are not encouraged in music.
Special imprints: Robert G. Merrick Editions.

Special series, joint imprints and/or copublishing
programs: Johns Hopkins: Poetry and Fiction; Ancient Society and
History; Parallax: Re-visions of Culture and Society; Johns
Hopkins Studies in Development; The American Moment; New
Studies in American Intellectual and Cultural History; Creating
the North American Landscape; Johns Hopkins Jewish Studies;
Perspectives in Security; Interpreting American Politics; Psychiatry
and the Humanities; Studies in Atlantic History and Culture; The
Johns Hopkins/AT&T Series in Telephone History; The Johns
Hopkins Studies in the History of Technology; Studies in Industry
and Society; New Series in NASA History; The Johns Hopkins
Symposia in Comparative History; The Johns Hopkins University
Studies in History and Political Science; The Henry E. Sigerist
Series in the History of Medicine; Documentary History of the
First Federal Congress; Early English Manuscripts in Facsimile;
The Johns Hopkins Studies in Earth and Space Sciences; The
Johns Hopkins Series in the Mathematical Sciences; The Papers of
Thomas A. Edison; The Papers of Dwight David Eisenhower; The
Papers of George Catlett Marshall; The Papers of Frederick Law
Olmsted; Foundations of Natural History; Early America: History,
Context, Culture; Reconfiguring American Political History;
Revisiting Rural America; The Johns Hopkins Series in
Hematology/Oncology; and The Johns Hopkins Series in
Psychiatry and Neuroscience.

The press is publisher for the World Bank, Inter-American
Development Bank, the International Food Policy Research
Institute; is copublisher with the Woodrow Wilson Center Press;
and is distributor for Resources for the Future, Inc.

University Press of Kansas

2501 West 15th Street

Lawrence, KS 66049-3904

(913) 864-4154

Fax: (913) 864-4586

Orders: (913) 864-4155

Internet: upkansas@kuhub.cc.ukans.edu

<u>Warehouse Address:</u>

2425-B West 15th Street

Lawrence, KS 66049

(913) 864-4156

<u>U.K./European Representative:</u>
Eurospan Group of Publishers

<u>Canadian Representative:</u>
Scholarly Book Services, Inc.

Director: Fred Woodward (864-4667)
Assistant Director: Susan Schott (864-4154)

Assistant to the Director: Sara Henderson White
Acquisitions Editorial: Cynthia Miller, Editor-in-Chief (American
     history, philosophy, sociology, women's studies) (864-
     4154)
     Acquisitions Editor: Michael Briggs (political science,
     military history, law)
     Editorial Assistant: Nancy Scott
Manuscript Editorial, Design and Production: TBA
     Production Editor: Megan Schoeck
     Designer: Janet Moore
     Assistant Editor: Dorothea Anderson
     Production Editorial Assistant: Susie Albers
Marketing: Susan Schott, Marketing Manager (864-4154)
     Promotion & Advertising Manager: Cathy Evans
     Direct Mail & Exhibits Manager: Debbie Gillispie
     Marketing Assistant: Suzanne Galle
Business: Sam Giannakis, Business Manager (864-4154)
     Order Fulfillment Clerks: Majella Wilder and Christina
     Flory
     Warehouse Manager: Chris Crutchfield (864-4156)

Full Member

Established: 1946   Admitted to AAUP: 1946
Title output 1992: 39   Title output 1993: 50
Titles currently in print: 347

Editorial Program

American history; women's studies; presidential studies; political
philosophy, ethics, and moral theory; political science and public
policy; military history; environmental studies; sociology; and
Kansas, the Great Plains, and the Midwest. The press does not
consider fiction, poetry, or festschriften for publication.

Special series, joint imprints and/or copublishing
programs: American Political Thought; The American Presidency
Series; Development of Western Resources; Modern War Studies;
Kansas Nature Guides; Landmark Law Cases and American
Society; Rural America; Studies in Government and Public Policy;
Studies in Historical Social Change; U.S. Army War College
Guides to Civil War Battles.

The press distributes the Brownings' Correspondence for
Wedgestone Press and a series of natural history handbooks for
the University of Kansas Museum of Natural History.

The Kent State University Press

P.O. Box 5190
Kent, OH 44242-0001
(216) 672-7913
Fax: (216) 672-3104

<u>Orders:</u>
(800) 247-6553
(419) 281-1802
Fax: (419) 281-6883

<u>U.K./European Representative:</u>
Eurospan Group of Publishers

<u>Canadian Representative:</u>
Scholarly Book Services, Inc.

Director: John T. Hubbell
Editorial: Julia J. Morton, Senior Editor
      Assistant Editor: Linda K. Cuckovich
      Editorial Assistant: Joanna Hildebrand
Marketing: Susan L. Wakefield, Manager
      Marketing Assistant: Charlene Ende
Design and Production: Will Underwood, Manager
      Production Assistant: Diana Gordy
Journals Circulation/Secretary: Sandra D. Clark
Bookkeeper: Norma E. Hubbell

Full Member

Established: 1965
Title output 1992: 22
Titles currently in print: 159

Admitted to AAUP: 1970
Title output 1993: 25
Journals published: 3

Editorial Program

History, including military, U.S. diplomatic, Civil War, American cultural, women's and art history; Ohio regional studies; American and British literature and criticism; biography; North American (particularly Midwestern) archaeology; and the following journals: *Civil War History*; *The Midcontinental Journal of Archaeology*; and *Extrapolation*.

Special series, joint imprints and/or copublishing programs: Special Papers of *The Midcontinental Journal of Archaeology*; Kent State University Research Papers in Archaeology; The Novels and Related Works of Charles Brockden Brown; Studies in American Diplomatic History; Literature and Medicine; Translation Studies; Salmon P. Chase Papers.

Special imprints: Black Squirrel Books (Ohio and Western Reserve reprints).

The University Press of Kentucky

---

663 South Limestone Street
Lexington, KY 40508-4008
(606) 257-2951
Fax: (606) 257-2984

<u>Mailing Address</u> (Orders Only):
P.O. Box 6525
Ithaca, NY 14851

<u>Orders and Customer Service</u>:
(800) 666-2211
Fax: (800) 688-2877

Director: Kenneth Cherry (257-8432)
    Assistant to the Director: Leila Salisbury (257-8150)
Acquisitions Editorial: Nancy Grayson Holmes, Editor–in–Chief
    (literature, gender studies, African-American studies,
    American history, Appalachian studies, folklore, Irish
    studies) (257-8434)
    Kenneth Cherry (military history, political science,
    international studies, film studies, Kentuckiana) (257-8432)
Manuscript Editorial: Georgiana Strickland, Managing Editor (257-8438)
    Assistant Editor: Angelique Galskis (257-8433)
Marketing: Mary Beth Haas, Marketing Manager (257-8442)
    Advertising, Exhibits, & Direct Mail Manager: Teresa Wells
    (257-5200)
    Marketing Assistant: Delores Hiles (257-5200)
Design and Production: Wilma Lange, Production Manager (257-8435)
    Production Assistants: Katherine Shaw (257-8439); Glenda
    King (257-4669)
Business: Craig R. Wilkie, Assistant Director for Finance (257-8436)
    Accounting Clerk: Barbara Miller (257-4249)
Journals: Katherine Shaw, Manager (257-8439)
Rights & Permissions: Craig R. Wilkie (257-8436)

Full Member

Established: 1943
Title output 1992: 49
Titles currently in print: 491

Admitted to AAUP: 1947
Title output 1993: 42
Journals published: 1

Editorial Program
Scholarly books in the fields of American and European history;
military history; American, English, and Romance literature and

criticism; gender studies; political science; international studies; folklore and material culture; anthropology; African-American studies; sociology; serious nonfiction of general interest. Regionally, the press maintains an interest in Kentucky and the Ohio Valley, the Appalachians, and the upper South. The press also publishes the journal *Southern Folklore.* Submissions are not invited in fiction, drama, or poetry.

Special series: The Blazer Lectures; The Clark Lectures; Comparative Legislative Studies Series; New Books for New Readers; New Perspectives on the South; The Ohio Valley Series; The Public Papers of the Governors of Kentucky; Studies in the English Renaissance; and Studies in Romance Languages.

Louisiana State University Press

Post Office Box 25053
Baton Rouge, LA 70894-5053
(504) 388-6294
Fax: (504) 388-6461

<u>Warehouse:</u>
Printing Building
3555 River Road
Baton Rouge, LA 70803

Director: L. E. Phillabaum (388-6294)
    Associate Director: Catherine Fry (388-6666)
    Assistant Director: Margaret F. Dalrymple (388-6618)
Acquisitions Editorial: Margaret F. Dalrymple, Editor-in-Chief
    (388-6618)
Manuscript Editorial: John Easterly, Managing Editor (388-
    6618)
    Editors: Barry Blose; Gerry Anders
Marketing: Catherine Fry, Manager (388-6666)
    Associate Marketing Manager: Michael Pinkston
    Sales Manager: Claudette Price
    Advertising and Publicity Manager: Margaret Hart
    Promotion Manager: Lisa Pemstein
    Marketing Designer: Jeff Walker
Design and Production: Laura Gleason, Manager (388-5912)
    Designers: Amanda Key; Glynnis Phoebe
    Production Assistant: Shannon Sandifer
Business: William M. Bossier, Manager (388-8271)
    Assistant Business Manager: Rebekah Brown
Warehouse: James Green, Manager (388-3248)

Full Member

Established: 1935   Admitted to AAUP: unknown
Title output 1992: 61   Title output 1993: 80
Titles currently in print: 876   Journals published: 1

Editorial Program

Humanities and social sciences (with special emphasis on
Southern history and literature); Southern studies; French studies;
Latin American studies; political science; poetry; music (especially
jazz); and *The Journal of Macroeconomics.*

Special series, joint imprints and/or copublishing
programs: A History of the South; Southern Biography Series;
Southern Literary Studies; Library of Southern Civilization; W. L.
Fleming Lectures in Southern History; Papers of Jefferson Davis;
Political Traditions in Foreign Policy Series; The Miller Center
Series on the American Presidency; Pennington Center Nutrition
Series; Modernist Studies; Eisenhower Center Studies on War and
Peace; Horizons in Theory and American Culture; The Pegasus
Prize for Literature; Voices of the South.

McGill–Queen's University Press

Montréal Office: Kingston Office:
3430 McTavish Street   Queen's University
Montréal, Québec   Kingston, Ontario
Canada H3A 1X9   Canada K7L 3N6
(514) 398-3750   (613) 545-2155
Fax: (514) 398-4333   Fax: (613) 545-6682
Cable Address:
MCGILL UNIV MTL
Internet: mqup@printing.lan.mcgill.ca

U.S. Warehouse Address: U.K. Distributor:
University of Toronto Press   UCL Press Ltd.
340 Nagel Drive   Marston Book Services Ltd.
Buffalo, NY 14225-4731
(716) 683-4547

Director: Philip J. Cercone (Montréal)
        Assistant to the Director: Dorothy Beaven (Montréal)
        Administrative Assistant: Diane Duttle (Kingston)
Editorial, Montréal Office:
        Editor-in-Chief: Philip J. Cercone

Acquisitions Editor: Peter B. Blaney
Manuscript Editor: Joan McGilvray
Editorial Assistant: Joanne Pisano
Editorial, Kingston Office:
Senior Editor: Donald H. Akenson
Acquisitions Editor: Joan Harcourt
Assistant Editor: Roger Martin
Marketing: Ann Quinn, Manager (Montréal)
Sales Manager: Roy Ward (Montréal)
Marketing Assistant: Elizabeth Myles (Montréal)
Promotion Assistant: Cheryl Peteherych (Montréal)
Design and Production: Susanne McAdam, Production Manager
(Montréal)
Production Assistant: Pamela Murray (Montréal)
Business: Arden Ford, Manager (Montréal)
Treasurer: Joe Cheng (Montréal)

Full Member

Established: 1969

Admitted to AAUP: 1963
(as McGill University Press)

Title output 1992: 61
Titles currently in print: 460

Title output 1993: 70

Editorial Program

Scholarly books and well-researched studies of general interest in
the humanities and social sciences, including Arctic and northern
studies; history and political science; political economy; ethnic
studies; anthropology, especially North American native peoples;
philosophy and religion; architecture; English and Canadian
literature; economics; political economy; geography; ecology;
sociology; administrative studies; law; education; photography;
health and society; folklore; and art history.

Special series, joint imprints and/or copublishing
programs: Canadian Public Administration Series; McGill–
Queen's Studies in the History of Ideas; Canadian Association of
Geographers Series in Canadian Geography; Critical Perspectives
on Public Affairs; McGill–Queen's Studies in Ethnic History;
McGill–Queen's Studies in the History of Religion; Canadian
Research Institute for the Advancement of Women Series;
McGill–Queen's Native and Northern Series; Rupert's Land
Record Society Series; Studies on the History of Quebec/Études
d'histoire du Québec; Comparative Charting of Social Change;
McGill-Queen's Series in Health and Society; CHORA, Intervals in
the Philosophy of Architecture.

The University of Massachusetts Press

Street Address:
505 East Pleasant Street
Amherst, MA 01002
(413) 545-2217
Fax: (413) 545-1226
Orders: (413) 545-2219

Mailing Address:
P.O. Box 429
Amherst, MA 01004
Internet: (user I.D.)@umpress.umass.edu

Boston Office:
Paul Wright
c/o Graduate Studies
U. of Massachusetts at Boston
Boston, MA 02125
(617) 287-5710
Fax: (617) 265-7173

Director: Bruce Wilcox (E-mail: wilcox)
    Administrative Assistant: Christina Hammel
Acquisitions Editorial: Clark Dougan, Senior Editor
    Boston Editor: Paul Wright (E-mail: wrightp@umbsky.
    cc.umb.edu)
    Associate Editor: Janet Benton
Manuscript Editorial: Pamela Wilkinson, Managing Editor
Marketing: Ralph Kaplan, Marketing Manager
    Promotion Manager: Catlin Murphy
Design and Production: Jack Harrison, Manager (E-mail: harrison)
    Designer & Assistant Production Manager: Edith Kearney
    Heath
Business: Richard Lozier, Business Manager
    Customer Services: Rachel Shumway
    Credit Manager: Beverly King
    Warehouse Manager: David Pierce

Full Member

Established: 1964

Title output 1992: 42

Titles currently in print: 550

Admitted to AAUP: 1966

Title output 1993: 46

Editorial Program

Scholarly books and works of general interest, including American studies and history; black and ethnic studies; cultural criticism; environmental design; literary criticism; poetry and short fiction; philosophy and intellectual history; policy and politics; sociology and social theory; women's and gender studies; and books of regional interest.

Special series, joint imprints and/or copublishing programs: The Juniper Prize (poetry); A.W.P. Award Series in Short Fiction; Critical Perspectives on Modern Culture; Massachusetts Studies in Early Modern Culture; Native Americans of the Northeast: Culture, History, and the Contemporary.

The MIT Press

55 Hayward Street
Cambridge, MA 02142-1399
(617) 253-5646 (general)
(617) 625-8481 (customer serv)
Fax: (617) 258-6779 (general)
Fax: (617) 625-6660 (orders)
Fax: (617) 253-1709 (marketing)
Cable: MITCAM
Telex: 92143
Pubnet: SAN #202-6414

<u>London Office (Marketing):</u>
MIT Press Ltd.
14 Bloomsbury Square
London WC1A 2LP, England
(071) 404-0712
Fax: (071) 404-0601

<u>Warehouse Address:</u>
Uniserv, Inc.
525 Great Road
P.O. Box 1034
Littleton, MA 01460
(508) 486-3582

Director: Frank Urbanowski (253-5242; E-mail: furb@mit.edu)
   Associate Director for Operations: Michael Leonard (253-5250; E-mail: leonardm@mit.edu)
   Assistant Director for Acquisitions: Laurence Cohen (science, philosophy and linguistics) (253-1693; E-mail: lcohen@mit.edu)
   Assistant to the Director: Cathy Silton (253-5255; E-mail: csilton@mit.edu)
   Manager, Network and Information Services: Darlene Fladager (258-6783; E-mail: fladager@mit.edu)
Acquisitions Editorial: Roger Conover (architecture & design arts) (207/879-0441); Teri Mendelsohn (Assistant Editor for Philosophy, Bradford Books) (253-1653; E-mail: mendel@mit.edu); Terry Ehling (computer science and AI) (253-1672; E-mail: ehling@mitvma.mit.edu); Amy Pierce (cognitive and brain science) (252-1636; E-mail: apierce@mit.edu); Robert Prior (computer science and AI) (253-1584; E-mail: prior@mitvma.mit.edu); Ann Sochi (Assistant Editor for Economics) (253-3757; E-mail: sochi@mit.edu); Henry and Elizabeth Stanton (Bradford

Books) (802/326-4471; E-mail: stanton@uvmvm); Fiona
    Stevens (neuroscience) (212/316-2090; E-mail:
    stevens@cns.nyu.edu); Madeline Sunley (environment)
    (253-4113; E-mail: sunley@mit.edu); Terry Vaughn
    (economics & management) (253-1605; E-mail:
    tdv@mit.edu)
Managing Editor: Michael Sims (253-2080; E-mail:
    msims@mit.edu)
Marketing: Thomas McCorkle, Manager (253-3172; E-mail:
    mccorkle@mit.edu)
        Sales Manager: David LePere (253-8838; E-mail: lepere@
        mit.edu)
        International Sales Manager: Don Stanford (253-2887; E-
        mail: dstanfor@mit.edu)
        Subsidiary Rights Manager: Cristina Sanmartin (253-0629; E-
        mail: csan@mit.edu)
        Promotion and Direct Marketing Manager: Brooke Stevens
        (253-5642; E-mail: bsteve@mit.edu)
        Publicity Manager: Gita Manaktala (253-5643; E-mail:
        manak@mit.edu)
        Advertising Manager: Elizabeth Gunderson (253-5642; E-
        mail: gundeliz@mit.edu)
        Direct Mail Manager: Astrid Baehrecke (253-7297; E-mail:
        baehreck@mit.edu)
        Texts Manager: Julia Sawabini (253-5642; E-mail:
        sawabini@mit.edu)
        Exhibits Manager: Martha Henry (253-5642; E-mail:
        mshenry@mit.edu)
Design and Production: Terry Lamoureux, Manager (253-2882; E-
        mail: terryl@mit.edu)
        Electronic Publishing Coordinator: Wendy Da (253-8189)
        Design Manager: Yasuyo Iguchi (253-1961; E-mail:
        iguchi@mit.edu)
Business: Michael Leonard, Associate Director for Operations
        Accounting Manager: Cornelius Kiely (253-6150)
        Manager, Order Fulfillment and Computer Operations:
        Barbara Pellechia (625-8013)
        Credit and Collections Manager: Charles Hale (625-8615)
Journals: Janet Fisher, Associate Director for Journals (253-2864; E-
        mail: fisher@mitvma.mit.edu)
        Assistant Journals Manager: June Desmarais-McCaull (253-
        2864)
        Journals Editorial and Production Manager: Anita
        Flanzbaum (253-2805; E-mail: anita@mitvma.mit.edu)
        Journals Direct Mail Manager: Kate Rubin (253-2866); E-
        mail: rubink@mit.edu)
        Journals Marketing Manager: Rebecca McLeod (253-2866; E-

mail: mcleod@mitvma.mit.edu)
Journals Circulation Manager: Dottie Devereaux (253-2889;
E-mail: deverea@mitvma.mit.edu)
Distribution Manager: Sheila Lilja (508/486-3582)
London Office: Ann Sexmith, Manager

Full Member

Established: 1961   Admitted to AAUP: 1961
Title output 1992: 176   Title output 1993: 163
Titles currently in print: 2,000   Journals published: 30

Editorial Program

Aesthetics; architecture/design arts/photography; critical theory; information-computation-cognition: (1) computer science and artificial intelligence; (2) cognitive science; (3) neuroscience; energy, environment, and ecology; economics and business; formal linguistics; general sciences (astronomy, biology, mathematics, physics); science and technology studies; natural history; social theory; and the following journals: *Adaptive Behavior; Artificial Life; Assemblage; Chicago Journal of Theoretical Computer Science; Computational Linguistics; Computer Music Journal; Computing Systems; Design Book Review; Design Issues; Design Quarterly; The Drama Review; The Ecologist; Evolutionary Computation; International Organization; International Security; Journal of Architectural Education; Journal of Cognitive Neuroscience; Journal of Economics and Management Strategy; Journal of Inter-Disciplinary History; Leonardo; Linguistic Inquiry; NBER Macroeconomics Annual; NBER Tax Policy Annual; Neural Computation; October; Presence; Quarterly Journal of Economics; International Journal of Robotics Research; International Journal of Supercomputer Applications and High Performance Computing; Thesis Eleven;* and *Washington Quarterly.*

Special series: Artificial Intelligence; Attention and Performance; Bradford Books; Complex Adaptive Systems; Cellular and Molecular Neuroscience; Contemporary German Social Thought; Computational Models of Cognition and Perception; Cognitive Neuroscience; Current Studies in Linguistics; Computer Systems; Foundations of Computing; Global Environmental Accords; History of Computing; Issues in the Biology of Language and Cognition; Information Systems; Inside Technology; Learning, Development, and Cognitive Change; Leonardo Books; Linguistic Inquiry Monographs; Logic Programming; New Liberal Arts; Neural Network Modeling and Connectionism; October Books; Regulation of Economic Activity; Representation and Mind; Scientific and Engineering

Computation; Technical Communications and Information.
Copublishing and distribution programs: AAAI Press; The
Architectural History Foundation; Canadian Centre for
Architecture; Zone Books.

The Metropolitan Museum of Art

1000 Fifth Avenue
New York, NY 10028
(212) 879-5500
Cable Address: METMUSART
Telex: 666676
Fax: (212) 472-8725

Editorial: John P. O'Neill, Editor-in-Chief
  Executive Editor: Barbara Burn
  Managing Editor: Teresa Egan
  Senior Editors: Margaret Aspinwall, Carol Fuerstein,
  Kathleen Howard, Emily Walter
  Editors: Pamela Barr, Ruth Kozodoy, Ann Lucke, Ellen
  Shultz
  Production Editor: Barbara Cavaliere
Editor-in-Chief, *Bulletin*: Joan K. Holt
  Associate Editor: Tonia Payne
Editor, The Robert Lehman Collection Catalogue: Sue Potter
Marketing:
  Scholarly Books Marketing Consultant: Marilyn Abel
  Manager, Retail and Institutional Sales: Suzanne Fonarow
  Manager, Institutional Sales: Linda Curley
Design and Production: Gwen Roginsky, Production Manager
  Production Assistants: Peter Antony, Rich Bonk, Matthew
  Pimm, Jay Reingold
  Design Consultants: Bruce Campbell, Elizabeth Finger, Abby
  Goldstein, Malcolm Grear, Michael Shroyer
Business: Connie Harper, Budget Coordinator, Publications
Controller, Merchandise: Thomas A. Dougherty

Full Member

Established: 1908	Admitted to AAUP: 1949
Title output 1992: 14	Title output 1993: 16
Titles currently in print: 249	Journals published: 2

Editorial Program
Catalogs of exhibitions and of the permanent collections
(including archaeology; primitive art; the fine arts; decorative arts;
musical instruments; the Costume Institute); scholarly and
popular publications based on objects in the museum's collections
or otherwise associated with the museum; art history. The
museum publishes two journals: *The Metropolitan Museum of
Art Bulletin* and the *Metropolitan Museum Journal*. Unsolicited
manuscripts are not invited, the only exception being that of
articles appropriate to the *Journal*, which may be submitted for
consideration to its editorial board.

The University of Michigan Press

<u>Street Address:</u>
839 Greene Street
Ann Arbor, MI 48106-1104
(313) 764-4399
Fax: (313) 936-0456
Internet: um_press@um.cc.
       umich.edu
Indiv: (user I.D.)@umich.edu

<u>Mailing Address:</u>
P.O. Box 1104
Ann Arbor, MI 48106-1104

<u>UK/European Representative:</u>
Trevor Brown Associates

Director: Colin Day (936-3636; E-mail: colinday)
    Assistant Director: Mary Erwin (764-4387; E-mail: merwin)
Acquisitions Editorial: LeAnn Fields, Executive Editor (literature,
    theater, women's studies) (747-2463; E-mail: lfields); Ellen
    Bauerle (classics, archaeology, history) (747-2463; E-mail:
    bauerle); Colin Day (economics) (936-3636); Mary Erwin
    (ESL, regional) (764-4387); Malcolm Litchfield (political
    science, law) (763-3419; E-mail: mlitchfi); Susan B. Whitlock
    (anthropology, Modernist literature, reprints) (936-0394; E-
    mail: whitlock)
    Editorial Assistants: Eve Trager (747-2463; E-mail: etrager);
    Laurie Ham (936-3636; E-mail: llham)
Manuscript Editorial: Christina Milton, Managing Editor (764-
    4390; E-mail: cmilton)
    Manuscript Editors: Ellen McCarthy (764-4447; E-mail:
    emcc); Christina Triezenberg (763-1526; E-mail: ctriezen);
    Nancy Vlahakis (747-4480; E-mail: nanmv)
    Editorial Assistant: Robin Moir (763-0170; E-mail: ramoir)
Marketing: Michael Kehoe, Marketing Director (764-4330; E-mail:
    mkehoe)

Exhibits Coordinator: Diane Piel (763-0163)
Promotion Supervisor: Margaret Haas (936-0389; E-mail:
    mhaas)
Publicist/Marketing Assistant: Joanna Rubiner (764-4330)
Design and Production: John Grucelski, Production Manager (764-
    4391; E-mail: jgrucel)
Production Assistant: Katherine Toy-Nau (764-4391; E-mail:
    kathytoy)
Production Coordinator: Mary Meade (763-1525; E-mail:
    mmeade)
Graphic Artists: Heidi Dailey; Ron Fraker (936-0453); Carol
    Novak (763-6417)
Business: Carol Boone, Manager (764-4394)
Warehouse Supervisor: Larry Gable (764-2468)
Electronic Manuscript Specialist: Lorrie LeJuene (763-3477; E-mail:
    lorrie)

Full Member

Established: 1930   Admitted to AAUP: 1963
Title output 1992: 107   Title output 1993: 135
Titles currently in print: 1,090

Editorial Program
Scholarly works in anthropology; classics; economics; history; law;
literature; music; political science; theater; women's studies.
Textbooks in English as a Second Language; regional trade titles.
Distributes works of the Kiel Institute of World Economics.

Special series: American Academy in Rome; Amherst
Series in Law, Jurisprudence and Social Thought; Ann Arbor
Paperbacks; Analytic Perspectives on Politics; Comparative Studies
in Society and History Book Series; Critical Perspectives on
Women and Gender; Economics; Cognition and Society; Editorial
Theory and Literary Criticism; English for Academic Purposes;
Great Lakes Environment Series; International Academy for
Research in Learning Disabilities; Jerome Lecture Series (Classics);
Kelsey Museum Studies; Law, Meaning, and Violence; Linking
Levels of Analysis; Michigan Monographs in Classical Antiquity;
Michigan Studies in International Political Economy; Michigan
Studies in Political Analysis; Middle English Dictionary; New
Texts from Ancient Cultures; Pitt Series in English as a Second
Language; Poets on Poetry; RATIO: Institute for the Humanities;
Recentiores: Later Latin Texts and Contexts; Society for Early
English and Norse Electronic Texts; Social History, Popular
Culture, and Politics in Germany; Studies in Literature and
Science; Studies in Medieval and Early Modern Civilization;
Stylus: Studies in Medieval Culture; The Body, in Theory:

Histories of Materialism in the Human Sciences; The Michigan
American Music Series; Theater; Theory/Text/Performance;
Under Discussion; Women and Culture Series; Yeats: Annual of
Critical and Textual Studies.

Michigan State University Press

1405 South Harrison Road,
Suite 25
Manly Miles Building
East Lansing, MI 48823-5202
(517) 355-9543
Fax in the U.S.: (800) 678-2120
Fax international and Lansing area: (517) 432-2611
Internet: msp02@msu.edu

UK/European Distributor and
Representative:
Gazelle Book Services, Ltd.

Director: Fred C. Bohm
Editorial: Julie L. Loehr, Editor-in-Chief/Assistant Director
Business and Marketing: Lori A. Lancour, Manager
        Promotion Coordinator: Victor M. Howard
Design and Production: Michael J. Brooks, Manager
Journals: Laura A. Luptowski, Manager
Distribution and Fulfillment: Jane A. Latham, Coordinator
Press Development: Naomi Revzin, Director (355-8257)

Full Member

Established: 1947

Admitted to AAUP: 1992

Title output 1992: 13

Title output 1993: 19

Titles currently in print: 265

Journals published: 3

Editorial Program
Scholarly books and general nonfiction with areas of special
interest in African studies; agriculture; American Indian studies;
American studies; biological science; business; Canadian studies;
criminology; Great Lakes regional studies; books relating to the
State of Michigan; sociology; the social and environmental
sciences; U.S. history; urban studies; women's studies; and the
following journals: *African Rural and Urban Studies, Journal of
International Marketing,* and *Northeast African Studies.*

Special series, joint imprints and/or copublishing
programs: African Series; African Historical Documents Series;
International Business Series; Lotus Poetry Series; Rhetoric and

Public Affairs Series; Schoolcraft Series; and the Canadian Series.
The press distributes the publications of the Kresge Art Museum and the Michigan State University African Studies Center.

University of Minnesota Press

---

111 Third Avenue South
Suite 290
Minneapolis, MN 55401-2552
(612) 627-1970
Fax: (612) 627-1980
Orders: (612) 627-1940
Internet: (user I.D.)@maroon.tc.umn.edu

<u>U.K. Representative:</u>
UCL Press Limited

Director: Lisa Freeman (627-1971; E-mail: lfreeman)
> Assistant to the Director, Rights and Permissions: Gretchen Asmussen (627-1972; E-mail: asmus001)
> Assistant Director and Test Division Manager: Beverly Kaemmer (627-1963; E-mail: keamm002)
> Assistant Director, Marketing: Neelum Chaudhry (627-1931; E-mail: chaud002)

Editorial: Janaki Bakhle (gay and lesbian studies, anthropology, communications) (627-1976; E-mail: bakhl001);
> Biodun Iginla (literary and cultural theory, philosophy) (627-1974; E-mail: iginl001)

Marketing and Sales:
> Direct Mail: Kathryn Grimes (627-1934; E-mail: grime002)
> Exhibits/Advertising: Jeni Hendrickson (627-1933; E-mail: jhen)
> Promotions/Publicity: Dan Verdick (627-1932; E-mail: verdi001)

Design and Production: Kathy Wolter, Manager (627-1981; E-mail: wolte003)
> Copyediting Manager: Mary Byers (627-1985; E-mail: byers004)

Business: Terry Mattocks, Fiscal Manager (627-1941; E-mail: matto001)
> Customer Service Supervisor/Order Fulfillment: Sandrah Heir (627-1946; E-mail: heirx001)

Computer Operations: Dan Efron (627-1944; E-mail: defron)

Full Member

Established: 1925
Title output 1992: 39
Titles currently in print: 514

Admitted to AAUP: 1937
Title output 1993: 49

Editorial Program
Literary and cultural theory; social and political theory;
communications/media; feminist studies; gay and lesbian studies;
biology and the earth sciences; personality assessment, clinical
psychology and psychiatry; philosophy; Upper Midwest studies.

Special series, joint imprints and/or copublishing
programs: Theory and History of Literature; American Culture;
Hispanic Issues; Medieval Culture; Cultural Politics; Emergent
Literatures; Concepts in Social Thought; MMPI-2 Monographs;
MMPI-A Monographs; Minnesota Studies in the Philosophy of
Science; Wildlife Habitats; Politics, Culture and Social Theory;
Pedagogy & Cultural Practice; Theory Out of Bounds; Media and
Society; Social Movements, Protest, and Contention; Borderlines;
Public Worlds.

University Press of Mississippi

3825 Ridgewood Road
Jackson, MS 39211-6492
(601) 982-6205
Fax: (601) 982-6217
Orders: (800) 737-7788
      (601) 982-6246
Internet: mpress
    @ms.ihl.ms.gov

<u>Warehouse Address:</u>
931 Highway 80 West
Jackson, MS 39204

<u>Canadian Representative:</u>
Scholarly Book Services, Inc.

<u>European Representative:</u>
Bill Bailey Publishers'
Representatives

<u>U.K. Representative:</u>
Roundhouse Publishing Ltd.

Director and Publisher: Richard M. Abel (982-6206)
    Assistant to the Director: Julie Bullock (982-6205)
Acquisitions Editorial: Seetha A-Srinivasan, Associate Director
    and Editor-in-Chief (Scholarly) (982-6275)
      Executive Editor: JoAnne Prichard (Trade) (982-6371)
      Assistant Editor: S. Anne Stascavage (982-6102)
Manuscript Editorial: Ginger L. Tucker, Managing Editor (982-
    6249)

Marketing: Hunter M. Cole, Associate Director and Marketing
     Manager (982-6695)
     Promotions Manager: Carrie Didlake (982-6424)
     Assistant Sales Manager: Tim Huggins (982-6459)
Design and Production: John A. Langston, Manager (982-6274)
     Assistant Manager: Sally Hamlin (982-6554)
Business: Isabel Metz, Assistant Director and Business Manager
     (982-6551)
     Customer Service Manager: Debbie Stobaugh (982-6272)
     Customer Service Representative: Wendy Henderson (982-
     6246)
     Fulfillment Manager: Clarence Stringer
     Fulfillment Clerk: Danny Walters (982-6393)

Full Member
Established: 1970   Admitted to AAUP: 1976
Title output 1992: 47   Title output 1993: 49
Titles currently in print: 350

Editorial Program
Scholarly and trade titles in African American studies; American
studies, literature, history, and culture; art and architecture; ethnic
studies; folklife; natural sciences; performance; photography;
popular culture; reference; social sciences; Southern studies;
women's studies; other liberal arts.

Special series: Author and Artist; Center for the Study of
Southern Culture; Chancellor's Symposium in Southern History;
Comparative Diaspora Studies; The Eudora Welty Prize; Faulkner
and Yoknapatawpha; Folk Art and Artists; Folklife in the South;
Literary Conversations; Natural History; Performance Studies in
Culture; Studies in Popular Culture.

Imprints: Banner Books; Muscadine Books.

University of Missouri Press

2910 LeMone Boulevard   <u>U.K. Representative:</u>
Columbia, MO 65201-8227   Eurospan
(314) 882-7641
Fax: (314) 884-4498   <u>Canadian Representative:</u>
Internet: (user I.D.)@bigcat.   Scholarly Book Services
     missouri.edu

Director: Beverly Jarrett
	Executive Staff Assistant: Marilynn Keil (E-mail: mkeil01)
	Assistant Director: Linda Frech (E-mail: lfrech)
Acquisitions Editorial: Beverly Jarrett, Editor-in-Chief
	Acquisitions Editor: Clair Willcox (E-mail: cwillcox)
Manuscript Editorial: Jane Lago, Managing Editor (E-mail: jlago1)
	Manuscript Editors: John Brenner, Sara Fefer, Gloria
	Thomas
	Editorial Secretary: Janice Smiley
Marketing: Karen Caplinger, Marketing Manager
	Assistant Marketing Manager: Kathryn Conrad (Sales &
	Publicity) ((E-mail: kconrad)
	Advertising Manager: Polly Law (Advertising, Direct Mail,
	Exhibits)
	Marketing Assistant: Laura Choukri
Design and Production: Dwight Browne, Production Manager
	Production Assistant: Nikki Waltz
	Senior Designer: Kristie Lee
	Designer: Stephanie Foley
Business: Linda Frech, Chief Financial Officer (E-mail: lfrech)
	Receptionist & Business Secretary: TBA
	Order Fulfillment Supervisor: Debbie Guilford
	Order Fulfillment/Accounting Assistant: Tracy Tritschler–
	Martinez
	Warehouse Manager: Carl Joseph
	Warehouse Clerk: TBA

Full Member

Established: 1958

Admitted to AAUP: 1960

Title output 1992: 51

Title output 1993: 51

Titles currently in print: 454

Editorial Program

American and European history, including intellectual history
and biography; African-American studies; women's studies;
American, British, and Latin American literary criticism;
journalism; political science, including foreign relations;
philosophy, particularly political philosophy and ethics; art
history; various regional studies of Missouri, the Midwest, and
south central United States; short fiction and creative nonfiction.

Special series: Missouri Biography Series; Southern
Women Series; Missouri Heritage Readers; and Paul Anthony
Brick Lectures.

Modern Language Association of America

10 Astor Place
New York, NY 10003-6481
(212) 475-9500
Fax: (212) 477-9863
Internet: mlaod@cuvmb.cc.columbia.edu
Bitnet: mlaod@cuvmb.bitnet

Executive Director: Phyllis Franklin (614-6301)
Director of Book Publications: Martha Noel Evans (614-6338)
Book Acquisitions & Development: Joseph Gibaldi (614-6312)
Managing Editor of MLA Publications: Judy Goulding (614-6306)
Editorial Coordinator of Book Publications: Elizabeth Holland
     (614-6307)
Promotions Coordinator: David C. Smith (614-6304)
Production Manager: Judith Altreuter (614-6303)

Associate Member

Established: 1883	Admitted to AAUP: 1992
Title output 1992: 11	Title output 1993: 14
Titles currently in print: 165	Journals published: 4

Editorial Program
Scholarly, pedagogical, and professional books on language and literature, plus the *MLA International Bibliography; PMLA; Profession; ADE and ADFL Bulletins; and MLA Newsletter.*

National Academy Press

Street Address:	Mailing Address:
2001 Wisconsin Ave., N.W.	2101 Constitution Ave., N.W.
Harris Bldg., Suite 384	Lockbox 285
Washington, DC 20007	Washington, DC 20055
Bookstore: (202) 334-2612	
Fax: (202) 334-2793	Orders: (800) 624-6242/(202)
Telex: 248664 NASW UR	334-3313/Fax (202) 334-2451
Cable Address: NARECO	E-mail Orders: amerchant@
Internet: slubeck@nas.edu	nas.edu

Director: Scott F. Lubeck (334-3324)
Executive Editor: Stephen M. Mautner (334-3336)
Marketing Director: Barbara A. Kline (334-3328)
International and Special Sales: Natalie Ambrose (334-3037)
Production Manager: Dawn M. Eichenlaub (334-3330)
Business Manager: Kathy N. Stein (334-3329)
Fulfillment Manager: Ann Merchant (334-3117)
Permissions Editor: Richard Morris (334-3335)
Director of Data Imaging: James M. Gormley (334-3325)

Associate Member
Established: 1864   Admitted to AAUP: 1988
Title output 1992: 98   Title output 1993: 80
Titles currently in print: 900

Editorial Program
Primarily professional-level, policy-oriented titles in agricultural
sciences, behavioral and social sciences; biology; chemistry;
computer sciences; earth sciences; economics; education; energy;
engineering; environmental issues; industry; international issues;
materials science; medicine; natural resources; nutrition; physical
sciences; public policy issues; statistics; transportation; and urban
and rural development. Publications are generally restricted to
material emanating from the National Academy of Sciences,
National Academy of Engineering, Institute of Medicine, and the
National Research Council. Occasional titles on scientific topics
for the general public.

National Gallery of Art

4th Street and Constitution Avenue, N.W.
Washington, DC 20565-0001
(202) 842-6200
Fax: (202) 408-8530

Editor-in-Chief: Frances P. Smyth
        Senior Editor and Editor, Systematic Catalogue: Mary
        Yakush
        Editors: Tam L. Curry, Susan Higman
        Editorial Assistant: Julie Warnement

Managing Editor, Studies in the History of Art: Carol Eron
        Editorial Assistant: Ulrike Mills
Design and Production: Chris Vogel, Manager
        Graphic Designers: Phyllis Hecht, Margaret Bauer
Assistant for Project Management: Maria Tousimis

Associate Member

Established: 1941

Title output 1992: 21

Titles currently in print: 119

Admitted to AAUP: 1992

Title output 1993: 21

Journals published: 1

Editorial Program

The National Gallery publishes catalogues of exhibitions and of the permanent collections (including Western art of the early Renaissance through the contemporary era); scholarly and popular publications based on objects in the museum's collections; a scholarly journal, *Studies in the History of Art,* in conjunction with the Center for Advanced Study in the Visual Arts; scholarly publications on conservation; and educational materials for use by the public and by teachers and schools. Unsolicited manuscripts are not invited at this time.

Naval Institute Press

---

118 Maryland Avenue
Annapolis, MD 21402-5035
(410) 268-6110
Fax: (410) 269-7940

<u>Warehouse Address:</u>
USNI Operations Center
2062 Generals Highway
Annapolis, MD 21401-6780
(410) 224-3378
(800) 233-8764
Fax: (410) 224-2406

<u>U.K./European Representative:</u>
Airlife Publishing Ltd.

<u>Canadian Representative:</u>
Vanwell Publishing Ltd.

Executive Director and Publisher: James A. Barber, Jr.
Press Director: Ron Chambers
        Administrative & Editorial Assistant: Eve Secunda
        Secretary & Administrative Assistant: Jean Tyson
Acquisitions Editorial: Paul W. Wilderson, Executive Editor
        Senior Acquisitions Editor: Mark Gatlin
        Acquisitions Editor: Anne Collier-Rehill

Manuscript Editorial: Mary Lou Kenney, Managing Editor
        Senior Manuscript Editor: Anthony F. Chiffolo
        Manuscript Editor: Linda O'Doughda
        Production Editor: J. Randall Baldini
Design and Production: John Cronin, Manager
        Senior Book Designer: Karen White
        Book Designer: Pamela Schnitter
        Production Coordinator: Charles E. Vance
Marketing: Tom Harnish, Director
        Publicity/Copy Manager: Susan Artigiani
        Exhibits Manager: TBA
        Advertising/Direct Mail Manager: Maureen Peterson
        Administrative & Promotion Assistant: Judy Heise
        Bookstore Manager: Virginia Schultz
        Customer Service Manager: Judy Macauley
Journals: Fred H. Rainbow, Editor-in-Chief, *Proceedings*
        Managing Editor, *Proceedings*: John G. Miller
        Editor, *Naval History*: Fred L. Schultz
Subsidiary Rights Editor/Permissions: Linda Cullen
Import Book Coordinator: Patricia A. Sappington

Full Member

Established: 1899	Admitted to AAUP: 1949
Title output 1992: 46	Title output 1993: 47
Titles currently in print: 525	Journals published: 2

Editorial Program

Joint and general military subjects; naval biography; naval history; oceanography; navigation; military law; naval science textbooks; sea power; shipbuilding; professional guides; nautical arts and lore; technical guides; and the journals *Proceedings* and *Naval History*.

Special series, joint imprints and/or copublishing programs: Studies in Military Science and Strategy; Fundamentals of Naval Science Series; Anatomy of the Ship Series; Classics of Naval Literature; Classics of Sea Power; Bluejacket Books (new paperback series).

University of Nebraska Press

901 North 17th Street
Lincoln, NE 68588-0520
(402) 472-3581
Fax: (402) 472-6214
Internet: (user I.D.)@unlinfo.unl.edu

<u>Orders:</u>
(402) 472-3584

Director: Willis G. Regier (472-5942; E-mail: wregier)
Editorial: Daniel Ross, Assistant Director and Editor-in-Chief
(472-5941; E-mail: dross)
Managing Editor: Deborah Oliver (472-0010; E-mail: doliver)
Science Editor: Nancy Rosen (472-5945; E-mail: nrosen)
Humanities Editor: Douglas Clayton (472-0011; E-mail: dclayton)
Reprint Editor: Jay Fultz (472-7709; E-mail: jfultz)
Production Editors: Stephen Barnett (472-0645); Jennifer Comeau (472-7703; E-mail: jcomeau)
Marketing: Sandra Johnson, Marketing Manager (472-5937; E-mail: sjohnson)
Publicity & Exhibits Manager: Annette Windhorn (472-5938; E-mail: awindhorn)
Advertising Manager: Sarah Walz (472-3588)
Direct Mail Manager: Jeanette Rivard (472-5949)
Design and Production: Debra Turner, Production Manager (472-5944; E-mail: dturner)
Designers: Richard Eckersley (472-5943); Dika Eckersley (472-7713); Andrea Shahan (472-7718)
Assistant Production Manager: Alison Rold (472-7706)
Electronic Media Manager: Michael Jensen (472-3541; E-mail: jensen)
Business: Pamela Hanson, Manager (472-5939)
Customer Services Manager: Kirtland C. Card (472-5946)
Credit Manager: Diane Hill (472-5948)
Rights & Permissions: Elaine Maruhn (472-7702; E-mail: emaruhn)

Full Member
Established: 1941
Title output 1992: 110　　Title output 1993: 117
Titles currently in print: 1,750　　Journals published: 3

Editorial Program
English literature; American literature; translation; political
science; music; the American West; the Great Plains; the
American Indian; food production and distribution; agriculture;
natural history; psychology; modern history of Western Europe;
Latin American studies; and the journal *Prairie Schooner*.
Submissions are not invited in original poetry or fiction.

Special imprints: Bison Books; Landmark Editions.

Special series, joint imprints and/or copublishing
programs: Regents Renaissance Drama Series; Regents Restoration
Drama Series; Nebraska Symposia on Motivation; Children, the
Law, and Social and Behavioral Sciences; State Histories; Latin
American Studies Series; Greek and Latin Music Theory; Studies
in the Anthropology of North American Indians; American
Indian Lives Series; Politics and Government of the American
States; American Tribal Religions; Women in the West; Modern
Scandinavian Literature in Translation; European Women
Writers; Latin American Women Writers; French Modernist
Library; Indians of the Southeast Series; Twentieth-Century
American West Series; Law in the American West; North
American Beethoven Studies; Brahms Studies; Texts and
Contexts; American Musicological Society Monographs; Cather
Studies; Our Sustainable Future.

Distributors and publishers of Mental Measurements
Yearbooks and other works of the Buros Institute of Mental
Measurement.

University of Nevada Press

Morrill Hall, Mailstop 166
Reno, NV 89557-0076
(702) 784-6573
Fax: (702) 784-6200

Warehouse Address:
Desert Research Institute
5625 Fox Avenue (Stead)
Reno, NV 89506

1621 E. Flamingo Road, Suite 15-A
Las Vegas, NV 89119
(702) 895-4080
Fax: (702) 895-4086

Canadian Representative:
University of
British Columbia Press

U.K. Representative:
U.C.L. Press, Ltd.

Director: Thomas R. Radko (E-mail: radko@scs.nevada.edu)
Editorial: TBA, Editor-in-Chief
     Acquistions Editor: Trudy McMurrin (E-mail:
     mcmurrin@nevada.edu)
     Editor: Sara Vélez Mallea (E-mail: velez@unr.edu)
Marketing: Sandy Crooms, Marketing and Sales Director (E-mail:
     crooms@scs.nevada.edu)
     Sales and Promotion Coordinator: Chris Patt (E-mail:
     cppatt@unr.edu)
Design and Production: Cameron R. Sutherland, Production
     Manager
     Senior Graphic Designer and Paperback Editor: Heather
     Goulding (E-mail: goulding@scs.nevada.edu)
Business: Sheryl Laguna, Business Manager
     Assistant Business Manager: Nancy Genrich
Office Manager: Charlotte E. Heatherly (E-mail:
     ceh@scs.nevada.edu)

Full Member

Established: 1961	Admitted to AAUP: 1982
Title output 1992: 15	Title output 1993: 27
Titles currently in print: 147	Journals published: 5

Editorial Program

Scholarly books and serious fiction and nonfiction, with special interests in the history, biography, anthropology, and natural history of Nevada and the West, and works dealing with the Basque peoples of Europe and the Americas. Additional interests include contemporary affairs; Native American studies; ethnonationalism; history; literature; film studies; photography; natural resources; women's studies; and gambling and commercial gaming.

Special series: Max C. Fleischmann Series in Great Basin Natural History; Basque Series; Wilbur S. Shepperson Series in History and Humanities; Western Literature Series; Vintage West Reprint Series; Ethnonationalism in Comparative Perspective Series; The Gambling Studies Series.

The press distributes publications of the University of Nevada Oral History Program, the Institute for the Study of Gambling and Commercial Gaming, Nevada Publications, Cachuma Press, Genny Smith Books, and the Black Rock Press.

University Press of New England

23 South Main Street
Hanover, NH 03755-2048
(603) 643-7100
Fax: (603) 643-1540
Internet: (user I.D.)@Dartmouth.edu

<u>Warehouse:</u>
37 Lafayette Street
Lebanon, NH 03766-1446

<u>U.K./European Representative:</u>
Trevor Brown Associates

<u>Canadian Representative:</u>
Scholarly Book Services

Director: Thomas L. McFarland (643-7100; E-mail:
    thomas.l.mcfarland)
    Associate Director, Operations: Thomas Johnson (643-7102;
    E-mail: thomas.m.johnson)
    Executive Secretary/Permissions: Patricia Kratz (643-7100)
Editorial: Phil Pochoda, Editorial Director (643-7103)
    Acquisitions: David Caffry (643-7108)
    Editorial Assistant: TBA
    Editor-in-Chief, Wesleyan: Eileen McWilliam (203/344-
    7918)
    Editorial Assistant, Wesleyan: Suzanna Tamminen (203/
    344-7918)
Manuscript Editorial: Mary Crittendon, Managing Editor (643-
    7115)
    Production Editor: Carol Sheehan (643-7115)
Marketing: Director TBA
    Marketing Manager: Nanine Hutchinson (643-7106)
    Publicist/Subsidiary Rights: John Landrigan (643-7107)
    Promotion Assistant: Beth Biathrow (643-7106)
Design and Production: Mike Burton, Assistant Director (643-7116;
    E-mail: michael.p.burton)
    Design and Production Assistant: Kathy Kimball (643-7117)
    Production Assistant: Douglas Tifft (643-7117)
Journals: Thomas Johnson, Manager (643-7102)
    Subscriptions: Jack Wingerter (643-7111)
Business: Sondra Farnham, Accounting Supervisor (643-7112)
    Accounting Clerk: Ingrid Knudsen (643-7110)
    Customer Service: Sherri Strickland (643-7110); Jack
    Wingerter (643-7112)
    Warehouse/Shipping: Anne Demers, Sara Williams

Full Member

Established: 1970   Admitted to AAUP: 1975
Title output 1992: 56   Title output 1993: 68
Titles currently in print: 648   Journals published: 4

University Press of New England publishes books under its own imprint and is the publisher for Brandeis University Press, Brown University Press, Dartmouth College, Middlebury College Press, University of New Hampshire, University of Rhode Island, Tufts University, University of Vermont, Wesleyan University Press and Salzburg Seminar.

Editorial Program

General and scholarly; American history and American studies; arts, media and pop culture; identity and communities; art history; Jewish studies; globalism and post-Cold War studies; nature and environment; New England history and ecology; poetry, fiction and literary criticism; social science and social problems; and the journals *International Environmental Affairs; New England Review: Middlebury Series; Jewish History.*

Wesleyan University Press: Cultural studies; interdisciplinary studies; American history; literature; women's studies; gender and gay studies; government and public issues; biography; poetry; and social and natural sciences.

Special series: Bibliographies of New England History; Brown University Slavic Reprint Series; Collected Writings of Jean-Jacques Rousseau; Hardscrabble Books—Fiction of New England; The Papers of Daniel Webster; Studies in the History of Art (National Gallery of Art); Brandeis Series in American Jewish History, Culture, and Life; Tauber Institute Series for the Study of European Jewry; Studies in Arctic Affairs; The Bread Loaf Anthology of Contemporary American Literature; Nelson A. Rockefeller Series in Social Science and Policy; Wesleyan Poetry; the Complete Works of Henry Fielding (with the Clarendon Press, Oxford); Wesleyan Music/Culture; American Furniture (Chipstone Foundation).

University of New Mexico Press

1720 Lomas Boulevard NE   <u>Warehouse:</u>
Albuquerque, NM 87131-1591   3721 Spirit Drive SE
(505) 277-2346   Albuquerque, NM 87106
Fax: (505) 277-9270   (505) 842-5181
Fax: (800) 622-8667 (orders)   Fax: (505) 842-5570

Fax: (505) 277-3350 (customer service)
Cable: UNMPRESS
Telex: 660-461 (include the words "UNM Press" in message)
Internet: unmpress@carina.unm.edu

<table>
<tr><td><u>U.K. Representative:</u>
John Ramsay Marketing</td><td><u>European Representative:</u>
Bill Bailey Publishers' Reps</td></tr>
</table>

Director and Senior Editor: Elizabeth C. Hadas
      Associate Director: David V. Holtby
      Secretary to the Director: Dianne Edwards
Acquisitions Editorial: David V. Holtby (history, Latin American studies); Dana Asbury (art, photography); Larry Durwood Ball (Western history, anthropology); Barbara Guth (American studies, women's studies)
      Editorial Assistant: Anne Tyler
Marketing: Peter Moulson, Director
      Associate Manager: Maureen Mills
      Advertising and Exhibits Manager: Nancy Coggeshall
      Graphic Designer: Nancy Woodard
      Marketing Assistant: Tam Davis
Sales: David K. Brown, Director
      Associate Sales/Remainder Manager: Sheri Hozier
Design and Production: Emmy Ezzell, Art and Production Manager
      Art Director: Kristina Kachele
      Graphic Designers: Linda Tratechaud, Sue Niewiarowski
      Reprint Manager and Production Assistant: Denise Johnson
Business: Lois Bursack, Assistant Director for Business
      Accountants: Junnetta Woodworth, Cheri Hernandez
      Accounting Assistants: Bruce Cummings, Sinikka Hinkkanen
      Customer Service Manager: Gordon Benson
      Customer Service Assistants: Mariamarta Nuñez, Janet Shelton
      Receptionist: Fonceal Pfeifenroth
Data Manager: Taylor Horst
Warehouse Manager: Rick Hays

Full Member

Established: 1929   Admitted to AAUP: 1937
Title output 1992: 63   Title output 1993: 63
Titles currently in print: 357

Editorial Program
Scholarly books and serious nonfiction, with special interests in social and cultural anthropology; ethnic studies; archaeology; American frontier history; Western American literature; Latin American history; history of photography; art and photography; books that deal with important aspects of the Southwest or the Rocky Mountain states, including natural history and land grant studies.

Special series, joint imprints and/or copublishing programs: American Poetry Series; Coyote Books; Histories of the American Frontier; New Mexico Natural History Series; New Mexico Land Grant Series; Historical Society of New Mexico; the Committee on Desert and Arid Zones Research (AAAS); Pasó por Aquí Series on the Nuevomexicano Literary Heritage.

New York University Press

70 Washington Square South
New York, NY 10012-1091
(212) 998-2575
Fax: (212) 995-3833
Internet: hammerj@elmer2.
      bobst.nyu.edu

European Representative:
Eurospan

Canadian Representative:
Kellington & Associates

Director: Colin H. Jones
      Assistant to the Director: Kathe Sweeney
Acquisitions Editorial: Niko Pfund, Editor-in-Chief (social sciences, law, history, women's and gender studies, Middle East and Jewish studies)
      Editor: Timothy Bartlett (behavioral sciences, literature, women's and gender studies)
      Assistant Editor: Jennifer Hammer (women's health, women and religion)
Manuscript Editorial: Despina P. Gimbel, Managing Editor
Marketing: Susan Conn, Sales and Marketing Manager
      Marketing Coordinator: Kathleen May
      Sales and Marketing Coordinator: Megan Murphy
Design and Production: Kenneth Venezio, Production Manager
Business: Farukh Farooqi, Manager, Budget & Operations
      Accounts Receivable Assistant: Brenda DiGarbo
Permissions: Kris Rubi, Editorial Assistant

Full Member

Established: 1916   Admitted to AAUP: 1937
Title output 1992: 216   Title output 1993: 153
Titles currently in print: 1,186

Editorial Program
Women's and gender studies; history; economics, psychology and psychiatry; politics; sociology; law; New York City and State regional affairs; Middle East studies; Judaica; literature and literary criticism.

Special imprints: Washington Mews Books; The Gotham Library.

Special series, joint imprints and/or copublishing programs: Essential Papers in Psychoanalysis; Psychoanalytic Crosscurrents; International Library of Critical Writings in Psychology; Clinical Gerontology; Elmer Holmes Bobst Awards for Emerging Writers; Feminist Crosscurrents; Women's Classics; The Cutting Edge: Lesbian Life and Literature; Readings in Political and Legal Theory; NOMOS; International Library of Essays in Law and Legal Theory; Reappraisals in Jewish Social and Intellectual History; Modern Jewish Masters Series; New Perspectives in Jewish Studies; Hagop Kevorkian Series in the Art and Architecture of the Near East; NYU Studies in Near Eastern Civilization; NYU Studies in French Culture and Civilization.

The press also distributes occasional book titles for The Council on Foreign Relations; The Trilateral Commission; The United Nations Association for the U.S.A.; The United Nations Population Fund; The International Economic Association; The International Fund for Economic Development; The Institute of Economic Affairs; and The Institute for International Economics.

The University of North Carolina Press

Street Address: Mailing Address:
116 South Boundary Street   P.O. Box 2288
Chapel Hill, NC 27514   Chapel Hill, NC 27515-2288
(919) 966-3561   (800) 848-6224 (orders)
Fax: (919) 966-3829   Fax: (800) 272-6817 (orders)
Internet: uncpress@unc.edu
Indiv: (user I.D.)@unc.edu

Director: Kate Douglas Torrey (962-4204; E-mail: kate_torrey)
     Assistant to the Director: TBA

Rights & Permissions Manager: Kathy Shaer (E-mail: kathy_shaer)

Acquistions Editorial: Barbara Hanrahan, Editor-in-Chief (962-4200; E-mail: barbara_hanrahan)

Assistant to the Editor-in-Chief: Sian Hunter White (962-4200; E-mail: sian_hunter-white)

Executive Editor: Lewis Bateman (history, classics) (962-4201; E-mail: lewis_bateman)

Editor: C. David Perry (regional trade, Latin American studies, folklore) (962-4203; E-mail: david_perry)

Assistant Editor, Paperback Coordinator: Sarah Nawrocki (E-mail: sarah_nawrocki)

Manuscript Editorial: Ron Maner, Managing Editor (E-mail: ron_maner)

Assistant Managing Editor/Electronic Manuscript Specialist: Pamela Upton (E-mail: pam_upton)

Editor: Christi Stanforth (E-mail: christi_stanforth)

Marketing: Kathleen Ketterman, Marketing Manager (962-4749; E-mail: kathleen_ketterman)

Sales Manager: Johanna Grimes (962-4197; E-mail: johanna_grimes)

Associate Marketing Manager: Katherine Reynolds (962-4198; E-mail: katherine_reynolds)

Assistant Marketing Manager/Publicity Manager: Lisa Dellwo (962-4199; E-mail: lisa_dellwo)

Associate Publicity Manager and Reprints Coordinator: Jessica Philyaw (962-4199; E-mail: jessica_philyaw)

Exhibits Manager & Assistant Sales Manager: Christine Egan (E-mail: chris_egan)

Design and Production: Production Telephone (966-5726)

Richard Hendel, Associate Director and Design and Production Manager (962-4196; E-mail: rich_hendel)

Assistant Production Manager/Printing & Binding: Heidi Perov (E-mail: perov)

Assistant Production Manager/Design: April Higgins (E-mail: april_higgins)

Composition Manager/Electronic Projects Coordinator: Marjorie Fowler (E-mail: marjorie_fowler)

Reprints Controller: Jackie Johnson (E-mail: jackie_johnson)

Journals: Barbara K. (Pat) Weeks, Journals Circulation Manager (E-mail: pat_weeks)

Business: Judith Bergman, Assistant Director and Controller (E-mail: judy_bergman)

Accounting Manager: Roy Alexander (E-mail: roy_alexander)

Customer Service Manager: Doris Goodwin (962-4205; E-mail: doris_goodwin)

Full Member

Established: 1922
Title output 1992: 69
Titles currently in print: 1,006

Admitted to AAUP: 1937
Title output 1993: 71
Journals published: 6

Editorial Program

American and European history; American and English literature; American studies; Southern studies; political science; folklore; religious studies; legal history; classics; women's studies; media studies; music; rural studies; urban studies; public policy; Latin American studies; anthropology; business and economic history; health care; regional trade; North Caroliniana; and the following journals: *Social Forces; The High School Journal; Studies in Philology; Early American Literature; Southern Literary Journal;* and *Journal for the Education of the Gifted.* Submissions are not invited in fiction, poetry, or drama.

Special series, joint imprints and/or copublishing programs: The Fred W. Morrison Series in Southern Studies; Cultural Studies of the United States; Gender and American Culture; Civil War America, Military Campaigns of the Civil War; Studies in Ancient History; Social Medicine; Studies in Rural Culture; Studies in Legal History; H. Eugene and Lillian Youngs Lehman Series; Thornton H. Brooks Series in American Law and Society; American Folklore Recordings; Chapel Hill Books; Dental Laboratory Technology Manuals; Dental Assisting Manuals; Old Salem Series; Supplementary Volumes to "The Papers of Woodrow Wilson"; James Sprunt Studies in History and Political Science; Studies in Comparative Literature; Studies in the Germanic Languages and Literatures; Studies in the Romance Languages and Literatures.

The press also publishes for the Institute of Early American History and Culture, sponsored by Colonial Williamsburg and the College of William and Mary; and for the American Society for Legal History. The press distributes books published by the North Carolina Museum of Art, Raleigh, and by the Museum of Early Southern Decorative Arts, Winston-Salem.

Northeastern University Press

Street Address:
271 Huntington Ave., Suite 272
Boston, MA 02115-5096
(617) 373-5480
Fax: (617) 373-5483
Internet: sbrassant@lynx.neu.edu

Mailing Address:
360 Huntington Ave – 272 HN
Boston, MA 02115-5096

U.K. Representative:
Academic & University
Publishers Group

Canadian Representative:
Cariad Ltd.

Director and Editor-in-Chief: William A. Frohlich (373-5476)
Associate Director: Jill Bahcall (373-5481)
Assistant to the Director: Scott Brassart (373-5482)
Staff Assistant: Jacqueline Gambarini (373-5480)
Acquisitions Editorial: John Weingartner, Senior Editor (373-5478)
Marketing: Christina Beck, Promotion Manager (373-5479)
Production: Ann Twombly, Director (373-5477)
Production Editor: Emily McKeigue (373-5475)

Full Member
Established: 1977
Title output 1992: 28
Titles currently in print: 189

Admitted to AAUP: 1984
Title output 1993: 25

Editorial Program
Scholarly books and serious nonfiction, with special interests in
American history, literature and literary criticism, music,
women's studies, and criminal justice.

Special series, joint imprints and/or copublishing
programs: Northeastern Classics Editions; The Northeastern
Library of Black Literature; The Northeastern Series in Feminist
Theory; the Samuel French Morse Poetry Prize; New England
Studies; Women's Life Writings from Around the World.

The press distributes books from the Massachusetts
Historical Society; the Montreal Museum of Fine Arts; the
Museum of Fine Arts, Boston; and the National Museum of
Women in the Arts.

Northern Illinois University Press

DeKalb, IL 60115-2854
(815) 753-1826
Fax: (815) 753-1845
Cable Address: HEARTLAND
Internet: s10bdb1@corn.cso.niu.edu

Director: Mary Lincoln (753-1826)
Acquisitions Editor: Dan Coran (753-1826)
Managing Editor: Susan Bean (753-1075)
Marketing: Wendy Warnken, Advertising & Marketing (753-1075)
Design and Production: Julia Fauci (753-1826)
Business: Barbara Berg, Bookkeeping/Customer Service (753-1826)

Full Member

Established: 1964   Admitted to AAUP: 1972
Title output 1992: 15   Title output 1993: 17
Titles currently in print: 215

Editorial Program

Anthropology; American history; European history; Russian
history; Latin American history; philosophy; political science;
British literature; American literature; and regional studies.

Special series, joint imprints and/or copublishing
programs: Russian Studies; Origins of Modern Mexico; Studies in
Modern America.

Northwestern University Press

625 Colfax Street   <u>Book Distribution Center:</u>
Evanston, IL 60208-4210   Northwestern University Press
(708) 491-5313   Chicago Distribution Center
Fax: (708) 491-8150   11030 S. Langley
                                    Chicago, IL 60628
                                    (800) 621-2736 (orders)
                                    Fax: (312) 660-2235

Director: Nicholas Weir-Williams (491-8114)
Editorial: Susan Harris, Managing Editor

Assistant Editor: Amy Schroeder (491-8112)
Editorial Assistant: Heather Kenny (491-7384)
Marketing: Kim Maselli, Marketing Manager (491-8111)
Publicity Coordinator: Tom Szidon (491-7420)
Sales: Sarah Welsch, Sales and Rights Manager (491-8113)
Design and Production: Jill Shimabukuro, Production and Design
Manager (491-3844)
Business: Kim Maselli, Manager
Business Office Coordinator: Karen Burke (491-8110)
Fufillment Coordinator: Bob Eliacin (491-5315)

Full Member

Established: 1959
Title output 1992: 29
Titles currently in print: 325

Admitted to AAUP: 1988
Title output 1993: 40
Journals published: 2

Editorial Program

Philosophy; literary criticism and theory; theater studies; drama; European literature; Jewish studies; law; literature in translation; psychology and psychiatry; and the following journals: *Renaissance Drama* and *YIVO Annual*.

Special series: Studies in Phenomenology and Existential Philosophy; The Writings of Herman Melville; Islam and Society in Africa; Russian Literature and Theory; Writings from an Unbound Europe; European Classics; Rethinking Theory; Psycho-Social Issues; Avant-Garde and Modernism.

Imprints: TriQuarterly Books.

Copublishing programs: American Bar Foundation; American Association of Teachers of Slavic and East European Languages.

University of Notre Dame Press

Street Address:
Maintenance Center
Notre Dame, IN 46556-5010
(219) 631-6346
Fax: (219) 631-8148
Cable Address: Du Lac
Telex: 6346

Mailing Address:
P.O. Box L
Notre Dame, IN 46556-5010

Director: James R. Langford

Associate Director: Jeff Gainey
Secretary to the Director: Gina Bixler
Acquisitions Editorial: Ann Rice, Executive Editor
Manuscript Editorial: Carole Roos, Jea Morgenroth, Editors
Marketing: Kathy Moore, Manager
Publicity Manager: Marcie Bates
Design and Production: Margaret Gloster, Design Manager
Production Manager: Thomas Ringenberg
Business: Diane Steele

Full Member

Established: 1949 — Admitted to AAUP: 1959
Title output 1992: 47 — Title output 1993: 41
Titles currently in print: 687 — Journals published: 1

Editorial Program

Philosophy; ethics; sociology; political science; history; theology; medieval studies; and other liberal arts; law and business; and the journal *Midwest Studies in Philosophy*. Submissions are not invited in the hard sciences, mathematics, or psychology.

Special series, joint imprints and/or copublishing programs: International Studies of the Committee on International Relations, University of Notre Dame; Publications of the Center for the Study of Christianity and Judaism in Antiquity, University of Notre Dame; Studies in American Catholicism; Studies in the Philosophy of Religion; Boston University Studies in Philosophy and Religion; Library of Religious Philosophy.

Ohio University Press

Scott Quadrangle
Athens, OH 45701-2979
(614) 593-1155
Fax: (614) 593-4536
Internet: (user I.D.)@ouvaxa.
cats.ohiou.edu

Book Distribution Center:
Ohio University Press
Chicago Distribution Center
11030 S. Langley Avenue
Chicago, IL 60628
(800) 621-2736
Fax: (312) 660-2235

U.K. and European Representative:
Academic & University Publishers Group

Director: Duane Schneider (E-mail: schneider)
        Associate Director: Holly Panich
        Editorial Assistant and Permissions: Nancy Basmajian
Acquisitions Editorial: Holly Panich, Executive Editor
        Editor for Reprints and Monographs in International
        Studies Series: Gillian Berchowitz (E-mail: berchowitz)
Marketing and Sales: Sharon Arnold, Manager (E-mail: arnold)
        Publicity: Nancy Basmajian
Production: Helen Gawthrop, Manager
Business: Bonnie Rand, Chief Financial Officer
        Customer Service: Judy Wilson

Full Member

Established: 1964   Admitted to AAUP: 1966
Title output 1992: 46   Title output 1993: 42
Titles currently in print: 650

Editorial Program

General scholarly nonfiction with particular strength in 19th-century British literature and literary criticism; history; 19th- and 20th-century continental philosophy; African studies; and Western Americana. Submissions are not invited in the hard sciences, poetry, or fiction.

Special imprints: The Swallow Press.

Special series, joint imprints and/or copublishing programs: Ohio University Center for International Studies Monographs, Africa Series, Latin America Series, Southeast Asia Series; Complete Works of Robert Browning, copublished with Baylor University; The Collected Letters of George Gissing; Continental Thought Series; and Eastern African Studies.

Ohio University Press distributes the publications of Ravan Press, Johannesburg, South Africa.

Ohio State University Press

180 Pressey Hall   <u>Warehouse:</u>
1070 Carmack Road   2578 Kenny Road
Columbus, OH 43210-1002   Columbus, OH 43210-1038
(614) 292-6930
Fax: (614) 292-2065
Internet: (user I.D.)@magnus.acs.ohio-state.edu

U.K. Representative:
Eurospan Group of Publishers

Director: Peter John Givler (292-6930; E-mail: pgivler)
Acquisitions Editor: Charlotte Dihoff (292-6930; E-mail: cdihoff)
    Acquisitions Assistant: Jean Staskevich (292-3664; E-mail: jstaskev)
Managing Editor: Ruth Melville (292-3667; E-mail: rmelvill)
    Assistant Editor: Ellen Satrom (292-3550)
Marketing: Marla Bucy, Manager (292-1462; E-mail: mbucy)
    Marketing Assistant: Gretchen Brandt (292-6824)
Design and Production: John Delaine, Production Manager (292-3686; E-mail: jdelaine)
    Assistant Production Manager: Victoria Althoff (292-6282; E-mail: valthoff)
Journals: Margaret Starbuck, Journals Manager (292-3666; E-mail: mstarbuc)
    Subscription Manager: Melodie McGrothers (292-1407; E-mail: mmcgroth)
Business: Tom Kangas, Manager (292-3692; E-mail: tkangas)
    Book Accounts Supervisor: Lisa Alwood (292-3701; E-mail: lalwood)
    Secretary: Priscilla Vitelli (292-6930)
    Warehouse Manager: Gloria Moore (292-8498)

Full Member

Established: 1957	Admitted to AAUP: 1961
Title output 1992: 30	Title output 1993: 28
Titles currently in print: 349	Journals published: 6

Editorial Program

Scholarly studies with special interests in business and economic history; criminology; fiction; literary criticism; political science; regional studies; Slavic and Eastern European studies; teaching and higher education; urban studies; Victorian studies; women's health; and women's studies.

Journals: *Geographical Analysis; Journal of Higher Education; Inks: Cartoon and Comic Art Studies; Journal of Money, Credit and Banking; Narrative;* and *The Russian Review.*

Special series: The History of Crime and Criminal Justice; Historical Perspectives on Business Enterprise; Parliamentary and Legislative Institutions and Politics; Studies in Victorian Life and Literature; The Theory and Interpretation of Narrative; Urban Life and Urban Landscape; Women and Health; The Centenary Edition of the Works of Nathaniel Hawthorne; The Complete Works of

Aphra Behn; The Ohio State University/*The Journal* Award in
Poetry; The Helen Hooven Santmyer Prize in Women's Studies;
and the Vascular Flora of Ohio.
Special imprint: Sandstone Press.

University of Oklahoma Press

1005 Asp Avenue
Norman, OK 73019-0445
(405) 325-5111
Fax: (405) 325-4000
Orders: (800) 627-7377
Fax: (405) 364-5798

Book Distribution Center:
4100 28th Avenue, N.W.
Norman, OK 73069-8218

Canadian Representative:
Scholarly Book Services

Director: George W. Bauer (325-5111)
Secretary to the Director: Yvonne C. Evans (325-3189)
Acquisitions Editorial: John N. Drayton, Assistant Director/Editor-in-Chief (325-5114)
Acquisitions Editor: Kimberly Wiar (325-2873)
Paperbacks Editor: Ron Chrisman
Manuscript Editorial: Sarah Nestor, Managing Editor (325-3248)
Manuscript Editors: Mildred Logan (325-3268); Sarah I. Morrison (325-3263); Alice K. Stanton (325-3251)
Marketing: Beverly Todd, Manager (325-3202)
Assistant Marketing Manager/Publicity: Lennie Draper (325-3198)
Direct Mail and Textbook Manager: Jo Ann Reece (325-3199)
Sales: Glenda Madden, Manager (325-3193)
Sales Assistant: Vicki Castro (325-3196)
Design and Production: Patsy Willcox, Manager (325-3186)
Assistant Production Manager: Will Austin (325-3185)
Designers: Bill Cason (325-3188); Cathy Imboden (325-3158)
Business: Lain Adkins, Assistant Director/Finance & Operations (325-3247)
Customer Service Supervisor: Glenda Glacken (325-2000)
Distribution and Operations Manager: Rick Stinchcomb (325-2013)
Distribution Supervisor: Helen Ward (325-6531)
Rights & Permissions: Suzanne Harrell (325-5132)

Full Member

Established: 1928   Admitted to AAUP: 1937
Title output 1992: 92   Title output 1993: 90
Titles currently in print: 1,001

Editorial Program
Scholarly books and general nonfiction with special interests in
Western U.S. history; American Indian studies; regional studies;
natural history; women's studies; classical studies; language and
literature; art and archaeology; and political science.

Special series: American Indian Literature and Critical
Studies; Civilization of the American Indian; Oklahoma Western
Biographies; American Exploration and Travel; Western Frontier
Library; Oklahoma Project for Discourse and Theory; Oklahoma
Series in Classical Culture; Animal Natural History; Oklahoma
Museum of Natural History Publications; Julian J. Rothbaum
Distinguished Lecture Series; Variorum Chaucer.

Oregon State University Press

---

101 Waldo Hall
Corvallis, OR 97331-6407
(503) 737-3166
Fax: (503) 737-3170

Director: Jeffrey Grass
Managing Editor: Jo Alexander
Marketing Manager: Tom Booth
Business Manager: Pennie Coe
Customer Service: Donna Atto

Affiliate Member

Established: 1961   Admitted to AAUP: 1991
Title output 1992: 5   Title output 1993: 7
Titles currently in print: 131

Editorial Program
The Oregon State University Press publishes scholarly and
specialized books in the following areas of emphasis and has a
special commitment to publishing works of importance to the
Pacific Northwest: history (environmental or regional) and
biography (regional); Pacific Northwest Studies; literature

(American/regional); natural resources and natural resource management.

Oxford University Press

Editorial Offices:
200 Madison Avenue
New York, NY 10016
(212) 679-7300
Fax: (212) 725-2972
Internet: (user I.D.)
    @rock.concert.net

Customer Service:
Orders/Prices: (800) 451-7556
Inquiries: (800) 445-9714
Journals: (800) 852-7323
Fax: (919) 677-1303

Canadian Office:
70 Wynford Drive
Don Mills, ONT
Canada M3C 1J9
(416) 441-2941
Fax: (416) 444-0427

Distribution Center:
2001 Evans Road
Cary, NC 27513
(919) 677-0977
Fax: (919) 677-8877

English Language Teaching:
(212) 684-1500
Fax: (212) 545-7924

U.K. Office:
Walton Street
Oxford OX2 6DP
England
(44) 865 56767
Fax: (44) 865 56646

President: Edward W. Barry
        Assistant to the President: Layla Voll
Acquisitions Editorial: Sheldon Meyer, Senior Vice President,
        Special Editorial
        Vice President, Executive Editor, Economics and Business:
        Herb Addison
        Vice President, Executive Editor, Humanities and Social
        Sciences: Helen McInnis
        Vice President, Executive Editor, Medicine: Jeffrey House
        Vice President, Executive Editor, Science and Medicine:
        Donald Jackson
        Vice President, Editor, Special Editorial: Leona Capeless
        Editorial Director, Academic Reference: Claude Conyers
        Executive Editor, Trade Reference: Linda Halvorson Morse
        Executive Editor, Children's and Young Adult Books:
        Nancy Toff
        Executive Editor, Music: Maribeth Payne

Manager, Music Department: Susan Brailove
Electronic Publishing Coordinator: Lillian Hastie
Managing Editor, American National Biography: Paul Betz
Acquiring Editors: Donald Kraus (bibles); Robert Rogers
(chemistry); Joyce Berry (geology, geography, art &
architecture); Kirk Jensen (life sciences); Elizabeth Maguire
(literary studies); Edith Barry (medicine); Linda Robbins
(paperbacks); Jeffrey Robbins (physical sciences); Joan
Bossert (psychology and medicine); Cynthia
Read (religion and linguistics); Nancy Lane (world
history); Robert Miller (philosophy and classics); Elizabeth
Barry (clinical medicine); Gioia Stevens (political science
and sociology)
Manuscript Editorial: Ellen Fuchs, Managing Editor
Assistant Managing Editor: Irene Pavitt
Copyright and Permissions Manager: Allison Crane
Development Editor: Susan Hannan
Production Editor: Dolores Oetting
Manuscript Editors: Stanley George, Henry Krawitz, Paul
Schlotthauer, Colby Stong, Melinda Wirkus
Marketing and Sales:
Vice President, Director, Trade Publishing: Laura Brown
Vice President, Marketing Director, Humanities & Social
Sciences: Karen Casey
Vice President, Marketing Director, Science and Medicine:
Barbara Wasserman
Vice President, Sales Director: Jonathan Weiss
Director, International Sales: L. D. Clepper
Director, Paperbacks: Ellen Chodosh
Director, Bible Sales: Hargis Thomas
Marketing Managers:
Academic Humanities: Michael Groseth
Academic Sciences: Peter Titus
Academic Social Sciences: Peter Knapp
Children's Books: Mary Ann Stafford
College Humanities and Social Sciences: Christopher
Johnson
College Science: Peter Ryttel/Medicine: Juliane Martinez
Design/Production, Trade & Desktop: Brice Hammack
Direct Mail, Humanities and Social Sciences: TBA
Direct Mail, Trade: T.J. Stiles
Electronic Publishing: Ursula Bollini
Exhibits: Jan Arrigo
Paperbacks: Kurt Hettler
Publicity: Susan Rotermund
Special Sales: Sam Testa
Subsidiary Rights: Marjorie Mueller

Telephone Sales: Richard Rocco (NC)
Trade Advertising & Promotion: Arthur Gilmartin
Trade Marketing: Amy Roberts
Trade Sales: Vera Plummer
Design and Production: Gerard Case, Vice President,
Manufacturing and Design
Manufacturing Director: John Shinkarick
Production Manager: Ellen Barrie
Production Manager/Monographs: Nancy Hoagland (NC)
Journals: Audrey Cook, Manager (NC)
Marketing Manager: Matthew Bedell (NC)
Customer Service Manager: Gloria Bruno (NC)
Business: Gerald Sussman, Senior Vice President, Administration
& Planning
Senior Vice President and Distribution Director: Thomas
McCarty (NC)
Vice President, Finance: Richard Gehringer (NC)
Director, Human Resources: Nancy O'Connor
Director, Information Systems: Randall Roch (NC)
Managers:
Accounting: Karen Lifsey (NC)
Budget and Financial Analysis: William Weinberg
Credit and Collections: Banks Honeycutt (NC)
Customer Service: Donna Jones (NC)
Human Resources: Eliza Franklin (NC)
Inventory: Kenneth Guerin (NC)
Publishing Database: Judith Lanham
Shipping Services: Cameron Shaw (NC)
English Language Teaching: Roy Gilbert, Director
Art Director: Lynn Luchetti
Editorial Manager: Susan Lanzano
Managing Editor: Rita Chabot
Production Manager: Abram Hall
Direct Marketing Manager: Margaret Kollitides

Full Member

Established: 1895   Admitted to AAUP: 1950
Title output 1992: 1,429   Title output 1993: 1,544
Titles currently in print: 11,956   Journals published (U. S. only): 18

Editorial Program

Scholarly monographs; general nonfiction; Bibles; college
textbooks; medical books; music; reference books; journals;
children's books; English language teaching. Submissions are not
invited in the area of fiction.

University of Pennsylvania Press

Blockley Hall
418 Service Drive
Philadelphia, PA 19104-6097
(215) 898-6261
Cable: PNSYL PRESS
Fax: (215) 898-0404
Internet: (user I.D.)
     @A1.quaker.upenn.edu

Warehouse & Returns Address:
P.O. Box 4836 Hampden Station
Baltimore, MD 21211

Canadian Representative:
Scholarly Book Services

U.K. Representative:
Academic & University Publishers Group

Director: Thomas M. Rotell (898-1672; E-mail: rotell)
     Associate Director/Editorial Director: Tim Clancy (898-1677;
     E-mail: clancy)
     Assistant Director: Jo Joslyn (898-5754)
     Assistant to the Director/Rights & Permissions: Eileen P.
     Hillman (898-6263; E-mail: mullen)
Acquisitions Editorial: Patricia Smith (anthropology, women's
     studies, nursing) (898-1709, E-mail: smith); Jerry
     Singerman (history, literature, music) (898-1681; E-mail:
     singerman); Jo Joslyn (art history, architecture) (898-5754);
     Tim Clancy (law, business, economics) (898-1677); Eileen
     Hillman (reprint series)
     Editorial Assistants: Ridley Hammer (898-6262); TBA
Manuscript Editorial: Alison Anderson, Managing Editor (898-
     1678; E-mail: anderson)
     Manuscript Editor: Mindy Brown (898-1679; E-mail: brown)
Marketing: Kathleen Moore, Manager (898-1673; E-mail: moore)
     Assistant Marketing Manager: Michael Waxman (898-1674)
     Marketing Assistant: Carol Gaines (898-6264; E-mail:
     cgaines)
Design and Production: Carl Gross, Manager (898-1675; E-mail:
     gross)
     Production Coordinator: Toni Kidwell (898-1676; E-mail:
     kidwell)
Business: Julie Schilling, Manager (898-1670; E-mail: schilling)
     Accountant: Kathy Ranalli (898-1682)
     Order Supervisor: Marlene DeBella (898-1671)

Full Member

Established: 1869
Title output 1992: 69
Titles currently in print: 770

Admitted to AAUP: 1967
Title output 1993: 79
Journals published: 1

Editorial Program

Scholarly books and serious nonfiction, with special interests in American, British and Medieval history; anthropology; archaeology, art and art history; architecture; biological sciences; business; computer science; economics; folklore; history of science, technology and medicine; law; linguistics; American and British literature; medicine; music theory; nursing; Pennsylvania regional studies; veterinary science; women's studies; and the following journal: *Nursing History Review*. Submissions are not invited in the areas of fiction, poetry, or self-help.

Special series, joint imprints, and/or copublishing programs: Architectural Theory; Chemical Sciences in Society; Conduct and Communication; Contemporary Ethnography; Health Economics; Classics in Biology and Medicine; History of Food; Developmental Biology; Ethnohistory; Innovation in Organizations; Law in Social Context; Lectura Dantis Americana; The Middle Ages; New Cultural Studies; Penn Studies in Contemporary Fiction; Pennsylvania Edition of Theodore Dreiser; Pennsylvania Studies in Human Rights; Pension Research Council; Publications Sponsored by the Shelby Collum Davis Center; Studies in the Criticism and Theory of Music; Studies in Health, Illness and Caregiving.

The press distributes books from the Philadelphia Museum of Art; Philadelphia Martime Museum; University of Pennsylvania Museum; Oral Traditions Project; The Walker Art Center; the National Gallery of Art; and Liverpool University Press.

The Pennsylvania State University Press

---

820 North University Drive
University Park, PA 16802-1003
(814) 865-1327
Fax: (814) 863-1408
Cable: UNIPRESS
Internet: (user I.D.)
    @psuvm.psu.edu

<u>U.K. Representative:</u>
TBA

<u>Canadian Representative:</u>
Michael Romano
Red Barn Booksellers

Director: Sanford G. Thatcher (E-mail: sgt3)
     Assistant to the Director: Jan Wilson
Acquisitions Editorial: Philip Winsor, Senior Editor (humanities)
     Editor: Peter J. Potter (history and social sciences)
     (E-mail: pjp8)
     Editorial Secretary: Georgia Homan
     Manuscript Editorial: Cherene Holland, Managing Editor
     (E-mail: cah8)
     Senior Manuscript Editor: Peggy Hoover
Marketing: TBA, Manager
     Assistant Marketing Manager: Lisa Bayer (E-mail: lmb2)
     Advertising Manager: Karen Walker
Design and Production: Janet L. Dietz, Manager
     Chief Designer: Steven Kress
     Production Assistant/Designer: Megan Youngquist
Business: Clifford Way, Jr., Supervisor, Accounting Operations
     (E-mail: cgw3)
     Billing Clerks: Kevin Trostle, Barbara Darlington
Journals: Mary Lou McMurtrie

Full Member

Established: 1956   Admitted to AAUP: 1960
Title output 1992: 70   Title output 1993: 66
Titles currently in print: 610   Journals published: 9

Editorial Program

Scholarly books in the humanities and social sciences, with
current emphasis on art history; literature; philosophy; religious
studies; Latin American studies; criminology; geography; law;
international relations; political theory; comparative politics; U.S.
politics; sociology; American and European history; medieval
studies; women's studies; science, technology, and society studies;
and the following journals: *The Chaucer Review; Philosophy and
Rhetoric; The Journal of General Education; Journal of Policy
History; Journal of Speculative Philosophy; Comparative
Literature Studies; Resources for American Literary Study;
SHAW: The Annual of Bernard Shaw Studies;* and *Legacy: A
Journal of American Women Writers.* Submissions are not
invited in fiction, poetry, or drama.

    Special imprints: Keystone Books.

    Special series: Literature and Philosophy; Penn State Studies
in Romance Literatures; Hermeneutics: Studies in the History of
Religions; Re-Reading the Canon: Feminist Interpretations of
Major Philosophers; Penn State Series in the History of the Book;
African American Authors Series; Studies of the Greater
Philadelphia Philosophy Consortium; Penn State Series in Lived

Religious Experience; Kenneth Scott Latourette Prize in Religion and Modern History.

University of Pittsburgh Press

---

127 North Bellefield Avenue
Pittsburgh, PA 15260
(412) 624-4110
Fax: (412) 624-7380

<u>European Distribution:</u>
Eurospan

<u>Distribution Center:</u>
CUP Services
Box 6525
750 Cascadilla
Ithaca, NY 14851
Orders only: (800) 666-2211
Fax: (607) 272-6292
Customer Service: (607) 277-2211

Acting Director: Peter Oresick (624-4112)
    Assistant to the Director: Mary Ellen Pearl (624-4112)
Editorial: Catherine Marshall, Assistant Director and Editor-in-Chief (composition, Latin American studies, Russian and East European studies, dance) (624-7386)
    Senior Manuscript Editor: Jane Flanders (political science) (624-7385)
    Production Editor: Kathleen McLaughlin (624-7387)
    Pitt Poetry Series Editor: Ed Ochester (624-7386)
    Editorial Assistant: Elizabeth Detwiler (nature series) (624-7386)
Marketing: Peter Oresick, Promotion and Marketing Manager (624-7392)
    Assistant Promotion & Marketing Manager: Frank Lehner (624-7391)
    Publicity Coordinator: Luisa Bonavita (624-4111)
    Direct Mail/Exhibits Coordinator: Jennifer Matesa (624-4517)
    Acting Production & Design Manager: Kathleen Plummer (624-7383)
Business: Cindy Wessels, Manager (624-7393)
    Assistant Business Manager: Colleen Salcius (624-7382)
    Business Assistant: Michelle Wright (624-7393)
Subsidiary Rights Manager: Margie K. Bachman (624-7378)

Full Member

Established: 1936

Admitted to AAUP: 1937

Title output 1992: 52

Title output 1993: 48

Titles currently in print: 557

Editorial Program

Humanities and social sciences. Submissions are not invited in the hard sciences.

Special series, joint imprints and/or copublishing programs: Pitt Poetry Series; Pitt Latin American Series; Colección Archivos; Pittsburgh Editions of Latin American Literature; Pittsburgh Series in Bibliography; Pitt Series in Policy and Institutional Studies; Pitt Series in Russian and East European Studies; Pittsburgh Series in Composition, Literacy, and Culture; Pitt Series in Social and Labor History; Milton Studies; the Papers of Robert Morris; the Agnes Lynch Starrett Poetry Prize; and the Drue Heinz Literature Prize.

The press distributes and copublishes selected titles of The Carnegie Museum of Art, The Carnegie Museum of Natural History, The Carnegie Library, The Helen Clay Frick Foundation, and the Historical Society of Western Pennsylvania.

Princeton University Press

<u>Executive Offices</u>:
41 William Street
Princeton, NJ 08540-5237
(609) 258-4900
Fax: (609) 258-6305
Telex: 510-685-2306
Internet: (firstname_lastname)
        @pupress.princeton.edu

<u>Order Fulfillment</u>:
California/Princeton
Fulfillment Services
1445 Lower Ferry Road
Ewing, NJ 08618
Customer Service: (800) 777-4726
(609) 883-1759
Fax: (609) 883-7413

<u>U.K./European Office</u>:
University Presses of California,
Columbia, and Princeton, Ltd.
1 Oldlands Way, Bognor Regis
West Sussex PO22 9SA England
Phone: (243) 842165
Fax: (243) 842167

Director: Walter H. Lippincott (258-4903)

> Administrative Assistant to the Director: Jennifer Mathews (258-4953)
>
> Associate Director and Controller: Patrick Carroll (258-2486)

Acquisitions Editorial: Emily Wilkinson, Science Publisher (biological sciences) (258-4893); Peter Dougherty, Social Science Publisher (economics) (258-6778); Ann Wald, Executive Editor/Department Administrator (philosophy, religion, political theory) (258-2928)

> Acquisitions Editors: Malcolm DeBevoise (political science, law, cognitive science) (258-4922); Trevor Lipscombe (physical sciences, mathematics) (258-5775); Mary Murrell (anthropology, film studies, literature, women's studies) (258-4916); Lauren Osborne (classics, history) (258-4935); Elizabeth Powers (fine arts, music) (258-4937); Sara Van Rheenen (life and earth sciences) (258-4930)

Manuscript Editorial: Janet Stern, Managing Editor (258-5715)

> Editorial Production Manager: Jane Low (258-5406)
>
> Electronic Manuscripts Manager: Gretchen Oberfranc (258-4909)

Marketing: Adam Fortgang, Marketing Director (258-4896)

> Advertising Manager: Ray Potter (258-4924)
>
> Promotion Manager: Leslie Nangle (258-5881)
>
> Exhibits and Text Promotion Manager: Anna Kwapien (258-4915)

Sales: Eric Rohmann, Sales Director (258-4898)

> Subsidiary Rights Director: Brigitta van Rheinberg (258-5121)
>
> Permissions Manager: Florence Slade (258-5045)
>
> Publicity Director: Nina Mehta (258-5714)
>
> Reprints Editor: Deborah Tegarden (258-1413)

Production Director: Anju Makhijani (258-4929)

Business: Patrick Carroll, Controller (258-2486)

> Associate Controller: Bert Young (896-2111) (no E-mail)

Information Systems: Chuck Creesy, Director of Computing and Publishing Technologies (258-5745)

> Electronic Publisher: Doug Kincade (258-2167)

Journals: Robert Brown, Managing Editor, *Philosophy and Public Affairs* (258-1411)

Full Member

Established: 1905	Admitted to AAUP: 1937
Title output 1992: 190	Title output 1993: 190
Titles currently in print: 3,500	Journals published: 2

Editorial Program

Humanities: American, Asian, Middle Eastern, Russian, and East European history; archaeology; classics; fine arts (art history, music, painting and sculpture); philosophy; political theory; literature; religious studies; science: astrophysics, biology, chemistry, computer science, engineering, geology, history of science (including medicine), mathematics, ornithology, physics; social science: anthropology, economics, ethnic studies, law (constitutional and international), political science, sociology (especially historical), urban studies. The press does not publish drama or fiction.

Journals: *Annals of Mathematics; Philosophy and Public Affairs.* The press publishes only journals closely connected by subject area to its book-publishing program. Subscription fulfillment is handled by The Johns Hopkins University Press, Baltimore, Maryland.

Special imprints: The Bollingen Series, established in 1941 by the Bollingen Foundation, has been published by Princeton University Press since 1967. The Series includes original contributions to scholarship, translations of works heretofore unavailable in English, and new editions of classics. Among its fields of interest are aesthetics, archaeology, cultural history, ethnology, literary criticism, mythology, philosophy, psychology, religion, and symbolism. The press is not accepting further contributions to the Series.

Special monograph series: Alix G. Mautner Memorial Lectures; Princeton Studies in American Politics; Historical, International, and Comparative Perspectives; Annals of Mathematics Studies; A.W. Mellon Lectures in the Fine Arts; Charles Beebe Martin Classical Lectures; Contemporary Japanese Nonfiction; Eliot Janeway Lectures on Historical Economics; History of Business and Technology; Literature in History Series; Mathematical Notes; Monographs in Behavior and Ecology; Monographs in Population Biology; Muslim Politics; Nonlinear Science: Theory and Applications; Physical Chemistry: Science and Engineering; Porter Lectures; Princeton Essays in Literature; Princeton Essays on the Arts; Princeton Monographs in Art and Archaeology; Princeton Opera Series; Princeton Series in Astrophysics; Princeton Series in Computer Science; Princeton Series in Geochemistry; Princeton Series in Geology and Paleontology; Princeton Series in Physics; Princeton Studies in Culture/Power/History; Princeton Studies in International History and Politics; Princeton Studies in Legal Theory; Princeton Studies in Mathematical Economics; Princeton Studies on the Near East; Studies in Church and State; Studies in Intellectual History and the History of Philosophy; Studies in Moral, Political, and Legal Philosophy.

Poetry series: The Lockert Library of Poetry in Translation.

Original source series: The Collected Papers of Albert Einstein; Collected Works of Spinoza; Complete Works of W.H. Auden; Encyclopedia of Indian Philosophies; Kierkegaard's Writings; Modern Classics in Near Eastern Studies; The Papers of Thomas Jefferson; The Papers of Woodrow Wilson; The Philosophical, Political, and Literary Works of David Hume; Princeton Library of Asian Translations; Selected Writings of Wilhelm Dilthey; The Writings of Henry D. Thoreau.

University of Puerto Rico Press

<u>Street Address:</u>
Cond. Vick Center
Avenida Muñoz Rivera #867
Oficina 304–Edificio D
Hato Rey, P.R. 00925
(809) 250-0550/0435/0599
Fax: (809) 753-9116/751-8785

<u>Mailing Address:</u>
Apartado 23322
Estación U.P.R.
San Juan, P.R. 00931-3322

Acting Director: Dalidia Colón-Pieretti (250-0550)
Acquisitions Editorial: Gloria Madrazo, Editor-in-Chief (250-0435)
    Production Manager: Juan L. Abascal (250-0435)
    Editors: Jesús Tomé (250-0599); Ana V. García San Inocencio (250-0550)
Marketing: Aracelis González, Director (250-0550)
Sales: José A. Burgos, Manager (758-6932)
Business: Nandy Vázquez, Manager (250-0615)
    Accounting: Agustín González (250-0435)
    Collections: Moraima Clavell (250-0550)
Journals: Yudit de Ferdinandy, Manager (751-0148)
    Journal Marketing: Nancy Torres (250-0725)

Full Member

Established: 1932
Title output 1992: 36
Titles currently in print: 800
Journals distribution: 4

Admitted to AAUP: 1977
Title output 1993: 37
Journals published: 1

Editorial Program
Scholarly studies on Puerto Rico, the Caribbean and Latin America (in the humanities and social sciences); literary works; Caribbean

Collection; Puerto Rican Classics (literature); Puerto Rican Poetry
Collection; San Pedrito Collection (children's books/ecology);
Colección Verde (ecological collection about Puerto Rico); Mujeres
de Palabra: Colección de Escritos sobre la mujer (literature/
women's studies). Children's books and other general interest
publications.

Journals: *La Torre* and *Revista de Estudios Hispánicos*
(Hispanic studies journals); *OP-CIT* and *Historia y Sociedad*
(Puerto Rican history); *Diálogo* (philosophy).

Purdue University Press

1532 South Campus Courts—B
West Lafayette, IN 47907-1532
(317) 494-2038
Fax: (317) 494-0793

U.K. Representative:
Academic & University
Publishers Group

Canadian Representative:
Scholarly Book Services, Inc.

Director: David Sanders (494-2038, E-mail: dsanders@mentor.cc.
    purdue.edu)
Editorial: Margaret Hunt, Managing Editor (494-6259)
Marketing, Design & Production: Carol McGrew, Manager
    (494-2035)
Business: Donna VanLeer, Office Manager (494-2038)
    Control Clerk: Beverly Carrell (494-2040)

Full Member
Established: 1960
Title output 1992: 7
Titles currently in print: 85

Admitted to AAUP: 1993
Title output 1993: 12

Editorial Program
Scholarly works in literary studies; regional studies; history;
philosophy and religion; social sciences; technology; and
agriculture. Submissions are not invited in fiction or textbooks.

Special series: Verna Emery Poetry Competition; Balkan
and Danubian Studies; History of Philosophy Series; Science and
Society Series; Purdue Studies in Romance Literatures; and the
History of Technology Series.

Resources for the Future

<table>
<tr><td>

1616 P Street, N.W.
Washington, DC 20036-1400
(202) 328-5000
Fax: (202) 939-3460
Cable Address: RESOURCE

</td><td>

<u>Book Orders and Customer Service:</u>
P.O. Box 4852
Hampden Station
Baltimore, MD 21211
(410) 516-6955
Fax: (410) 516-6998

</td></tr>
</table>

Director of Publications: Richard Getrich (328-5085)
Production Editor: Betsy Kulamer (328-5026)
Editor/Writer: Melissa Edeburn (328-5113)
Book Marketing Manager: Shirley McDermott (328-5086)

Associate Member

Established: 1952

Admitted to AAUP: 1988

Title output 1992: 5

Title output 1993: 6

Titles currently in print: 125

Editorial Program

Resources for the Future (RFF) publishes books principally in the field of natural resources and environmental economics. Its books are the results of research carried out by staff research fellows and by those, such as RFF grantees and visiting fellows, whose work has been sponsored in whole or part by the organization.

Among the specialized topics currently represented by RFF books in print are the following: agriculture; energy; environmental economics and policy; forestry; international environmental studies; land use; minerals; political science; resource economics and policy; U.S. regional issues; water resources; space economics; risk management; and climate resources. RFF books embody both theoretical and applied approaches to their topics and often deal with public policy issues.

Rice University Press

Street Address:
6100 S. Main, Entrance #7
Admin. Annex
Houston, TX 77005
(713) 527-6035
(713) 285-5236
Fax: (713) 285-5276

Mailing Address:
P.O. Box 1892
Houston, TX 77251

Distributors:
Texas A&M University Press
Drawer C
College Station, TX 77843

Faculty Editor: Fred von der Mehden
Acquiring/Managing Editor: Susan Bielstein
Marketing Manager: Caitlin Wood
Editorial Assistants: Zing Koh, Ryan Hess
Accountant: Dixie Griffin

Affiliate Member
Established: 1981
Title output 1992: 6
Titles currently in print: 48

Admitted to AAUP: 1987
Title output 1993: 6

Editorial Program
Literary theory and criticism; photography; art and architecture; regional (Texas); ethnic studies; Latin America; history; nature; history of science; urban studies; African-American studies; business; fiction reprints. Submissions are not invited in unpublished fiction or poetry. The press distributes back issues of the journal *Rice University Studies*. The press also publishes a fiction reprint series.

The Rockefeller University Press

222 East 70th Street
New York, NY 10021-5405
(212) 327-7938
Fax: (212) 327-7944
Telex: 710-581-4146
Internet: (user I.D.)@rockvax.rockefeller.edu

Interim Director: Raymond Fastiggi (327-8567; E-mail: fastigg)
  Assistant to the Director: Stephanie Gregerman
  (327-8880; E-mail: jcb)
Editorial: Dianne Mitchell, Managing Editor (327-8568; E-mail:
  mitched)
Design and Production: Heather Leahy, Manager (327-8569;
  E-mail: leahy)
  Designer: Jody Miller (327-8569; E-mail: millerj)
Journals: Leslie Grundfest, Production–Editorial Manager (327-
  8545; Fax: 327-8513; E-mail: grund)
Business: Raymond Fastiggi, Interim Director

Affiliate Member

Established: 1958	Admitted to AAUP: 1982
Title output 1992: 1	Title output 1993: 0
Titles currently in print: 37	Journals published: 4

Editorial Program

Scholarly works on scientific subjects under study at the
Rockefeller University, primarily in the biomedical sciences.
Interested in related subjects, such as historical, philosophical or
biographical studies, that illuminate the goals of our scientific
frontiers, along with problems and opportunities that this
research poses. Manuscripts from nonscientific fields are unlikely
to be considered. The press publishes the following four journals:
*The Journal of Cell Biology; The Journal of Clinical Investigation;
The Journal of Experimental Medicine;* and *The Journal of
General Physiology.* Occasionally a book is published under a
joint imprint and/or copublishing arrangement. Copublication
with W.H. Freeman: A Guided Tour of the Living Cell, Christian
DeDuve (Scientific American Library).

Russell Sage Foundation

112 East 64th Street
New York, NY 10021
(212) 750-6000
Fax: (212) 371-4761
Internet: lisa@rsage.org

<u>U.K. Representative:</u>
University Presses Marketing

Director of Publications: Lisa Nachtigall (750-6037)
   Assistant to the Director: Susan Hoseth (750-6038)
Exhibits Manager: Sara Beckman (750-6030)
Permissions Editor: Sara Beckman
Foundation President: Eric Wanner

Associate Member

Established: 1907
Title output 1992: 12
Titles currently in print: 209

Admitted to AAUP: 1989
Title output 1993: 16

Editorial Program
Scholarly books on current research and policy issues in the social sciences.

Rutgers University Press

109 Church Street
New Brunswick, NJ 08901-1242
(908) 932-7762
Fax: (908) 932-7039
Internet: (user I.D.)@
   zodiac.rutgers.edu.

<u>Warehouse, Fulfillment,
and Customer Service:</u>
(908) 932-1970
Fax: (908) 932-1974
(800) 446-9323

<u>U.K. Representatives:</u>
John Ramsay Marketing Ltd.
Bill Bailey Publishers Reps

<u>Canadian Representative:</u>
Kellington & Associates

Acting Director: Stephen D. Maikowski (932-7762; E-mail:
   maikowski)
   Secretary to the Director: Christina Lindeman (932-7762)
Acquisitions Editorial: Leslie Mitchner, Editor-in-Chief

(humanities, literature, art, film) (932-7782)
Editor: TBA (social sciences, history, regional) (932-7763)
Editor: Karen Reeds (sciences, biology, history of science)
(932-8174; E-mail: reeds)
Manuscript Editorial & Production: Marilyn Campbell, Managing
Editor (932-7396)
Senior Editor/Electronic Manuscripts Manager: Kate Harrie
(932-7365; E-mail: harrie)
Assistant Manager, Production: Tricia Politi (932-7546)
Assistant Manager, Reprints and Production Services:
Susan Dermody (932-7546)
Marketing: Stephen Maikowski, Assistant Director, Marketing and
Sales (932-7764)
Publicity and Domestic Subsidiary Rights Manager: Beth
Salamon (932-7764)
Promotion Manager: TBA (932-7764)
Marketing Assistant: Arlene Bacher (932-7765)
Business: Prospero Hernandez, Associate Director and Chief
Operations Officer (932-7038)
Business Manager: Rona Tenenbaum (932-7038)
Accounting: Eileen Kornberg (932-7037)
Fulfillment: Barbara Reid, Supervisor and Customer
Service (932-1969)
Credit and Collection Manager: John Reid (932-1968)
Order Entry: Penny Borden (932-1967)

Full Member

Established: 1936   Admitted to AAUP: 1937
Title output 1992: 70   Title output 1993: 71
Titles currently in print: 665

Editorial Program

Books of general interest; fiction; literary criticism; film; art history
and criticism; American history; women's studies; anthropology;
sociology; geography; life and health sciences; history of
science/technology; books of regional interest; pioneering
textbooks; black studies and literature; biography.

Special series, joint imprints and/or copublishing
programs: Perspectives on the Sixties; American Women Writers
Series (fiction reprints); Rutgers Films in Print; Depth of Field:
Topics in Film and Visual Culture; Crime, Law, and Deviance
Series; Adolescence in a Changing World; Women Writers: Texts
and Contexts; Health and Medicine in American Society;
Communications: A Multidisciplinary Approach; Lives of
Women in Science; joint imprints with The Jane Voorhees
Zimmerli Museum and the Museum of the City of New York.

The press also distributes publications of the New Jersey Historical Society.

Scandinavian University Press
(formerly Universitetsforlaget)

Kolstadgaten 1
N-0608 Oslo, Norway
Phone: 47-22 57 54 00
Fax: 47-22 57 53 55

<u>Mailing Address:</u>
P.O. Box 2959 Toyen
N-0608 Oslo, Norway

Scandinavian University Press North America
875-84 Massachusetts Avenue
Cambridge, MA 02139, USA
Phone: (617) 497-6515
(800) 498-2877
Fax: (617) 354-6875

Chairman of the Board: Professor Inge Lonning
Managing Director: Trygve Ramberg
     Deputy Managing Director: Petter A. Knudsen
Scholarly Books, University Textbooks, and General:
     Editorial Director: Randi Bauer
     Editor-in-Chief: Lars Alldén
     Marketing Manager: Unni Fjesme
Secondary School Textbooks:
     Editorial Director: Marit Landsem Berntsen
     Section Heads: Per Bakken (general education, business & physical training); Vegard Rian (technology and vocational training)
Marketing Manager: Inger Føyner
Personnel Manager: Per-Kristian Paulsboe
Foreign Rights Manager: Elisabet W. Middlethon
Sales Manager: Sissel Henriksen
Journals: Editorial Director: Terje Sorlie
     Editors: Sophie Gabbe Nygaard, Agnete Schjonsby, Hakan Parup (Stockholm office)
     Marketing Manager: Harald Joa
Warehouse, Shipping, Orders: Ray Abiad (Books); Alessandro De Paoli (Subscription Journals); Aud Arvesen Larsen (Single Copies Journals)

International Member

Established: 1950   Admitted to AAUP: 1970
Title output 1992: 382   Title output 1993: 390
Titles currently in print: 4,500   Journals published: 110

Editorial Program

Scholarly works by Norwegian scholars in all fields, particularly in the humanities and social sciences; textbooks in all subjects for students at the universities and other higher education institutions; textbooks for primary and secondary education and in all subjects for vocational schools. Submissions are not invited in fiction, poetry or elementary-level textbooks. Works from foreign authors are considered for journals, series, and trade books.

The press publishes a total of 102 journals, 50 of which are in English, and 15 of which are in Scandinavian languages with English summaries: *Acta Sociologica; Acta Odontologica Scandinavia; Boreas; Cephalalgia; Cooperation and Conflict; Geografiska Annaler—Series A and B; Inquiry; Lethaia; Norwegian Archaeological Review; Norwegian Journal of Geology; Norwegian Journal of Geography; Nordic Journal of Linguistics; Scandinavian Journal of Gastroenterology; Scandinavian Political Studies; Symbolae Osloenses; Acta Chirurgica—The European Journal of Surgery; Acta Dermato-Venerologica; Acta Obstetricia et Gynecologica Scandinavica; Acta Oncologica; Acta Oto-Laryngologica; Acta Paediatrica Scandinavica; Alcohol, Drugs and Traffic Safety; European Journal of Experimental Musculoskeletal Research; European Journal of Public Health; Scandinavian Audology; Scandinavian Journal of Caring Sciences; Scandinavian Journal of Infectious Diseases; Scandinavian Journal of Plastic and Reconstructive Surgery and Hand Surgery; Scandinavian Journal of Primary Health Care; Scandinavian Journal of Rehabilitation Medicine; Scandinavian Journal of Rheumatology; Scandinavian Journal of Social Medicine; Scandinavian Journal of Thoracic and Cardiovascular Surgery; Scandinavian Journal of Urology and Nephrology; Upsala Journal of Medical Sciences; Scandinavian Journal of Forest Research; Swedish Journal of Agriculture Research; Scandinavian Journal of History; Studia Neophilologica; Grana; Ethnos; Scandinavian Journal of Housing and Planning Research; Scandinavian Journal of Psychology; Scandinavian Actuarial Journal; Acta Orthopaedica Scandinavica; Blood Pressure; CMI News Letter & Yearbook; Culture & History; Eranos; European Journal of Endocrinology; Fossils and Strata; International Forum of Psychoanalysis; Konsthistorisk Tidsskrift; Nora; Nordic Journal of Psychiatry; Scandinavian Journal of Clinical and Laboratory Investigation; Scandinavian Journal of Logopedics and Phoniatrics; Scandinavian Journal of Occupational Therapy;*

Scandinavian Journal of Rehabilitation Medicine; Scandinavian Journal of the Old Testament; Studies on Crime and Crime Prevention; World Pollen and Spore Flora.

The press is also publisher to the Norwegian Academy of Sciences and Letters, the Institute for Comparative Research in Human Cultures, and many other academic and government institutions.

Smithsonian Institution Press

Smithsonian Institution
470 L'Enfant Plaza, S.W.
Suite 7100
Washington, DC 20560
(202) 287-3738
Fax: (202) 287-3184
        (202) 287-3637
Cable: SMITHSONIA WSH
Telex: 264729

Director: TBA (ext. 377)
> Deputy Director: Vincent L. MacDonnell (ext. 363)
> Administrative Officer: Ann Garvey (ext. 352)

Acquisitions Editorial: Daniel H. Goodwin, Director, University Press (social sciences) (ext. 312)
> Acquisitions Editors: Amy Pastan (general humanities) (ext. 375); Mark G. Hirsch (history and American studies) (ext. 346); Peter F. Cannell (natural sciences) (ext. 328)

Manuscript Editorial: Ruth W. Spiegel, Assistant Director and Managing Editor (ext. 376)
> Staff Editors: Duke Johns, Jack Kirshbaum, Jenelle Walthour, Deborah Sanders
> Federal Series Editors: John T. Korytowski, Diane M. Tyler, Jonathan Craig Warren

Marketing: Hilary Reeves, Manager (ext. 374)
> Publicity: Lisa Mincey (ext. 343)

Design and Production: Kenneth Sabol, Production Manager (ext. 370)
> Design Manager: Alan C. Carter (ext. 371)
> Designers: Linda McKnight, Kathleen Sims, Janice Wheeler

Permissions: Cheryl Anderson (ext. 388)
Rights and Sub-Rights: Diane Cooke (ext. 365)
Business: John R. Ouellette, Assistant Director, Finance (ext. 354)

Assistant Financial Manager: Brenda Green (ext. 337)

Other Programs:
Smithsonian Books Division: Patricia A. Gallagher, Assistant
      Director and Editor-in-Chief (ext. 317)
New Media: Caroline S. Newman, Director (ext. 362)
Smithsonian Video Collection: Andrew B. Ferguson, Acquisitions
      Editor (287-3081)
Smithsonian Collection of Recordings: Bruce Talbot, Executive
      Producer (ext. 367)

Full Member

Established: 1846   Admitted to AAUP: 1966
Title output 1992: 110   Title output 1993: 103
Titles currently in print: 715

Editorial Program

Publications related to air and space; American cultural history;
history of science and technology; natural history; anthropology
and archaeology; the arts/art history; conservation; and
evolutionary biology. Submissions are not invited in fiction or
poetry.

Special series, joint imprints and/or copublishing
programs: Smithsonian Series in Ethnographic Inquiry; New
Directions in American Art; The Smithsonian Library of the Solar
System; Famous Aircraft of the National Air and Space Museum
Series; History of Aviation Series; Smithsonian Series in
Archaeological Inquiry; Comparative Evolutionary Biology Series;
Smithsonian Studies in History and Technology; Studies in the
History of Film and Television; Biological Diversity Series;
Classics of Smithsonian Anthropology; Smithsonian Nature Book
Series; Handbook of North American Indians; Smithsonian
Studies in Native American Literature; The Papers of Joseph
Henry; and Smithsonian Contributions to: Anthropology,
Astrophysics, Botany, Earth Sciences, Folklife Studies, Marine
Biology, Paleobiology, and Zoology.

Nonbook publications (recordings): The Smithsonian
Collection of Recordings produces archival jazz, musical theater,
and popular song recordings, as well as classical recordings played
by Smithsonian performing arts groups on original instruments.

Nonbook publications (video): High-quality modern and
classical works developed or cosponsored by Smithsonian and
other academic institutions.

University of South Carolina Press

Street Address:
1716 College Street
Columbia, SC 29208
(803) 777-5243
Fax: (803) 777-0160
Internet:
(user I.D.)@uscpress.scarolina.edu

Business Office and Warehouse:
205 Pickens Street
Columbia, SC 29208
(800) 768-2500
Fax: (800) 868-0740

U.K. Representative:
John Ramsay Marketing Ltd.

Canadian Representative:
Scholarly Book Services

Director: TBA (777-4858)

Assistant Director: Robin Sumner Asbury (777-2217; E-mail: robin)

Assistant to the Director: Pat Busbee (777-5245; E-mail: pat)

Acquisitions Editorial:

Acquisitions Editors: Warren Slesinger (rhetoric and speech communication, contemporary literature, military and maritime history, American history, regional trade books) (777-5207; E-mail: warren); Joyce Harrison (religious studies, political science, business and economics) (777-5244; E-mail: joyce)

Acquisitions Assistant: Thelma Davis (777-5244; E-mail: thelma)

Manuscript Editorial: Peggy Hill, Managing Editor (777-5877; E-mail: peggy)

Assistant Managing Editor: Jamie Browne (777-9055; E-mail: jamie)

Marketing: Robin Sumner Asbury, Sales and Marketing Manager (777-2217; E-mail: robin)

Marketing Manager: Linda Fogle (777-4848; E-mail: linda)

Publicity/Rights Manager: Lee Gaither (777-2021; E-mail: lee)

Assistant Marketing Manager: TBA (777-5231)

Secretary, Permissions: TBA (777-5029)

Design and Production: Rebecca Blakeney, Manager (777-2238; E-mail: rebecca)

Assistant Design and Production: Michelle Myers (777-2449; E-mail: michelle)

Designer: Carleton Giles (777-3579; E-mail: carleton)

Business: Dianne Smith, Manager (251-6308)

Credit Manager: Vicki Leach (251-6311)

Customer Service: Libby Mack (251-6309); Carol Dibble (251-6310)
Warehouse Manager: Fred Eaddy (251-6312)
Warehouse Assistant: Eddie Hill (251-6312)
Computer Operations: Gary Sharpe, Information Resources Coordinator (777-0254; E-mail: gary)

Full Member

Established: 1944	Admitted to AAUP: 1948
Title output 1992: 53	Title output 1993: 52
Titles currently in print: 351	

Editorial Program

Rhetoric and speech communication; religious studies; music; social work; international relations; contemporary literature; southern history and culture; military history; maritime history; international business; industrial relations; health; marine science. The press does not normally publish fiction, poetry, symposia, or festschriften.

Special series, joint imprints and/or copublishing programs: The Papers of John C. Calhoun; The Papers of Henry Laurens; The Belle W. Baruch Library in Marine Science.

Southern Illinois University Press

<u>Street/Warehouse Address</u>:	<u>Mailing Address</u>:
McLafferty Road	P.O. Box 3697
Carbondale, IL 62901	Carbondale, IL 62902-3697
(618) 453-2281	
Fax: (618) 453-1221	

<u>U.K. Representative</u>:	<u>Canadian Representative</u>:
Baker & Taylor International	Scholarly Book Services, Inc.

Director: John F. Stetter (453-6615)
Executive Assistant to the Director/Rights and Permissions: Gipsey Hicks (453-6616)
Acquisitions Editorial: Curtis L. Clark, Associate Director (453-6629)
Acquisitions Editor: TBA
Editorial Assistant: Kathy Smiley (453-6626)
Manuscript Editorial: Susan H. Wilson, Managing Editor (453-

6627)
     Manuscript Editors: Teresa White (453-6620); Stephen W.
          Smith (453-6631); Carol A. Burns (453-6628)
Marketing: James D. Simmons, Associate Director (453-6623)
     Marketing Assistant: Patti Shands (453-6624)
     Associate Marketing Manager: Dan Seiters (453-6633)
     Direct Mail Manager: Gordon Pruett (453-6634)
Design and Production: Natalia Nadraga, Associate Director
     (453-6614)
     Assistant Design and Production Director: Duane Perkins
     (453-6613)
     Design and Production Coordinator: Robyn Laur Clark
     (453-6612)
Business: Walter Kent, Executive Associate Director and Chief
     Financial Officer (453-6617)
     EDP Manager: Lisa McMannis (453-6610)
     Order Entry: Mona Wilson (453-6619); Tonya Persinger (453-
     6618)
     Warehouse Manager: Kenneth Crowell (453-6621)
     Storekeeper, Warehouse: Dave Robinson (453-6621)

Full Member

Established: 1956   Admitted to AAUP: 1980
Title output 1992: 54   Title output 1993: 58
Titles currently in print: 1,295

Editorial Program

Scholarly books, especially in the humanities and social sciences.
Particular strengths lie in American and English literature;
architecture; film and theater; philosophy; speech, rhetoric, and
composition studies; and First Amendment studies. Lists also in
some of the behavioral and social sciences, including journalism
and education, as well as certain sciences, including botany and
zoology.

Special series, joint imprints and/or copublishing
programs: Crosscurrents/Modern Critiques; Landmarks in
Rhetoric and Public Address; Philosophical Explorations; Studies
in Writing and Rhetoric; Ad Feminan: Women and Literature;
American Civil Liberties Union Handbooks; Library of
Renaissance Humanism; John Dewey: The Early Works, The
Middle Works, The Later Works; The Papers of Ulysses S. Grant.

Southern Methodist University Press

Street Address:
314 Fondren Library West
Dallas, TX 75275
(214) 768-1430
Fax: (214) 768-1428

Mailing Address:
Box 415
Dallas, TX 75275-0415

Director: Keith Gregory (768-1432)
Acquisitions Editor: Kathryn M. Lang (768-1433)
Manuscript Editor: Freddie Jane Goff (768-1434)

Full Member
Established: 1937
Title output 1992: 12
Titles currently in print: 122

Admitted to AAUP: 1946
Title output 1993: 13

Editorial Program
Ethics and human values; fiction; film and theater; medical humanities; religion and theology; Southwestern studies.
  Special series, joint imprints and/or copublishing programs: The DeGolyer Library Publication Series and Southwest Life and Letters.

Stanford University Press

Stanford, CA 94305-2235
(415) 723-9434
Fax: (415) 725-3457
Cable Address: STANPRESS

Director: Norris Pope (725-0827))
     Assistant to the Director, Rights and Contracts: Henrietta Bensussen (725-0815)
     Permissions: Nettie DeBill (725-0845)
Acquisitions Editorial: Norris Pope, Editor-in-Chief (725-0827)
     Senior Editors: Muriel Bell (Asian studies and behavioral sciences) (725-0824); Helen Tartar (humanities) (725-0825); John R. Ziemer (Asian thought and literature) (725-0834)
Manuscript Editorial: Julia Johnson Zafferano, Managing Editor

(725-0833)
Associate Editors: John S. Feneron (725-0828); Jan Johnson (723-3077); Peter J. Kahn (725-0832); Amy Klatzkin (725-0836); Ellen F. Smith (725-0835); Lynn Stewart (725-0816); John R. Ziemer (725-0834)
Marketing: Robert S. Lloyd, Manager (725-0826)
Promotion Manager: Wes Peverieri (725-0823)
Advertising Manager: Gregory G. Kajfez (725-0821)
Design and Production: Copenhaver Cumpston, Manager (725-0842)
Business: Carl Stempin, Manager (723-2272)
Order Fulfillment Manager: Christie B. Cochrell (725-0816)

Full Member

Established: 1925   Admitted to AAUP: 1937
Title output 1992: 92   Title output 1993: 87
Titles currently in print: 1,300

Editorial Program
Scholarly titles in most areas of the humanities and social sciences, and in the natural sciences and law. Particular interests in anthropology; health policy; history; literary criticism and theory; linguistics; political science; psychology; sociology; and women's studies; and in China, Japan, Latin America, and the Soviet Union.

State University of New York Press

State University Plaza
Albany, NY 12246
(518) 472-5000
Fax: (518) 472-5038
Cable Address: SUNYCA

Orders:
State University
of New York Press
P.O. Box 6525
Ithaca, NY 14850

Warehouse:
State University of New York Press
750 Cascadilla Street
Ithaca, NY 14850

Director: William D. Eastman
Assistant to the Director: Leslie Frank-Hass
Acquisitions Editorial: Lois Patton, Associate Director & Editor-in-

Chief
Editors: Carola Sautter, Priscilla Ross, Clay Morgan,
Christine Worden
Marketing: Dana Yanulavich, Director
Marketing Managers: Bernadette LaManna, Francine
Keneston, Terry Swierzowski, Nancy Farrell
Exhibits: Hannah Hazen
Production Editors: Marilyn Semerad, Elizabeth Moore,
Diane Ganeles, Ruth Fisher, Megeen Mulholland, Christine
Lynch
Business: Mary Nicholson, Manager
Customer Services Manager: Janice Heidrich
Accountant: Debbie O'Connor
Royalties: Kathleen Johnson
Secretaries: Julie Waterman, Judy Spevack, Beverly Venable, Debi
Hill

Full Member

Established: 1966   Admitted to AAUP: 1970
Title output 1992: 228   Title output 1993: 231
Titles currently in print: 1,261   Journal published: 1

Editorial Program
Philosophy; religion; Middle East studies; Jewish studies; Asian
studies; work and labor studies; women; linguistics; education.
The press also publishes the journal *Dante Studies*.

Syracuse University Press

1600 Jamesville Avenue   <u>U.K. Distributor:</u>
Syracuse, NY 13244-5160   Drake Marketing Services
(315) 443-5534
Fax: (315) 443-5545

<u>Canadian Sales Representative:</u>
Cariad Ltd.

Director: Robert Mandel (443-5534)
Assistant to the Director: Andrea Garza Pflug (443-5534)
Acquisitions Editorial: Cynthia Maude-Gembler, Executive Editor
(443-5543)
Manuscript Editorial: Joyce Atwood, Managing Editor (443-5544)

Assistant Managing Editor: John Fruehwirth (443-5542)
Copy Editor: Dorothy J. Whyte
Marketing: Thomas Lavoie, Marketing Manager/Assistant
    Director (443-5546)
    Assistant Marketing Manager: Theresa A. Litz (443-5547)
    Promotion Assistant: Andrews Kurian (443-5547)
Design and Production: Mary Peterson Moore, Manager (443-5540)
    Associate Designer: Victoria Lane (443-5540)
Business: Alice Randel Pfeiffer, Manager (443-5539)
    Accountant: Patricia Sanborn (443-5539)
    Credit Manager: Susan DeMar (443-5539)
    Office Assistant, Orders: Rosalie Beccheria (443-2597)
    Order Supervisor: Carol Holava (443-5538)
    Warehouse Manager: Fred Wellner (443-5537)
    Warehouse Assistant: Jeff McManus (443-5537)

Full Member

Established: 1943	Admitted to AAUP: 1946
Title output 1992: 43	Title output 1993: 30
Titles currently in print: 650	

Editorial Program

Contemporary Middle East; international affairs; Irish studies; medieval and renaissance studies, especially the role of women; New York State and the region; Iroquois studies; American history; special education; environmental management studies; peace studies and conflict resolution; utopian and communal societies. Submissions are not invited in fiction or poetry, hard sciences, mathematics, technical law and medicine, ancient history, or the classics.

Special series, joint imprints and/or copublishing programs: The Adirondack Museum/Syracuse University Press; Contemporary Issues in the Middle East; Mohammed El-Hindi Series on Arab Culture and Islamic Civilization; A Critical Bibliography of French Literature; Irish Studies; Iroquois and Their Neighbors; New York State Studies; York State Books; New York Classics; Utopianism and Communitarianism; Syracuse Studies on Peace and Conflict Resolution.

The press distributes books bearing the imprints of: American University of Beirut, Dayan Center for Middle Eastern and African Studies (Tel-Aviv University), Union College Press, the New Netherland Project, The Adirondack Museum, St. Lawrence University, the National Library of Ireland, Colgate University Press, and various departments of Syracuse University.

Teachers College Press

1234 Amsterdam Avenue
New York, NY 10027-6696
(212) 678-3929
Fax: (212) 678-4149
Internet: (user I.D.)@
    columbia.edu

Warehouse:
Teachers College Press
P.O. Box 20
Williston, VT 05495-0020
(800) 488-2665
Fax: (802) 864-7626

Returns:
64 Depot Road
Colchester, VT 05446-2102

Canadian Representative:
Guidance Centre

European Representative:
Eurospan Group of Publishers

Director: Carole Pogrebin Saltz (678-3927; E-mail: cps8)
    Assistant Director/Editorial Production Manager: Sandra
    Pak (678-3926)
    Assistant to Director: Térèse Parisi (678-3965)
    Administrative Assistant: Michael McGann (678-3919)
Acquisitions Editorial: Fay Zucker, Managing Acquisitions Editor
    (Athene, language and literacy) (678-3905)
    Senior Acquisitions Editor: Brian Ellerbeck (administration,
    school change, leadership, policy, special & gifted education,
    curriculum studies, psychology) (678-3908)
    Acquisitions Editor: Susan Liddicoat (early childhood
    education, sociology, educational research, philosophy,
    teacher education/foundations) (678-3928)
    Acquisitions/Development Editor: Carol Collins (infancy,
    counseling) (678-3909)
    Rights and Permissions Manager/Assistant Acquisitions
    Editor: Micah Kleit (678-3827)
Marketing: Mel Berk, Marketing Manager (678-3915; E-mail:
    mb237)
    Marketing Assistant: Justin Mayhew (678-3963)
    Graphic Arts Manager: Dave Strauss (678-3982)
    Publicity Manager/Computer Operations: Leyli Shayegan
    (678-3919; E-mail: ls175)
Production: Peter Sieger, Senior Production Editor (678-3806;
    E-mail: prs7)
    Production Editors: Cynthia Fairbanks (678-3902); Karl
    Nyberg (678-3945); Neil Stillman (678-3907)
    Assistant Production Editor: Patrick Mousseau (678-3914)

Production Assistant: Kim Nelson (678-3911)
Business: Mary Lynch, Business Manager (678-3913)
Business Assistant: Adriane Butler (678-3917)
Secretary/Receptionist: Evelyn Reddick (678-3929)

Full Member

Established: 1904

Admitted to AAUP: 1971

Title output 1992: 57

Title output 1993: 57

Titles currently in print: 550

Editorial Program

Scholarly, professional, text, and trade books on education, related areas, and feminist studies (Athene Series). Multimedia instructional materials and tests and evaluation materials for classroom use at all levels of education.

Specific areas of interest in education are: curriculum; early childhood; school administration and educational policy; counseling and guidance; mathematics; philosophy; psychology; language and literacy; science; sociology; special education; social studies; teacher education; all areas of women's studies.

Special series: Advances in Contemporary Educational Thought; Counseling and Development; Critical Issues in Curriculum; Critical Issues in Educational Leadership; Early Childhood Education; Education and Psychology of the Gifted; Institute for Research on Teaching; John Dewey Lecture Society; Language and Literacy; On Essential Schooling; Politics of Identity and Education; Professional Development and Practice; Professional Ethics in Education; Reflective History; Research Issues in Special Education; Sociology of Education; Special Education; Ways of Knowing in Science; Yearbook in Early Childhood Education; and the Athene Series–An International Collection of Feminist Books.

Temple University Press

Broad and Oxford Streets
Philadelphia, PA 19122
(215) 204-8787
Fax: (215) 204-4719
Cable:
TEMPRESS, PHILADELPHIA

<u>Warehouse:</u>
Temple University Press
Warehouse, 7th floor
Broad and Lehigh
Philadelphia, PA 19132

Director: David M. Bartlett
Acquisitions Editorial: Michael Ames, Editor-in-Chief & Assistant
     Director
          Senior Executive Editor: Janet M. Francendese
          Senior Acquisitions Editor: Doris B. Braendel
Manuscript Editorial: Charles H. E. Ault, Managing Editor and
     Assistant Director
Marketing Director and Assistant Director: Ann-Marie Anderson
          Advertising and Promotion Manager: TBA
          Marketing Associate: Henna Remstein
          Promotions Coordinator: Sam Reynolds
Production: Mary Denham Capouya, Senior Production Editor
          Production Editors: Jennifer French, Richard Gilbertie, Joan
          Polsky Vidal
Business: Barry N. Morrill, Assistant Director, Business
          Operations
          Business Manager: Lauren Ingster
          Accountant/Assistant Business Manager: Steven Cameron
          Warehouse Manager: Howard Morton

Full Member

Established: 1969   Admitted to AAUP: 1972
Title output 1992: 114   Title output 1993: 92
Titles currently in print: 790

Editorial Program

American studies and history; sociology; policy and politics; health
care; women's studies; philosophy; photography; ethics; work;
political economy; urban studies; race and ethnicity; educational
policy; Philadelphia regional studies; anthropology; Latin
American studies; law and society; film theory; gender studies; gay
and lesbian studies.

Special series: American Civilization; Conflicts in Urban and
Regional Development; Ethics and Action; Health, Society &
Policy; Labor and Social Change; Visual Studies; Women in the
Political Economy; The Arts and Their Philosophies; Critical
Perspectives on the Past; Culture and the Moving Image; Asian
American History and Culture; Border Lines: Works in
Translation; Animals and Society; Themes in the History of
Philosophy; Africans in the Diaspora; Environmental Ethics,
Values, and Policy.

The University of Tennessee Press

293 Communications Building
Knoxville, TN 37996-0325
(615) 974-3321
Fax: (615) 974-3724
Internet: (user I.D.)@utkvx.utk.edu

Director: Jennifer Siler
Acquisitions Editorial: Meredith Morris-Babb, Acquisitions Editor
     Acquisitions Assistant: Kimberly Scarbrough
Manuscript Editorial: Stanley Ivester, Managing Editor
     Manuscript Editor: Scot Danforth
     Editorial Assistant: June Hussey
Marketing: Gene Adair, Marketing Manager
     Exhibits/Publicity Coordinator: Wendy Morris
Design and Production: Kay Jursik, Design/Production Manager
     Assistant Design/Production Manager: Cindy Wallace
Business: Jackie Hurst, Manager

Full Member

Established: 1940   Admitted to AAUP: 1964
Title output 1992: 31   Title output 1993: 26
Titles currently in print: 407

Editorial Program

American studies: women's studies, African-American studies, ethnomusicology, history, religion, anthropology, folklore, political science, vernacular architecture and material culture, literature; Native American studies; cultural and ethnic studies; studies in most disciplines on Appalachia and the Southeast; Caribbean studies. Submissions are not invited in poetry or original fiction.

Special series, joint imprints and/or copublishing programs: The Papers of Andrew Johnson; The Papers of Andrew Jackson; Correspondence of James K. Polk; Tennesseana Editions; Three Star Books; Tennessee Studies in Literature; Outdoor Tennessee; Voices of the Civil War; and New Perspectives in American Politics.

University of Texas Press

Street Address:
2100 Comal Street
Austin, TX 78722
(512) 471-7233
Fax: (512) 320-0668
Internet: (first name)
      @utpress.ppb.utexas.edu

Mailing Address:
P.O. Box 7819
Austin, TX 78713-7819

Director: Joanna Hitchcock (471-5708)
    Assistant to the Director: Sherry Solomon
    Special Projects Coordinator: Louise Saxon
    Receptionists: Amjad Khan, Martin Vasquez
Acquisitions Editorial (471-4278): Theresa May, Assistant Director
    & Executive Editor (social sciences)
    Acquisitions Editors: Shannon Davies (sciences); Ali
    Hossaini (humanities)
    Associate Editor: Tayron Cutter
    Editorial Assistant: Charlotte Harris
Manuscript Editorial: Carolyn Wylie, Managing Editor
    Manuscript Editors: Bruce Bethell, Jan McInroy
Marketing (471-4032): David Cohen, Marketing Manager
    Sales: Darrell Windham, Gretchen Webb
    Direct Mail Manager: Nancy Bryan
    Advertising and Publicity Manager: Amy Root
    Marketing Designer: Jonell Clardy
    Assistant to the Marketing Manager: Edwina Rawlins
Design and Production (471-5721): David Cavazos, Production
    Manager
    Designers: Karen Crowther, Ellen McKie, Teresa Wingfield
    Proofreader: Leslie Tingle
    Production Assistant: Peggy Gough
Journals (471-4531): Madeleine Vernezze, Journals Manager
    Journals Promotion Manager: Leah Dixon
    Journals Production Manager: Susan Hausmann
    Journals Production Assistant: Susannah Frishman
    Journals Circulation Manager: Paulette Curtis
    Journals Circulation Assistant: Sarah Marden
Business (471-4034): Joyce Lewandowski, Financial Officer
    Accounts Receivable: Margaret Cano
    Accounts Payable: Linda Ramirez
    Business Assistant: Laura Bost
    Computer Operations: William Braddock

Accountant: Patricia Thompson
Orders (471-4034): Shirley Stewart, Fulfillment Manager
Customer Service: Frances Renteria
Warehouse Manager: Donald Martinez
Warehouse Staff: George Mill, Michael Murillo, Rogelio Rocha, Jr., Luis Martinez
Rights and Permissions (471-5556): Zora Molitor, Rights and Permissions Manager
Rights and Permissions Assistant: Clare Hagerty
Publishing Fellow: Eliza Esquivel

Full Member

Established: 1950   Admitted to AAUP: 1954
Title output 1992: 84   Title output 1993: 92
Titles currently in print: 1,350   Journals published: 13

Editorial Program

Scholarly books in the humanities, social sciences, and natural and physical sciences; serious nonfiction of general interest; regional books; translations of Latin American and Middle Eastern literature; classics; art and architecture; film and media studies; American studies; Latin American studies; Mexican American studies; Middle Eastern studies; Native American studies; and the following journals: *American Short Fiction; Center: A Journal for Architecture in America; Cinema Journal; Conservation Administration News; Individual Psychology; The Journal of Politics; Joyce Studies Annual; Latin American Music Review; Libraries and Culture; Sociological Inquiry; Social Science Quarterly; Texas Studies in Literature and Language;* and *The Velvet Light Trap.* Unsolicited poetry manuscripts and children's books are not invited.

Special series, joint imprints and/or copublishing programs: Film Studies Series; Literary Modernism Series; Texas Pan American Series; Texas Press Sourcebooks in Anthropology; M. K. Brown Range Life Series; Modern Middle East Series; Supplement to the Handbook of Latin American Studies; Texas Field Guides; Corrie Herring Hooks Series; Texas History Center Series; Texas Archaeology and Ethnohistory Series; Handbook of Latin American Studies; Mexican American Monographs; New Interpretations of Latin America Series; Critical Reflections on Latin America Series; Inquiries into Latin America Series; Translations from Latin America Series.

The press distributes publications for the Center for Middle Eastern Studies, Center for Mexican American Studies, Institute of Latin American Studies, Institute for Mesoamerican Studies (SUNY/Albany), and Menil Foundation.

Texas A & M University Press

<table>
<tr><td>Street Address:</td><td>Mailing Address:</td></tr>
<tr><td>Lindsey Building</td><td>Drawer C</td></tr>
<tr><td>Lewis Street</td><td>College Station, TX</td></tr>
<tr><td>College Station, TX 77843-4354</td><td>77843-4354</td></tr>
<tr><td>(409) 845-1436</td><td></td></tr>
<tr><td>Fax: (409) 847-8752</td><td></td></tr>
<tr><td>Orders: (800) 826-8911</td><td></td></tr>
<tr><td>Internet: fdl@tampress.tamu.edu</td><td></td></tr>
</table>

Director: TBA
    Assistant to the Director: Joyce C. Smith
Acquisitions Editorial: Noel R. Parsons, Editor-in-Chief
    (humanities and social sciences)
    Acquisitions Editor: Camille North (natural sciences)
Manuscript Editorial: Mary Lenn Dixon, Managing Editor
    Associate Editor: Bonnie Lyons
    Editorial Assistant: Diana Vance
Marketing: Gayla Christiansen, Marketing Manager
    Assistant Marketing Manager: Mary Ann Jacob
    Publicity/Reprints Manager: Maureen Creamer
    Sales Manager: Steve Griffis
    Promotion Assistant: Joan McHugh
Design and Production: Susan Pearce, Production Manager
    Production Assistant: Angela Stanton
Business: Dianna Hein, Financial Manager
    Accountant: Johnny Ruiz
    Business Operations Manager: Sharon Pavlas
    Order Processing: Sandy Santana, Jackie Thornton
    Accounts Receivable and Collections: Wynona Davis
    Warehouse Manager: Steve Griffis
    Warehouse Supervisor: Michael Martin

Full Member

Established: 1974	Admitted to AAUP: 1977
Title output 1992: 32	Title output 1993: 32
Titles currently in print: 440	

Editorial Program
Books dealing with Texas and the Southwest; American and western history; natural history; the environment; women's studies; military history; economics; business; architecture; art;

veterinary medicine. Submissions are not invited in poetry.

Special series, joint imprints and/or copublishing programs: Joe and Betty Moore Texas Art Series; Kenneth E. Montague Business and Oil History Series; Centennial Series of the Association of Former Students; Texas A&M Economics Series; W. L. Moody, Jr. Natural History Series; Louise Lindsey Merrick Texas Environment Series; Elma Dill Russell Spencer Foundation Series (essays on the history of the West); Environmental History Series; Nautical Archaeology Series; Wardlaw Books; Tarleton State University Southwestern Studies in the Humanities Series; Texas A&M Southwestern Studies; Clayton Wheat Williams Texas Life Series; Texas A&M Military History Series; Charles and Elizabeth Prothro Texas Photography Series; Carolyn and Ernest Fay Series in Analytical Psychology; Studies in Architecture and Culture; and Sara and John H. Lindsey Series in the Arts and Humanities.

Texas Christian University Press

Box 30783
Fort Worth, TX 76129
(817) 921-7822
Fax: (817) 921-7822

Director: Judy Alter
Editor: Tracy Row

Affiliate Member

Established: 1966	Admitted to AAUP: 1982
Title output 1992: 8	Title output 1993: 8
Titles currently in print: 110	

Editorial Program

Humanities and social sciences, with special emphasis on Texas and Southwestern history and literature; American studies; fiction and young adult books, with special emphasis on Texas and the Southwest.

Special series, joint imprints and/or copublishing programs: The Chisholm Trail Series; The Texas Tradition Series; Chaparral Books for Young Readers.

Texas Tech University Press

Admin. Bldg. West Basement
Box 41037
Lubbock, TX 79409-1037
(806) 742-2982
Fax: (806) 742-2979
Orders: (806) 742-2982
      (800) 832-4042
Internet: aqtup@ttuvm1.ttu.edu

<u>Mailing Address:</u>
Box 41037
Lubbock, TX 79409-1037

Director: Wendell W. Broom
Editorial: Carole J. Young, Managing Editor (sciences)
      Judith A. Keeling (humanities)
        Assistant: Fran Kennedy
Marketing: Sandy Glass, Manager
Production: Marilyn M. Steinborn, Manager
Business: Joel Nichols, Manager
      Orders: Celia A. Smith
      Warehouse: Gordon Gentry

Full Member

Established: 1971
Title output 1992: 27
Titles currently in print: 237

Admitted to AAUP: 1987
Title output 1993: 17
Journals published: 3

Editorial Program

Biography and memoir; biological sciences; costume and textile history; environment and conservation; folklore; earth sciences; museum science; regional studies; classical studies; history; literary criticism, history and theory; poetry and fiction; popular culture. The press also publishes the following journals: *The Eighteenth Century; Conradiana;* and *Helios.*

Special series: TTUP Poetry Award Series; Special Publications, The Museum, Texas Tech University; Occasional Papers, The Museum, Texas Tech University; Museology; Studies in Comparative Literature; SRA Monographs.

The press distributes publications of the International Center for Arid and Semi-Arid Land Studies.

Texas Western Press

Street Address:
Corner of Wiggins & Rim Rd.
El Paso, TX 79902
(915) 747-5688
Fax: (915) 747-5969
Orders: (800) 488-3789

Mailing Address:
University of Texas at El Paso
El Paso, TX 79968-0633

Acting Director: John R. Bristol
       Assistant Director: Marcia Daudistel
Acquisitions Editor: TBA
Marketing: Marcia Daudistel
Production: Lisa Miller
Business: Marcia Daudistel, Assistant Director
       Accounts Supervisor: Patti Love

Full Member
Established: 1952
Title output 1992: 8
Titles currently in print: 136

Admitted to AAUP: 1986
Title output 1993: 8

Editorial Program
Scholarly books and serious nonfiction with special interests in the history and cultures of the Southwest; selected art and photography; U.S.-Mexico border studies; environmental studies; and the following series: Southwestern Studies and The Carl Hertzog Lecture Series.

University of Tokyo Press

7-3-1 Hongo, Bunkyo-ku
Tokyo 113, Japan
(03) 3811-0964
Fax: (03) 3814-9458, (03) 3812-6958
Cable Address: UNIVERSITYPRESS

U.S. Representative:
Columbia University Press

U.K. Representative:
Academic & University
Publishers Group

President: Hiroyuki Yoshikawa
Chairman of the Board: Takeshi Yoro
Managing Director: Tadashi Yamashita
Associate Director & Editor-in-Chief: Isao Watanabe
Controller: Kazuhiko Kurata
Manager, International Publications: Etsuko Hamao
Editors: Nina Raj, Susan Schmidt

International Member

Established: 1951   Admitted to AAUP: 1970
Title output 1992: 119 (8 in English)
Title output 1993: 126 (8 in English)
Titles currently in print: 3,776

Editorial Program

Titles published in Japanese reflect the research carried out in the University in the humanities, social sciences, and natural sciences.

Special series, joint imprints and/or copublishing programs: Continuing series are published in biology, earth sciences, and Japanese historical studies. Special projects include publication of textbooks and reprinting of historical source materials.

English-language publishing began in 1960; its aim is to disseminate Japanese scholarship in the social and natural sciences to an international audience. Areas of special strength include Japanese and Asian studies (including history, economics, law, and sociology). English-language publications also include translations of historical and important literary works and diaries.

University of Toronto Press, Inc.

Scholarly Publishing Division
10 St. Mary Street, Suite 700
Toronto, Ontario
Canada M4Y 2W8
(416) 978-2239
Fax: (416) 978-4738

<u>Orders/Customer Service:</u>
5201 Dufferin Street
North York, Ontario M3H 5T8
(800) 565-9523 or (416) 667-7791
Fax: (416) 667-7832

<u>U.S. Warehouse:</u>
340 Nagel Drive
Cheektowaga, NY 14225
(716) 852-0342

President and Publisher: George Meadows (978-2233)
    Vice President Communications & Special Projects: Hamish Cameron (978-2232)
    Vice President Scholarly Publishing: Bill Harnum (978-8457)
    Vice President Administration and Secretary: Kathryn Bennett (978-5850)
    Vice President Bookstores: Ron Johnson (978-7964)
    Vice President Order Fulfillment: Paul Kerys (667-7848)
Acquisitions Editorial: Ron Schoeffel, Editor-in-Chief (modern languages, Erasmus) (978-8432); Virgil Duff, Executive Editor (social sciences) (978-8431); Anne Forte, Managing Editor (978-6739); Joan Bulger, Editor (art & classics) (978-2416); Gerald Hallowell, Editor (history & literature) (902/634-4280); Suzanne Rancourt, Editor (medieval and Renaissance studies, English language and literature) (978-8435); Elizabeth Lumley (directories) (978-8651); Editorial Department Inquiries (978-5171)
Marketing: Carolyn Wood, Manager (978-3987)
    Sales Manager: Joan Yolleck (978-2228)
    Publicity and Promotion: Valerie Hatton (978-2234)
    Foreign Rights: (Ms.) Charley LaRose (978-6817)
    Marketing Department Inquiries: (978-8458)
Production and Design: Sandy Meadow, Production Coordinator (978-2501)
Journals: Anne Marie Corrigan, Manager (667-7781)
Business: Paul McCracken, Director of Finance (667-7905)
    Controller: Miles Hawkins (667-7765)
    MIS Manager: Ron Mar (667-7773)
    Credit Manager: Clive Williams (667-7774)
Printing Division: Peter Mania, Manufacturing Manager (667-7836)
    Manager, The Design Office: Patrick McGovern (978-3686)

Full Member

Established: 1901	Admitted to AAUP: 1937
Title output 1992: 114	Title output 1993: 130
Titles currently in print: 1,000	Journals published: 12

Editorial Program

Classical studies; medieval studies; Renaissance studies; Slavic studies; environmental studies; Erasmian studies; Victorian studies; English literature; Canadian studies; Canadian literature; literary theory and criticism; modern languages and literatures; philosophy; political science; law and criminology; religion and theology; education; music; art history; geography; Canadian and international history; sociology; anthropology; native studies; social work; and women's studies. The press also publishes the following journals: *Canadian Historical Review; Cartographica; University of Toronto Law Journal; Scholarly Publishing; Canadian Theatre Review; University of Toronto Quarterly; Canadian Journal of Economics; Clinical and Investigative Medicine; Physics Essays; Modern Drama; The Canadian Journal of Information Sciences;* and *The Tocqueville Review/La Revue Tocqueville.* Submissions are not invited in poetry or fiction.

Special series, joint imprints and/or copublishing programs: Dictionary of Canadian Biography; Benjamin Disraeli Letters; Collected Works of E.J. Pratt; Collected Works of A.M. Klein; Collected Works of Erasmus; Collected Works of John Stuart Mill; Erasmus Studies; Collected Works of Bernard Lonergan; Lonergan Studies; Historical Atlas of Canada; McMaster Old English Studies and Texts; Medieval Academy Reprints for Teaching; Ontario Historical Studies Series; Phoenix Supplementary Volumes; Publications of the Osgoode Society; Records of Early English Drama; Royal Inscriptions of Mesopotamia; State and Economic Life Series; Studies in Social History; Toronto Medieval Bibliographies; Toronto Medieval Texts and Translations; Toronto Old English Series; University of Toronto Romance Series; University of Toronto Ukrainian Studies; Reprints in Canadian History; Anthropological Horizons; Theory/Culture; Toronto Studies in Philosophy; Italian Linguistics and Language Pedagogy.

Universidad Nacional Autónoma de México (UNAM)

Av. del Imán #5
Ciudad Universitaria
México D.F. 04510
México
5-665-2653
Fax: 5-665-2778

Director: Mario Mendoza Castañeda (665-2653)
Technical Assistant Manager: Francisco Allende Morales (622-6573)
Sales Assistant Manager: Leonardo Dueñas Garcia (622-6570)
Journal Production: Rosa Margarita Guerrero Alonso (622-6576)

Book Selling: Guillermo Velázquez Valadez (622-6583)
Business: Eduardo Domínguez González (622-6582 tel./fax)
Rights and Permissions: Arturo Flores Maldonado (622-6587)
Administration: Manuel Ricardo Campos (622-6580)
General Services: Victor Alvarez Ortíz (622-6587)
General Supplies: Juan Acuña Guzmán (622-6579)
Accounting: José Rojo Uribe (622-6584)
Budget: Luis Gerardo Revueltas Cisneros (622-6586)
Operations and Control: Irma Delgado Hernández (622-6574)
Warehouse: Mario Gutiérrez Rendón (622-6572)

International Member

Established: 1921   Admitted to AAUP: 1991
Title output 1992: Not reported Title output 1993: Not reported
Titles in print: Not reported   Journals published: 80

Editorial Program

American studies; anthropology (cultural, physical); archaeology;
architecture; art & art history (art criticism, art history, decorative
arts, design & graphics, printing and sculpture); astronomy;
bibliography & reference; biography; biological sciences (botany,
genetics, marine biology, microbiology, zoology); business; child
development; classics; communications (broadcast media,
journalism); computer science; democracy; demography; drama;
earth sciences (geochemistry, geology, oceanography); economics
(history, theory); education (history, learning disabilities, theory &
method); engineering; environment conservation; ethnic studies;
foreign affairs; gender studies; geography; history (American, Latin
American, ancient/classical, medieval, modern); history of
science; human rights; law; language (language arts, linguistics,
speech); Latin American studies; library science; literature (literary
criticism, literary history, literary theory, American, classical,
European, medieval, renaissance, modern, contemporary folklore,
mythology, translations); maritime studies; mathematics;
medicine (general, history); music (history, theory); performing
arts (dance, music, theatre); philosophy (ethics, history of
philosophy, logic, metaphysics); physical science; poetry; political
science/public affairs; psychology; publishing; regional studies;
religion; social work; sociology; urban studies; veterinary sciences;
women's studies.

The University of Mexico publishes more than eighty
refereed academic journals produced by different colleges, schools,
centres, and research institutes. Some of these are: *Revista
Universidad Nacional; Gaceta UNAM; Voices; Nuestra América;
Revista de Artes Plásticas; Revista Mexicana de Física*, etc. Journal
subjects cover humanities, arts, natural and physical sciences,

technology, and social sciences. Additional information on each journal is available on request.

United States Institute of Peace Press

1550 M Street, N.W., Suite 700
Washington, DC 20005-1708
(202) 429-3814
Fax: (202) 429-6063
Internet:
dan_snodderly@usip.org

<u>Customer Service:</u>
P.O. Box 88
Arlington, VA 22210-0088
(800) 537-9359
Fax: (703) 243-2489

<u>U.K./European Representative:</u>
University Presses Marketing

Director: TBA
Editorial: Dan Snodderly (429-3814)
Marketing: Kay Hechler (429-3816)
Production: Joan Engelhardt (429-3813)

Associate Member
Established: 1991
Title output 1992: 5
Titles currently in print: 29

Admitted to AAUP: 1993
Title output 1993: 7

Editorial Program
Manuscripts generally derived from Institute-funded research. Serious nonfiction ranging across the entire spectrum of international relations: conflict management and resolution; international law; diplomacy and negotiation; human rights; arms control; mediation and facilitation; foreign policy; ethnopolitics; rule of law; and religion and ethics. The books often deal with public policy issues.

University of Utah Press

---

101 University Services Building
Salt Lake City, UT 84112
(801) 581-6771
Fax: (801) 581-3365

Telex: Graphnet 3789459 Univ Utah SLC
Internet: (user I.D.)@media.utah.edu

<u>Canadian Distributor:</u>
University of British Columbia Press

Director: Nana L. Anderson (E-mail: nanderson)
    Editorial Assistant/Permissions Editor: Glenda Cotter
Associate Director/Acquisitions Editor: Jeffrey Grathwohl (E-mail:
    jgrathwohl)
Marketing Manager: Max Keele (E-mail: mkeele)
    Marketing Assistant/Exhibits Manager: Lyn Marshal
Editorial and Production Manager: Rodger Reynolds (E-mail:
    rreynolds)
Operations/Customer Service: Sydney Grubb (E-mail: sgrubb)
    Warehouse: Vicky Lemay

Full Member

Established: 1949   Admitted to AAUP: 1979
Title output 1992: 26   Title output 1993: 25
Titles currently in print: 195

Editorial Program

Anthropology and archaeology; Western history; regional studies;
linguistics; Mormon studies; Mesoamerica; Middle East studies;
nature writing and criticism; ethics.

Special series: University of Utah Anthropological Papers;
Tanner Lectures on Human Values; Publications in the American
West; Utah Centennial Series; Publications in Mormon Studies;
Ethics in a Changing World.

Utah State University Press

Utah State University
Logan, UT 84322-7800
(801) 750-1362
Fax: (801) 750-1541
Internet: mspooner@cc.usu.edu

Director: Michael Spooner
Executive Editor: John R. Alley, Jr.

Marketing Manager: Mary Donahue
Business Manager: Cathy Tarbet

Affiliate Member

Established: 1972   Admitted to AAUP: 1984
Title output 1992: 8   Title output 1993: 7
Titles currently in print: 54

Editorial Program

Scholarly books with special emphasis on folklore; Western regional studies including environment, society, culture, history, economy; agricultural history; biography; and political science. By invitation only in the areas of fiction, drama, poetry, and literary criticism.

Special series, joint imprints, and/or copublishing programs: The Western Experience Series; The Western Folklife Series.

Vanderbilt University Press

Street Address:
112 21st Avenue South
Suite 201, University Plaza
Nashville, TN 37203
(615) 322-3585
Fax: (615) 343-8823
Internet:
vupress@vanderbilt.edu

Mailing Address:
Box 1813, Station B
Nashville, TN 37235

U.K./European Representative:
Trevor Brown Associates

Canadian Representative:
Michael Romano

Director: Charles Backus
Assistant to the Director: Martha Gerdeman
Editorial: Bard Young, Editor
Marketing: Laurie Parker Duren, Manager
Business and Production: Jane C. Tinsley, Manager

Affiliate Member

Established: 1940   Admitted to AAUP: 1993
Title output 1992: 2   Title output 1993: 7
Titles currently in print: 83

Editorial Program
Scholarly books and serious nonfiction in most areas of the
humanities, the social sciences, medicine, and education. Special
interests include philosophy; religion; anthropology; Latin
American studies; history; literary criticism; natural history; and
titles of regional interest.

The University Press of Virginia

<u>Street Address:</u>
Bemiss House
210 Sprigg Lane
Charlottesville, VA 22903-0608
(804) 924-3468
Fax: (804) 982-2655
Internet: upressva@virginia.edu
Indiv: (user I.D.)@virginia.edu

<u>Warehouse Address:</u>
500 Edgemont Road
Charlottesville, VA 22903-0608
(804) 924-6305
Fax: (804) 982-2655

<u>Mailing Address:</u>
Box 3608, University Station
Charlottesville, VA 22903-0608

<u>Canadian Representative:</u>
Rex Williams, Cariad Ltd.

<u>U.K. and European
Representative:</u>
Eurospan Group of Publishers

Director: Nancy C. Essig (924-3131; E-mail: nce6x)
    Assistant to the Director: Carol M. Mitchell (924-3361;
    E-mail: cmm2m)
Acquisitions Editorial: Cathie Brettschneider (humanities) (982-
    3033); Richard K. Holway (history & social sciences) (924-
    7301; E-mail: rkh2a)
    Editorial Assistant: Boyd Zenner (924-4725; E-mail: bz2v)
Manuscript Editors: Susan Lee Foard (924-6067; E-mail:
    slf9d); Cynthia Foote (924-6065; E-mail: chf); Gerald Trett
    (924-6066; E-mail: glt6h)
Marketing: Nancy Mills, Manager (924-6070; E-mail: njm8j)
    Sales & Publicity Manager: Mary Kathryn Hassett (924-6064;
    E-mail: mkh2w)
    Exhibits Manager: Julie Stowe (924-1450; E-mail: jls9m)
Design and Production: Janet Anderson (924-3585; E-mail: jma7u)
    Production Assistant: Teresa Lowe (924-6069; E-mail: tml3s)
Business: Richard S. Becker, Chief Financial Officer and
    Operations Manager (924-1373; E-mail: rbecker)
    Accountant: Roger L. Deane (924-6068; E-mail: rld7m)

Customer Service: Brenda Fitzgerald (924-3469; E-mail: bwf)
Warehouse Manager: Johnny Tyler (924-6305; E-mail: jrt3u)

Full Member

Established: 1963

Title output 1992: 51

Titles currently in print: 759

Admitted to AAUP: 1964

Title output 1993: 49

Editorial Program

General scholarly nonfiction with particular strength in literature; U.S. history; women's studies; African and Caribbean studies; Victorian studies; religion; constitutionalism; and cultural studies.

Special series: CARAF BOOKS (Caribbean and African Literature translated from French); Feminist Issues—Practice, Politics, Theory; Victorian Literature and Culture; Studies in Religion and Culture; Knowledge: Disciplinarity and Beyond; the Carter G. Woodson Institute Series in Black Studies; History of Early Modern Germany; Minds of the New South; A Nation Divided: New Studies in Civil War History; Southern Texts Society Series; Constitutionalism and Democracy; New World Studies; Age Studies; Race and Ethnicity in Urban Politics; and Reconsiderations in Southern African History.

The press is publisher for Colonial Williamsburg Foundation, Winterthur Museum, Thomas Jefferson Memorial Foundation, U.S. Capitol Historical Society, American Antiquarian Society, Colonial Society of Massachusetts, and the Bibliographic Society of the University of Virginia.

University of Washington Press

Street Address:

1326 Fifth Avenue, Suite 555

Seattle, WA 98101-2604

(206) 543-4050 (General)

(206) 543-8870 (Orders)

Fax: (206) 543-3932 (General)

       (206) 685-3460 (Business Office)

       (800) 669-7993 (Orders)

Internet: (user I.D.)@u.washington.edu

Mailing Address:

P.O. Box 50096

Seattle, WA 98145-5096

U.K. Representative:

Trevor Brown Associates

Director: Donald R. Ellegood (E-mail: ellegood)
  Assistant to the Director and Subsidiary Rights Manager:
  Jessica Lind (E-mail: jlind)
Editorial: Naomi B. Pascal, Associate Director and Editor-in-Chief
  (E-mail: nbpasc)
  Managing Editor: Julidta C. Tarver (E-mail: jctarv)
  Assistant Managing Editor: Marilyn Trueblood
  Editors: Gretchen Van Meter (E-mail: gvanm), Lorri
  Hagman, Pamela Bruton
  Editorial Assistant: Kathleen Pike Timko (E-mail: kptimko)
Marketing and Sales: Patrick Soden, Associate Director & General
  Manager (E-mail: patsoden)
  Sales Manager & Exhibits: Marcy Pirsch
  Publicists: Alice Herbig, Cynthia Wilke (E-mail: cynthiaw)
  Advertising: Mary Anderson
Design and Production: Veronica Seyd, Manager (E-mail: vseyd)
  Assistant Production Manager: Pamela Chaus (E-mail:
  pamchaus)
  Production Assistant: Denise Clark
  Art Director: Audrey Meyer
  Graphic Designer: Robert Hutchins
Business: Dorothy Anthony, Assistant Director and Manager (543-
  2857; E-mail: djabooks)
  Credit and Accounts Receivable Manager: Linda Tom
  (543-8658; E-mail: lindatom)
  Order Fulfillment Manager: Patricia Kain (685-3286; E-mail:
  pkain)
  Accounting and Administrative Support Supervisor:
  Robert Ross (543-2856; E-mail: bobross)
  MIS Manager: Debra Whitney (543-2862; E-mail: dwhitney)
  Warehouse Manager: Eric Ramhorst (543-4342; E-mail:
  amhort)
  Multimedia: Robert Hutchins, Manager (E-mail: bobhutch)
Development: Nina Ventura, Development Officer
  Development Assistant: Cynthia Wilke (E-mail: cynthiaw)

Full Member

Established: 1909   Admitted to AAUP: ca. 1937
Title output 1992: 147   Title output 1993: 115
Titles currently in print: 1,300

Editorial Program

Anthropology; Asian-American studies; Asian studies; art;
aviation history; environmental studies; forest history; marine
sciences; music; regional and general art history; history and

culture of the Northwest; Native American studies; Scandinavian
studies. Submissions are not invited in poetry, fiction,
mathematics, or law.

Special series, joint imprints and/or copublishing
programs: Asian Law Series; the Geo. S. Long Publication Series in
Forestry; History of East Central Europe Series; Jessie and John
Danz Lecture Series; Publications on Near Eastern Studies; Henry
M. Jackson Lectures on Modern Chinese Studies and Publications
in Korean Studies; the Jackson School Publications in
International Studies; Jacob Lawrence Series on American Artists;
McLellan Books; Emil and Kathleen Sick Series in Western
History and Biography; The Samuel and Althea Stroum Lectures
in Jewish History; Samuel and Althea Stroum Books; Thomas
Burke Memorial Washington State Museum Monographs;
Washington Sea Grant Publications; Weyerhaeuser
Environmental Books. Nonbook publications include diagnostic
tests and audiovisual materials.

Washington State University Press

Cooper Publications Building
Pullman, WA   99164-5910
(509) 335-3518
(800) 354-7360
Fax: (509) 335-8568

Director: Thomas H. Sanders
        Assistant Director: Mary B. Read
Editorial: Glen Lindeman, Keith Petersen, Editors
        Copy Editor: Jean Taylor
Marketing: Beth DeWeese, Marketing and Promotion
        Coordinator
Journals: Nancy Grunewald, Coordinator
Business: Mary B. Read, Assistant Director
        Order Fulfillment: Arline Lyons

Affiliate Member
Established: 1927   Admitted to AAUP: 1987
Title output 1992: 7   Title output 1993: 9
Titles currently in print: 63   Journals published: 6

Editorial Program
Pacific Northwest; prehistory, history, and culture relating to the region; Western American history; ethnic studies; Asian-American studies; Native American studies; women's studies; and environmental issues. The press distributes publications for the Washington State University Museum of Art. The press also publishes the following journals: *ESQ: A Journal of the American Renaissance; International Education Forum; Northwest Science; Northwest Theatre Review; Poe Studies; Western Journal of Black Studies.*

Wayne State University Press

4809 Woodward Avenue
Detroit, MI 48201-1309
(313) 577-4600
Fax: (313) 577-6131
Bitnet: kwildfo@waynest1
Internet: kwildfo@cms.cc.wayne.edu

<u>Canadian Representative:</u>
Scholarly Book Services

Director: Arthur B. Evans (577-4606)
    Assistant to the Director: Barbara D. Muzzin (577-4607)
Acquisitions Editorial: Arthur B. Evans, Director (577-4606)
    Acquisitions Assistant: Mary Beth O'Sullivan (577-6127)
Manuscript Editorial: Kathryn Wildfong, Assistant Director (577-4604)
    Manuscript Editors: Lynn Trease (577-6128); TBA
Marketing: Ann Schwartz, Assistant Director (577-4603)
    Sales Manager: Frank B. Ware (577-6077)
    Promotion Manager: Stacy Lieberman (577-2109)
Design and Production: Alice M. Nigoghosian, Associate Director (577-6130)
Journals: Darlene K. Maxey, Journals & Reprints Manager (577-4626)
Business: Theresa Mahoney, Manager
    Order Fulfillment: Theresa Martinelli (577-6126)
    Warehouse Manager: Al Fisher (577-4619)
Rights and Permissions: Mary Garcia (577-6257)

Full Member

Established: 1941   Admitted to AAUP: 1956
Title output 1992: 46   Title output 1993: 38
Titles currently in print: 529   Journals published: 4

Editorial Program

Scholarly books and serious nonfiction, with special interests in
African-American studies; Judaica; classics; folklore; literary
criticism and theory; film and television studies; urban and labor
studies; health sciences; regional and local history; ethnic studies;
and speech pathology. The press publishes the following journals
and annual volumes: *Annals of Scholarship; Criticism; Merrill-
Palmer Quarterly; Human Biology; Lessing Yearbook* (annual).

Special imprints: Great Lakes Books.

Special series, joint imprints and/or copublishing
programs: Detroit Institute of Arts (distribution and co-
publication): African-American Life; American Jewish
Civilization; Classics in Folklore; Classical Studies: Pedagogy;
Contemporary Film and Television; Great Lakes Books; Humor in
Life and Letters; Jewish Folklore and Anthropology; Kritik:
German Literary Theory and Cultural Studies; Henry Ford
Museum and Greenfield Village (distribution); Labor Economics
and Labor Policy; Latin American Literature and Culture; Men
Who Wrote about Women; William Beaumont Hospital Studies
in Speech and Language Pathology.

Wilfrid Laurier University Press

Waterloo, Ontario   <u>U.S. Distribution:</u>
Canada N2L 3C5   Humanities Press International
(519) 884-0710, Ext. 6124
Fax: (519) 725-1399   <u>U.K., Ireland, and European</u>
Internet: press@mach1.wlu.ca   <u>Representative:</u>
                                     Trevor Brown Associates

Director: Sandra Woolfrey (ext. 6123)
        Secretary to the Director: Bev Beitz (ext. 6519)
Manuscript Editorial: Maura Brown, Managing Editor (ext. 6119)
Marketing: Maura Brown, Marketing Manager (ext. 6119)
        Promotions Assistant: Leslie Macredie (ext. 6281)
Design and Production: Doreen Armbruster, Production
        Coordinator (ext. 6120)
        Electronics Coordinator: Steve Izma (ext. 6125)

Journals: Leslie Macredie, Journals Coordinator (ext. 6281)
Business: Jeff Bennett, Financial Supervisor (ext. 6121)

Full Member

Established: 1974   Admitted to AAUP: 1986
Title output 1992: 10   Title output 1993: 13
Titles currently in print: 126   Journals published: 10

Editorial Program

Religious studies; history; literature; philosophy; sociology/anthropology; communication studies; political science; environment/conservation; film studies; art and art history; women's studies. The press publishes the following journals: *Canadian Journal of Political Science; Canadian Social Work Review; Dialogue: Canadian Philosophical Review; Anthropologica; Studies in Religion; Canadian Bulletin of Medical History; Horizons; Toronto Journal of Theology; Canadian Journal of Communication;* and *Journal of Applied Recreation Research.*

Special series and joint imprints: Canadian Corporation for Studies in Religion Series: Editions SR; Dissertations SR; SR Supplements; Studies in Christianity and Judaism; The Study of Religion in Canada; Comparative Ethics. Other series: The Library of the Canadian Review of Comparative Literature.

Copublications with: Calgary Institute for the Humanities; Canadian Corporation for Studies in Religion; and the Kitchener-Waterloo Art Gallery.

University of Wisconsin Press

<u>Street Address:</u>   <u>Mailing Address:</u>
807 West Dayton Street   114 North Murray Street
Madison, WI 53715-1199   Madison, WI 53715-1199
(608) 262-4928
Orders and Customer Service: <u>Europe, Middle East, Africa:</u>
(608) 262-8782   Eurospan Group of Publishers
Fax: (608) 262-7560

Director: Allen N. Fitchen (262-4924)
     Associate Director: Ezra S. Diman (262-4927)
     Assistant to the Director & Associate Director: Colleen Heinkel (262-4928)

Acquisitions Editorial: Rosalie Robertson, Senior Acquisitions
    Editor (262-4922/2-0504)
    Assistant Acquisitions Editor: Mary E. Braun (262-0496)
Manuscript Editorial: Elizabeth A. Steinberg, Assistant Director
    and Chief Editor (262-8905)
    Manuscript Editors: Raphael Kadushin (262-8906); Carol
    Olsen (262-8810)
Marketing: James S. Sanford, Assistant Director and Manager (262-
    4750/2-5379)
    Assistant Marketing Manager: Sheila Leary (262-6438)
    Direct Mail Manager: Charles G. Evenson (262-5384)
    Publicity: (262-5379)
Design and Production: Gardner R. Wills, Production Manager
    (262-4978)
    Assistant Production Manager: Terry Emmrich (262-8977)
Business: Rod Knutson, Assistant Director and Manager (262-4929)
    Shipping & Warehouse Manager: Lee Hosking (262-4951)
    Customer Service: (265-2792) or (262-2994)
    Accounts Receivable: (262-4850)
    Credit Manager: (262-4929)
    Accountants: Melody Bakken, Books (262-7919); Anne
    Herger, Journals (262-0681)
Journals: Stephen M. Miller, Manager (262-4950)
    Assistant Journals Managers: Susan Kau, John Motoviloff
    (262-8909)
    Publicity and Advertising: Adrienne Omen (262-5839)
    Subscriptions: Rita Emmert, Judith Choles (262-4952)
Rights and Permissions: Margaret A. Walsh (262-4925)

Full Member

Established: 1937	Admitted to AAUP: 1945
Title output 1992: 39	Title output 1993: 49
Titles currently in print: 1,129	Journals published: 14

Editorial Program
General scholarly titles and serious nonfiction with special
interest in African-American studies; anthropology; cinema
studies; classics and humanities; environmental studies;
literature; political science; regional studies; social sciences;
women's studies; and the following journals: *The American
Orthoptic Journal* (annual); *Arctic Anthropology; The Journal of
Consumer Affairs; Contemporary Literature; The Journal of
Aesthetics and Art Criticism; The Journal of Human Resources;
Land Economics; Landscape Journal; Luso-Brazilian Review; The
Modern Language Journal; Monatshefte; Restoration and
Management Notes; Substance;* and *Urban and Regional*

Information Systems Journal (URISA). Submissions are not invited in fiction, drama, festschriften, poetry (except for specific submissions to the poetry competition listed below), and unrevised doctoral dissertations.

Special series, joint imprints and/or copublishing programs: Wisconsin Studies in American Autobiography; The Brittingham Prize in Poetry and the Felix Pollak Prize in Poetry; History of American Thought and Culture; History of Anthropology; La Follette Public Policy; Life Course Studies; New Directions in Anthropological Writing; North Coast Books; Rhetoric of the Human Sciences; Social Demography; Science and Literature; Wisconsin Project on American Writers; Wisconsin Studies in Classics; Wisconsin Studies in Film.

The Woodrow Wilson Center Press

Woodrow Wilson International Center for Scholars
370 L'Enfant Promenade, Suite 704
Washington, DC 20024-2518
(202) 287-3000
Fax: (202) 287-3772
Telex: 264729
Internet: wwcem144@sivm.si.edu

Director: Joseph Brinley (ext. 304)
Administrative Assistant: Pamela J. Moore (ext. 218)
Editor: Carolee Belkin Walker (ext. 229)

Associate Member

Established: 1987   Admitted to AAUP: 1992
Title output 1992: 8   Title output 1993: 13
Titles currently in print: 62

Editorial Program
The press publishes the best work produced by the Fellows and Guest Scholars and program activities of the Woodrow Wilson International Center for Scholars and only works that have their genesis at the Center. The Woodrow Wilson Center is an institute for advanced study, supported by both public and private funds, that brings scholars, public officials, and professionals from around the world to Washington D.C. to undertake individual research and encourages discourse among disciplines and

professions through meetings and conferences.

The Center's interests range throughout the humanities and social sciences, and the press has published in African studies, American studies, U.S. history, European history, international affairs, print and broadcast journalism, labor history, Eastern and Western Europe, Russia, Asia, architecture, Latin America, political science, economics, religion, and urban studies. Three prospective areas of concentration reflecting the Center's newest activities are ethnicity, governance, and urban studies. The press also publishes *The Woodrow Wilson Center Report* five times a year and advises and collaborates with other parts of the Center, including *The Wilson Quarterly* and the radio show "Dialogue" (syndicated on American Public Radio), on outreach projects.

Copublishing programs: The press publishes all its titles through copublishing programs, principally with Cambridge University Press and Johns Hopkins University Press.

Special series: Woodrow Wilson Center Special Studies; Scholars' Guides to Washington D.C.

Yale University Press

Office Address:
302 Temple Street
New Haven, CT 06511
(203) 432-0960
Fax: (203) 432-0948 (Main)
    (203) 432-2394 (Editorial)
    (203) 432-4061 (Production)

Mailing Address:
P.O. Box 209040
New Haven, CT 06520-9040

London Office:
23 Pond Street, Hampstead
London NW3 2PN, England
(071) 431-4422
Fax: (071) 431-3755
Cable: YALEPRESS, London
Telex: 896075

Director: John G. Ryden (432-0933)
    Associate Director: Tina C. Weiner (432-0962)
    Assistant Director & Controller: John D. Rollins (432-0938)
    Assistant to the Director: Dennis Danaher (432-0936)
    Secretary to the Director: Pamela H. Roche (432-0934)
Acquisitions Editorial: Charles Grench, Executive Editor
    (anthropology, archaeology, history, Judaic studies, religion,
    women's studies) (432-0904); Jean E. Thomson Black
    (science and medicine) (432-7534); Jonathan Brent (classics,
    literature, philosophy, poetry) (432-0905); Judith Calvert

(editions and series, languages) (432-0935); John S. Covell
(economics, law, political science) (432-0902); Harry Haskell
(music and performing arts) (432-0916); Fred Kameny
(reference books) (432-0909); Judy Metro (art and
architectural history, geography, landscape studies) (432-
0927); Gladys Topkis (education, psychiatry, psychoanalysis,
psychology, sociology) (432-0924)
    Assistant Editor: Otto Bohlmann (432-0921)
Manuscript Editorial: Meryl Lanning, Managing Editor (432-0913)
    Assistant Managing Editor: Laura Jones Dooley (432-0915)
    Editors: Harry Haskell (432-0916); Dan Heaton (432-1017);
Jane Hedges (432-0917); Lawrence Kenney (432-0908); Susan
Laity (432-0922); Heidi Myers (432-0903); Richard Miller (432-
0919); Noreen O'Connor (432-0923); Mary Pasti (432-0911);
Cynthia Wells (432-0920)
Marketing: Tina C. Weiner, Marketing Director (432-0962)
    Assistant Marketing Director: Sarah F. Clark (432-0965)
    Sales Manager: Susan Donnelly (432-0967)
    Advertising Manager: Ruth R. Sachs (432-0974)
    Publicists: Catherine Gysin (432-0972); Mary Kate Maco (432-
0971)
    Advertising Assistant: Ruth Kramer (432-0975)
    Promotion Designer: Thomas Strong (432-7993)
    Direct Mail Manager: Debra Bozzi (432-0959)
    Special Projects Coordinator: Mary Coleman (432-0912)
    Special Sales: Beth Ineson (432-7350)
    Exhibits: Stanford Forrester (432-0958)
    Sales Representative: R. Stephen Hulburt (432-0968)
Design and Production: Paul Royster, Manager (432-4062)
    Assistant Production Manager: Maureen Noonan (432-4064)
    Production Controllers: Cele Syrotiak (432-4063); Genevieve
Przygocki (432-4060)
    Designers: Nancy Ovedovitz (432-4067); James L. Johnson
(432-4068); Sonia Scanlon (432-4066); Deborah Dutton (432-
4065)
Business: John D. Rollins, Controller (432-0938)
    Customer Service Manager: Jim Stritch (432-0939)
    Credit Manager: Heidi Nissen (432-0942)
    Warehouse and Shipping Manager: Jeff Kazzi (481-4444)
Computer Services: Joan L. Bernstein, Manager (432-0937)
Permissions: Donna Anstey (432-0932)

<u>London Office:</u>
Managing Director and Acquisitions Editor: John Nicoll
Acquisitions Editors: Robert Baldock, Gillian Malpass
Marketing Manager: Kate Pocock
Foreign Rights: Linden Lawson

Full Member

Established: 1908   Admitted to AAUP: 1937
Title output 1992: 208   Title output 1993: 222
Titles currently in print: 2,450   Journals published: 1

Editorial Program

Humanities, social and behavioral sciences, natural sciences, and a journal, *Yale French Studies*. Poetry is not accepted except for submissions to the Yale Series of Younger Poets contest, held annually. Festschriften and collections of previously published articles are not invited and very rarely accepted.

Special series, joint imprints and/or copublishing programs: Collections in the Yale University Art Gallery; Yale Publications in the History of Art; Babylonian Inscriptions in the Collection of James B. Nies; The Bibliography of American Literature; Bio-Origins Series; Cassirer Lectures; The Castle Lectures; *Children's Literature*; The Culture and Civilization of China; Early Chinese Civilization; Documents of Communism; Composers of the Twentieth Century; Cowles Foundation Monographs; Yale Studies on White-Collar Crime; A History of Modern Criticism, 1750-1950; The Frederick Douglass Papers; Economic Growth Center Publications; Yale Series in Economic History; The Works of Jonathan Edwards; The Yale Edition of the George Eliot Letters; Elizabethan Club Series; Yale Studies in English; Yale Fastbacks; The Papers of Benjamin Franklin; The Freud Lectures at Yale; Hermes Books; Yale Historical Publications; Human Rights Watch Books; The Yale Edition of the Works of Samuel Johnson; The Yale Ben Jonson; Yale Judaica Series; Yale Language Series; The Papers of Benjamin Henry Latrobe; Complete Prose Works of John Milton; The Yale Edition of the Complete Works of St. Thomas More; Selected Works of St. Thomas More; Yale Studies in the History of Music; Yale Music Theory Translation Series; Yale Near Eastern Researches; Yale Oriental Series, Babylonian Texts; The Selected Papers of Charles Willson Peale and His Family; The Planetary Exloration Series; Yale Series of Younger Poets; Proceedings in Parliament; Psychoactive Plants of the World; The Psychoanalytic Study of the Child; The Silliman Memorial Lectures; Sport and History Series; The Henry L. Stimson Lectures; The Storrs Lectures; The Yale Edition of The Swinburne Letters; The Terry Lectures; The Yale Edition of Horace Walpole's Correspondence; Yale Western Americana Series; Yale College Series; The Yale Scene: University Series. Yale University Press also publishes some titles with the Paul Mellon Centre for Studies in British Art.

SALES AGENTS: CANADA, U.K., EUROPE

Academic & University Publishers Group
1 Gower Street
London WC1E 6HA
England
Tel: (071) 636-6005
Fax: (071) 580-3995

Airlife Publishing Ltd.
101 Longden Road
Shrewsbury SY3 9EB
Shropshire, England
Tel: (0743) 235651
Fax: (0743) 232944

Airlift Book Company
26/28 Eden Grove
London N7 8EF
England
Tel: (071) 607-5792
Fax: (071) 607-6714

Baker & Taylor International
652 East Main Street
Bridgewater, NJ 08807-0920
Tel: (908) 218-0400
Fax: (908) 707-4387

Bill Bailey Publishers' Representatives
16 Devon Square
Newton Abbot
Devon TQ12 2HR
England
Tel: (0626) 331079
Fax: (0626) 331080

University of British Columbia Press
6344 Memorial Road
Vancouver, British Columbia
Canada V6T 1Z2
Tel: (604) 822-3259
Fax: (604) 822-6083

Cariad Ltd.
89 Isabella Street, Suite #1103
Toronto, Ontario
Canada M4Y 1N8
Tel: (416) 924-1918

Cassandra Book Sales
44 Walmer Road, #407
Toronto, Ontario
Canada M5R 2X5
Tel: (416) 964-0376
Fax: (416) 964-0116

Drake Marketing Services
St. Fagan's Rd.
Fairwater, Cardiff
Wales

Eurospan Group of Publishers
3 Henrietta Street, Covent Garden
London WC2E 8LU
England
Tel: (071) 240-0856
Fax: (071) 379-0609

Gazelle Book Services
Falcon House, Queen Square
Lancaster LA1 1RN
England
Tel: (0) 524-68765
Fax: (0) 524-63232

Guidance Centre
712 Gordon Baker Road
Toronto, Ontario
Canada M2H 3R7
Tel: (416) 502-1262
Fax: (416) 502-1101

Hill/Martin Associates
756 Collier Drive
San Leandro, CA 94577
Tel: (510) 483-2939
Fax: (510) 614-0477

Humanities Press International, Inc.
Atlantic Highlands, NJ 07716
Tel: (908) 872-1441
Fax: (908) 872-0717

Kellington & Associates
88 Mutual Street
Toronto, Ontario
Canada M5B 2N3
Tel: (416) 368-3737
Fax: (416) 368-3380

Kuperard Ltd
No 9, Hampstead West
224 Iverson Road
West Hampstead
London NW6 2HL
England
Tel: (71) 372-4722
Fax: (71) 372-4599

Lavis Marketing
73 Lime Walk
Headington, Oxford OX3 7AD
England

Mosby-Yearbook, Ltd
5240 Finch Avenue East
Scarborough, Ontario
Canada M1S 5A2
Tel: (416) 298-1588 or (800) 268-4178
Fax: (416) 298-8071

Open University Press
Celtic Court, 22 Ballmoor
Buckingham MK18 1XW
England
Tel: (0280) 823388
Fax: (0280) 823233

Oxford University Press, Canada
70 Wynford Drive
Don Mills, Ontario
Canada M3C 1J9

John Ramsay Marketing, Ltd.
31 Oakdale Glen, Harrogate
North Yorkshire HG1 2JV
England
Tel: (0423) 568313
Fax: (0423) 531292

Michael R. Romano
Red Barn Booksellers
481 Peruville Road
Groton, NY 13073
Tel: (607) 277-2338
Fax: (607) 277-2374

Roundhouse Publishing Ltd.
Alan Goodworth
P.O. Box 140
Oxford OX2 7SF
England
Tel: (0865) 512682
Fax: (0865) 59594

Scandinavian University Press North America
875-84 Massachusetts Avenue
Cambridge, MA 02139
Tel: (617) 497-6515
     (800) 498-2877
Fax: (617) 354-6875

Scholarly Book Services Inc.
77 Mowat Avenue
Suite 403
Toronto, Ontario
Canada M6K 3E3
Tel: (416) 533-5490
Fax: (416) 533-5652

Trevor Brown Associates
First Floor, Dilke House
Malet Street
London WC1E 7JA
England
Tel: (071) 436-1874
Fax: (071) 436-1868

UCL Press, Ltd.
University College London
Gower Street
London WC1E 6BT
England
Tel: (071) 380-7707
Fax: (071) 413 8392

The University Press Group
164 Hillsdale Avenue, East
Toronto, Ontario M4S 1T5
Canada
Tel: (416) 484-8296
Fax: (416) 484-0602

University Presses Marketing
The Old Mill
Mill Street
Wantage, Oxon OX12 9AB
England
Tel: (235) 766662
Fax: (235) 766545

Vanwell Publishing Ltd.
1 Northrup Crescent
P.O. Box 2131
St. Catharines, Ontario
Canada L2M 6P5
Tel: (905) 937-3100
Fax: (905) 937-1760

The Association

The Association of American University Presses (AAUP) was established by a small group of university presses in 1937. In the subsequent fifty-seven years, the Association has grown steadily. Today the AAUP consists of 114 member presses, ranging in size from those publishing a handful of titles each year to those publishing several hundred.

The AAUP is a nonprofit organization. Its sources of financing are limited to membership dues and to revenues derived from such activities as organizing national conferences and seminars, producing publishing-related books and catalogues, and operating cooperative marketing programs. In addition, grants provided by foundations and government bodies help to finance special projects.

AAUP's member presses provide much of the personnel who guide the Association and carry out its work. A twelve-member board of directors sets policy for the organization. More than 100 individuals serve on twenty committees and task forces. Their activities reflect the diverse concerns of the membership, including emerging electronic publishing technologies, the First Amendment, production and analysis of industry statistics, computer innovations such as desktop editing and design, copyright protection, professional development, the creation of editorial guidelines for bias-free usage, equal employment opportunity, relations with government and private institutions, national and international marketing, cooperation with libraries, and scholarly journals publishing.

The AAUP "Central Office," located in New York City, consists of an executive director and a small professional staff. The office manages member programs and coordinates the work of the board and committees.

AAUP members fall into four categories—full, affiliate, international, and associate. For a complete description of membership requirements, consult the "Guidelines on Admission to Membership and Maintenance of Membership," reproduced elsewhere in this publication.

1994-95 AAUP BOARD OF DIRECTORS

Bruce Wilcox, University of Massachusetts Press, President (1994-95)

Fred Woodward, University Press of Kansas, President-elect (1994-95)

Colin Day, University of Michigan Press, Past-President (1994-95)

John Ouellette, Smithsonian Institution Press, Treasurer (1994-95)

Veronica Quinn, Columbia University Press, Treasurer-elect (1994-95)

Joan Catapano, Indiana University Press (1994-97)

Janet Fisher, The MIT Press (1994-97)

Karen Orchard, University of Georgia Press (1993-96)

Willis Regier, University of Nebraska Press (1992-95)

Thomas Rotell, University of Pennsylvania Press (1992-95)

Kate D. Torrey, University of North Carolina Press (1992-95)

Tina Weiner, Yale University Press (1993-96)

Peter C. Grenquist, AAUP Central Office, ex officio

AAUP COMMITTEES

Admissions and Standards

Beverly Jarrett, Missouri, Chair
Dorothy Anthony, Washington
John Ackerman, Cornell
Charles Grench, Yale
Leslie Mitchner, Rutgers
Thomas Radko, Nevada

Annual Meeting

Barbara Hanrahan, North Carolina, Chair
Joan Catapano, Indiana
Laurie Parker Duren, Vanderbilt
Susan Harris, Northwestern
Taylor Horst, New Mexico
John Langston, Mississippi
William Lindsay, Harvard
Hilary Reeves, Smithsonian

Business Handbook Task Force

Judith Bergman, North Carolina, Chair
Charles Apostolik, Georgia
Linda Frech, Missouri
Thomas Johnson, New England

Business Systems

David J. McGonagle, Catholic, Chair
Robert Dircks, Johns Hopkins
Michael Leonard, MIT
John Rollins, Yale

Computer

Bruce Barton, Chicago, Co-Chair
Charles Creesy, Princeton, Co-Chair
Michael Boudreau, Illinois
Marjorie Fowler, North Carolina
Steven Kress, Penn State
Jane Lago, Missouri
Lorrie LeJeune, Michigan
Jane-Ellen Long, California
Pamela Upton, North Carolina

Copyright

James Alexander, Cambridge, Chair
Linda Morse, Oxford
Sanford Thatcher, Pennsylvania State

Creative Writing Task Force

Les Phillabaum, Louisiana, Chair
Malcolm L. Call, Georgia
Peter Oresick, Pittsburgh

Design and Production

Mary Mendell, Duke, Chair
Anthony Crouch, California
Dika Eckersly, Nebraska
Steven Renick, California

Development

Thomas McFarland, New England, Chair
Jennifer Crewe, Columbia
J. G. Goellner, Johns Hopkins
Norris Pope, Stanford

Equal Opportunity

Catherine Fry, Louisiana, Chair
Sandy W. Adams, Johns Hopkins
Carol Burns, Southern Illinois
William Mayo, Howard
Sara Velez Mallea, Nevada

First Amendment

Paul Zimmer, Iowa, Chair
Naomi Pascal, Washington
Wendy Strothman, Beacon

International

John Moore, Columbia, Chair
Jonathan Brent, Yale
Prospero Hernandez, Rutgers
William Sisler, Harvard
Arnold C. Tovell, Cairo
Tadashi Yamashita, Tokyo

Library/University Press Relations

Nancy Essig, Virginia, Chair
Ann Marie Anderson, Temple
Charlotte Dihoff, Ohio State
Pat Soden, Washington
Sandra Whisler, California

Marketing

Hunter Cole, Mississippi, Chair
Paul Adams, Harvard
Kathryn Conrad, Missouri
Susan Donnelly, Yale
Amy Root, Texas
Beverly Todd, Oklahoma

Nominating

David Bartlett, Temple, Chair
Allen Fitchen, Wisconsin
Elizabeth Hadas, New Mexico
Seetha A-Srinivasan, Mississippi

Professional Development

Douglas Armato, Johns Hopkins, Chair
Sheila Levine, California
Anne McCoy, Columbia
Susan Schott, Kansas
Elizabeth Swain, Arizona
Paul Wilderson, Naval Institute

Public Policy

Lisa Freeman, Minnesota, Chair
Colin Day, Michigan
Robert Faherty, Brookings
Peter Givler, Ohio State
Peter Grenquist, AAUP
Bruce Wilcox, Massachusetts
Fred Woodward, Kansas

Public Relations Task Force

Peter Givler, Ohio State, Chair
David Bartlett, Temple
Kathryn Grimes, Minnesota
William Hamilton, Hawaii
Susan Rotermund, Oxford

Scholarly Journals

Barbara Berlin Caplan, Johns Hopkins, Chair
Anne Marie Corrigan, Toronto
June McCall, MIT
JoAnn Tenorio, Hawaii
Trish Thomas, Duke
Madeleine Vernezze, Texas

CENTRAL OFFICE STAFF

Executive Director: Peter C. Grenquist

Associate Executive Director: Hollis A. Holmes

Publications Manager & Special Projects Coordinator:
Chris Terry

Exhibits Manager: Jacqueline Philpotts

Accountant: Allan Katronetsky

Executive Assistant: Joan Roney

Program Assistant: Alka Velayudam

Exhibits Assistant: Arlene Eisenberg

Administrative Assistant: Kasheba Marshall

Mail Room Coordinator: A. Leon Hodge

BY-LAWS (Revised as of April 15, 1994)

ARTICLE I: PREAMBLE

This Corporation, existing under the Not-for-Profit Corporation Law of the State of New York, shall be known as the Association of American University Presses, Inc. (hereinafter referred to as the "Association").   The Association expects members to recruit, employ, train, compensate, and promote their employees without regard to race, ethnic background, national origin, status as a veteran or handicapped individual, age, religion, gender, marital status, or sexual preference.

ARTICLE II: PURPOSES

The purposes of the Association shall be:

a)   To encourage dissemination of the fruits of research and to support university presses in their endeavor to make widely available the best of scholarly knowledge and the most important results of scholarly research;

b)   To provide an organization through which the exchange of ideas relating to university presses and their functions may be facilitated;

c)   To afford technical advice and assistance to learned bodies, scholarly associations, and institutions of higher learning; and

d)   To do all things incidental to and in furtherance of the foregoing purposes without extending the same.

ARTICLE III: MEMBERSHIP AND AFFILIATION

Section 1:   Definition of Membership.
The membership of the Association shall consist of those members who were in good standing at the time of the incorporation of the Association in 1964, except those who have since resigned or whose membership has been otherwise terminated, and all other members who have since been admitted in accordance with the procedures set forth in Section 3 of this Article.

Section 2:   Definition of a University Press.
A university press is hereby defined as the scholarly publishing arm of a university or college, or of a group of such institutions within a state or geographic region located within the Americas. A university press as here defined must be an integral part of one

or more such colleges and universities, and should be so recognized in the manual of organization, catalogue, or other official publication of at least one such parent institution. The organization and functions of the university press must lie within the prescription of its parent institution or institutions.

Section 3:   Eligibility for Membership.
Any university press satisfying the requirements set forth in the "Guidelines on Admission to Membership and Maintenance of Membership" (hereinafter, the "Guidelines") that are in force at the time of application shall be eligible for election to membership in the Association. A university press shall be elected to membership by a majority vote of the membership on the recommendation of the Board of Directors at the Annual or a Special Meeting of the membership. Such action shall be taken by the Board only on the prior recommendation of the Committee on Admissions and Standards, which shall be responsible for determining that the applying university press satisfies the minimum requirements for membership.

Section 4:   Voting and Other Privileges.
Each member of the Association shall be entitled to one vote in such business as may come before the Association. Only members in good standing shall be entitled to vote or otherwise enjoy the privileges of membership in the Association. In these By-Laws the use of the term "member," "member of the Association," or "membership" shall mean university presses which have become members of the Association in accordance with Sections 1 or 3 of this Article III.

Section 5:   Cancellation of Membership and Resignation.
A university press, by its very nature, must be devoted to scholarly and educational ends; the failure of a university press to pursue such ends as its fundamental business shall constitute grounds for canceling its membership in the Association. Membership may also be canceled for nonpayment of dues or for continued failure, after admission to membership, to meet the minimum requirements set forth in the Guidelines. Cancellation of membership shall be effected, on recommendation of the Board of Directors, by a two-thirds vote of the members present and voting at the Annual Meeting or a Special Meeting, a quorum being present.

Any member may resign at any time if its current annual dues are paid, provided its resignation is confirmed in a written communication to the President of the Association from a responsible officer or group of officers of the parent institution or institutions. Should a member resign after the due date of the annual dues payment and before the next annual dues payment date, the member is responsible for the payment of such dues at the time of resignation.

Section 6:   International Membership.
At the invitation of the Board of Directors, international membership may be applied for by (a) university-affiliated scholarly book publishers in parts of the world not embraced by the Americas and (b) such presses within the Americas that publish primarily in languages other than English. To qualify for international membership in the Association, a publisher in either class must submit a formal application and provide such materials as requested by the Committee on Admissions and Standards, making evident its scholarly publishing program. Admission to international membership shall be by a majority vote of the membership at an Annual or Special Meeting, a quorum being present, on the prior recommendation of the Committee on Admissions and Standards and the Board of Directors.

International membership may be canceled on recommendation of the Board of Directors by a two-thirds vote of the members present and voting at an Annual Meeting or Special Meeting, a quorum being present. International members shall enjoy all rights and privileges of membership except the right to vote in any business being conducted by the Association, the Board of Directors, or the membership. Any reference elsewhere in these By-Laws to a voting right, therefore, shall be read so as to exclude international members. Dues for international members shall be set from time to time by the Board.

Section 7:   Affiliate Status.
At the invitation of the Board of Directors, university presses within the Americas may apply for affiliate status provided they satisfy all the requirements set forth in Section C of the Guidelines except for the number of books published and in regard to staffing.

Admission to affiliate status shall be by a majority vote of the membership at an Annual or Special Meeting, a quorum being present, on the prior recommendation of the Committee on Admissions and Standards and the Board of Directors.

Affiliate status may be canceled by a two-thirds majority vote of the membership at an Annual or Special Meeting, a quorum being present. Affiliates shall enjoy such rights and privileges as determined by the Board of Directors, but in no event shall their rights and privileges extend to service on the Board of Directors or on the Standing Committees of the Association or voting on any business conducted by the Association, the Board of Directors, or the membership. Any reference elsewhere in the By-Laws to a voting right shall be read so as to exclude affiliates. Annual fees for the maintenance of affiliate status shall be set from time to time by the Board of Directors.

Section 8:   Associate Status.
At the invitation of the Board of Directors, presses of non-degree-granting scholarly institutions and associations may apply for associate status, providing those institutions are incorporated as not-for-profit and that the presses satisfy the requirements for affiliate membership, except that the auspices and structures of the parent organizations of such presses will in all instances be those of non-degree-granting institutions or scholarly associations rather than those of universities. In the absence of an editorial committee or board, an applicant for associate membership shall observe commonly accepted standards of editorial review.

Admission to associate status shall be by a majority vote of the membership at an Annual or Special Meeting, a quorum being present, on the prior recommendation of the Committee on Admissions and Standards and the Board of Directors. Associate members shall enjoy such rights and privileges as determined by the Board of Directors, but in no event shall their rights and privileges extend to serving on the Board of Directors or on the Standing Committees of the Association or to voting on any business conducted by the Association, the Board of Directors, or the membership. Any reference elsewhere in the By-Laws to a voting right, therefore, shall be read so as to exclude associates. Associates shall not be eligible to participate in the Association's statistical programs. Annual fees for associates shall be set from time to time by the Board of Directors. Associates may number no more than thirty percent of the full members of the Association. Associate status may be canceled at any time by a two-thirds vote of the membership at an Annual or Special Meeting, a quorum being present.

ARTICLE IV: MEMBERSHIP MEETINGS

Section 1:   The Annual Meeting.
The Annual Meeting of members shall be held at such time and place within or without the State of New York as may be designated by the Board of Directors after giving due weight to preferences expressed by members. Such meetings shall be held for the purpose of electing the Board of Directors, approving the annual budget, and transacting such other business as may be properly brought before the meeting. At each Annual Meeting of members, the Board of Directors shall cause to be presented to the membership a report verified by the President and the Treasurer, or by a majority of the Board, in accordance with the requirements of Section 519 of the New York Not-for-Profit Corporation Law.

Section 2:   Special Meetings.
Special Meetings of the members shall be held at such time and place within or without the State of New York as may be designated by the Board of Directors. Such meetings may be called by (a) the Board of Directors; or (b) the Executive Committee; or (c) the President, the President-elect, or the Executive Director acting on a request received in writing that states the purpose or purposes of the meeting and is signed by 30 percent or more of the members of the Association.

Section 3:   Notice of Meetings.
Notice of the purpose or purposes and of the time and place of every meeting of members of the Association shall be in writing and signed by the President, President-elect, or the Executive Director, and a copy thereof shall be delivered personally or by the U.S. Postal Service not less than ten or more than fifty days before the meeting, to each member entitled to vote at such meeting.

Section 4:   Representation by Proxy.
A member may authorize a person or persons to act by proxy on all matters in which a member is entitled to participate. No proxy shall be valid after the expiration of eleven months from the date thereof unless otherwise provided in the proxy. Every proxy shall be revocable at the pleasure of the member executing it.

Section 5:   Quorum.
Except for a special election of Directors pursuant to Section 604 of the New York Not-for-Profit Corporation Law, the presence at a meeting in person or by proxy of a majority of the members entitled to vote thereat shall constitute a quorum for the

transaction of any business, except that the members present may adjourn the meeting even if there is no quorum.

Section 6: Voting.
In the election of members of the Board of Directors and the election of Officers, a plurality of the votes cast at an Annual Meeting shall elect. Any other action requires a majority of votes cast except as otherwise specifically provided in these By-Laws. A vote may be taken without a meeting if a majority of the members in good standing submit written votes in response to a request to this effect from the President, the President-elect, or the Executive Director.

ARTICLE V: DIRECTORS AND OFFICERS

Section 1: The Board of Directors.
The Association shall be managed by its Board of Directors, and, in this connection, the Board of Directors shall establish the policies of the Association while considering the wishes of the membership and the constituency of the Association (which constituency consists of the employees of the member presses), and shall evaluate the performance of the Executive Director. The Board of Directors shall meet at least three times each year, once in the fall and once in the winter and in conjunction with the Annual Meeting of the membership of the Association. The Board of Directors shall consist of not fewer than nine or more than twelve Directors, all of whom shall be at least nineteen years of age, at least two-thirds of whom shall be citizens of the United States, four of whom shall be the elected Officers of the Association, and at least one of whom shall be both a citizen of the United States and a resident of the State of New York. Directors other than Officers (Directors-at-Large), like Officers, must be on the staff of a member press, except that the Executive Director is an ex officio (nonvoting) member of the Board of Directors and the Executive Committee.

Section 2: Election Procedure and Term of Office.
Directors shall be elected by a plurality vote of the members present at the Annual Meeting. Candidates may be nominated by the Nominating Committee appointed by the Executive Committee, or from the floor. Officers shall be elected for a one-year term and Directors-at-Large for a three-year term. Directors shall not succeed themselves except that (a) Directors who are elected Officers shall continue as Directors as long as they remain Officers, and (b) the President and the Treasurer may be elected as

Directors during the year following their terms of office as President and Treasurer. Each newly elected Director and Officer shall assume office at the close of the Annual Meeting at which the election is held. Any Director or Officer may resign by notifying the President, the President-elect, or the Executive Director. The resignation shall take effect at the time therein specified. Except as provided for in Article IX ("The Executive Director"), Directors shall not receive any compensation for serving as Directors. However, nothing herein shall be construed to prevent a Director from serving the Association in another capacity for which compensation may be received.

Section 3:   Officers.
The elected Officers of the Association, each of whom must be on the staff of a member press, shall be a President, a President-elect, a Treasurer, and a Treasurer-elect, each to be elected for a one-year term by a plurality vote of the members present at the Annual Meeting. Between Annual Meetings of members, a Special Meeting of members may elect, by a plurality vote of the members present, an Officer to complete the term of an Officer who has resigned or otherwise ceased to act as an Officer.

Section 4:   Duties of Officers.
The President shall serve as presiding officer at all meetings of the membership and all meetings of the Board of Directors and the Executive Committee. The President, with the Executive Director, serves as spokesperson for the Association. At the Annual Meeting of members, the President and the President-elect shall provide a forum for the Association membership and constituency to discuss and assess the Association's program. The President-elect shall discharge the duties of the President in the President's absence, and shall succeed to the office of President in the event of a vacancy in that office, filling out the unexpired term as well as the term to which he or she is elected President.

The Treasurer shall be custodian of the Association's funds, shall be responsible for the preparation of its financial records as the basis for an annual audit, and shall report at the Annual Meeting of members on the Association's financial condition. The Treasurer-elect shall discharge the duties of the Treasurer in the Treasurer's absence, and shall succeed to the office of Treasurer in the event of a vacancy in that office, filling out the unexpired term as well as the term to which he or she is elected Treasurer.

Section 5:   Removal from Office and Replacement.
Any Director or elected Officer may be removed from office at any time, for cause or without cause, by a majority vote of the membership or may be removed for cause by a majority vote of the Board acting at a meeting duly assembled, a quorum being present. If one or more vacancies should occur on the Board for any reason, the remaining members of the Board, although less than a quorum, may by majority vote elect a successor or successors for the unexpired term.

Section 6:   Board Meetings.
Meetings of the Board of Directors shall be held at such place within or without the State of New York as may from time to time be fixed by resolution of the Board, or as may be specified in the notice of the meeting. Notice of any meeting of the Board need not be given to any Director who submits a signed waiver of such notice. Special Meetings of the Board may be held at any time upon the call of the Executive Committee, the Executive Director, the President, or the President-elect.

Section 7:   Board Quorum.
A majority of the members of the Board of Directors then acting, but in no event less than one-half of the entire board of Directors, acting at a meeting duly assembled, shall constitute a quorum for the transaction of business. If at any meeting of the Board there shall be less than a quorum present, a majority of those present may adjourn the meeting without further notice from time to time until a quorum shall have been obtained. The "entire Board of Directors" shall mean the total number of Directors that the Association would have if there were no vacancies.

Section 8:   Board Voting.
Except as otherwise specified in these By-Laws, all decisions of the Board shall be by majority vote of the Directors in attendance, a quorum being present. Any Board action may be taken without a meeting if all members of the Board or committee thereof consent in writing to the adoption of a resolution authorizing the action. The resolution and the written consents thereto shall be filed with the minutes of the proceedings of the Board. Any member of the Board or of any committee thereof may participate in a meeting of such Board or committee thereof by means of a telephone or similar communications equipment allowing all persons participating in the meeting to hear each other at the same time. Participation by such means shall constitute presence in person at a meeting.

ARTICLE VI: EXECUTIVE COMMITTEE

The Executive Committee of the Board of Directors shall consist of the Past-President and President of the Association and the President-elect, Treasurer, Treasurer-elect, and the Executive Director (ex officio, nonvoting). The Executive Committee shall advise and confer with the Executive Director, call Special Meetings of the Board of Directors as necessary, appoint committee members not otherwise appointed pursuant to these By-Laws, and serve as the investment committee for the Association. The Executive Committee shall, if necessary, act for the full Board of Directors between meetings of the Board, but only in those matters not establishing policy or not requiring a vote of more than a majority of Directors in attendance.

ARTICLE VII: STANDING COMMITTEES

The Standing Committees of the Association (in addition to the Executive Committee) shall be the Committee on Admissions and Standards, the Committee on the Annual Meeting Program, and the Nominating Committee. The Committee on Admissions and Standards shall be constituted as provided in the Guidelines, and the Nominating Committee shall be appointed by the Executive Committee and confirmed by a vote of the Board of Directors. Appointments to the Committee on the Annual Meeting Program shall be made in accordance with Article VIII of these By-Laws.

ARTICLE VIII: OTHER COMMITTEES

Other committees may be established at the Executive Director's discretion. The Executive Committee shall appoint chairs of said committees (and the Standing Committees) and such of their members as the Executive Committee may care to designate. The Executive Director shall charge the said committees with such duties, including reporting duties, as he or she may deem appropriate. Reports of standing and all other committees shall be made to the Board of Directors, in writing or orally, as requested by the Executive Director.

ARTICLE IX: THE EXECUTIVE DIRECTOR

The Board of Directors may appoint at such times, and for such terms as it may prescribe, an Executive Director of the Association who shall report to the Board of Directors and who is responsible for implementing policy through fiscally sound programs; establishing, charging, and monitoring the work of committees and task forces; and managing the Central Office (such Central Office consisting of salaried employees hired by the Executive Director in order to carry out the business of the Association). The Executive Director shall prepare an operating plan and budget and shall participate in meetings of the Board of Directors and Executive Committee in an ex officio nonvoting capacity as appropriate. Under the authority of the Board of Directors, the Executive Director shall have responsibility for the execution of Association policy, for the furtherance of the Association's interests, and for the day-to-day operation of the Association's business and programs. The Executive Director shall act as secretary at all Board meetings, Executive Committee meetings, and Annual and Special Meetings of the Association, and shall prepare and distribute minutes of the same. The Executive Director shall serve as Corporate Secretary. The Executive Director's salary shall be fixed annually by the Board.

ARTICLE X: REGIONAL ORGANIZATIONS

The Board of Directors may recognize geographical regions within which members of the Association and others may organize themselves for regional meetings to further the aims of the Association.

ARTICLE XI: DUES

The amount of the annual dues payment by members shall be voted each year at the Annual Meeting on recommendation of the Board of Directors. The fiscal year of the Association shall be April 1 to March 31. Dues shall be payable by September 30, at which time any member press that has not paid its dues shall be subject to suspension at the Board's discretion. When a member is suspended for nonpayment of dues, the President of the Association shall so notify the director of the said member and the responsible officer or officers of its parent institution or group of institutions, and shall further advise them that if such member has not paid its dues by the end of the Association's fiscal year its membership shall be subject to cancellation.

ARTICLE XII: BOOKS AND RECORDS

The Association shall keep at its office within the State of New York correct and complete books and records of account; minutes of meetings of the members, of the Board of Directors, and of the Executive Committee; and an up-to-date list of the names and addresses of all members. These books and records may be in written form or in any other form capable of being converted to written form within a reasonable time.

ARTICLE XIII: CHANGES IN BY-LAWS AND GUIDELINES

The members may amend or repeal these By-Laws by two-thirds of the votes cast at any Annual or Special Meeting called for that purpose at which a quorum is present. The members may revise, amend, or repeal the Guidelines by a majority of votes cast at any Annual or Special Meeting of members called for that purpose at which a quorum is present. Whenever there is a conflict between these By-Laws and the Guidelines, any Statement of Governance, or a resolution of the membership, Board of Directors, or Executive Committee, or any other document published by the Association, these By-Laws shall prevail.

GUIDELINES ON ADMISSION TO MEMBERSHIP AND MAINTENANCE OF MEMBERSHIP

Revised as of April 15, 1994

A. Preamble

The purposes of the Association are to encourage dissemination of the fruits of research and to support university presses in their endeavor to make widely available the best of scholarly knowledge and the most important results of scholarly research; to provide an organization through which the exchange of ideas relating to university presses and their functions may be facilitated; to afford technical advice and assistance to learned bodies, scholarly associations, and institutions of higher learning; and to do all things incidental to and in furtherance of the foregoing purposes without extending the same.

B. Membership, Associate Membership, and Affiliation

The membership of the Association shall consist of those members who were in good standing at the time of the incorporation of the Association in 1964, except those who have since resigned or whose membership has otherwise been terminated, and all other members who have since been admitted.

A university press is defined as the scholarly publishing arm of a university or college, or a group of such institutions within a state or geographic region located within the Americas. It must be an integral part of one or more such colleges and universities, and should be so recognized in the manual of organization, catalogue, or other official publication of at least one such parent institution. The organization and functions of the university press must lie within the prescription of its parent institution or institutions.

Any press satisfying these requirements shall be eligible in principle for election to membership in the Association. A press shall be elected to membership by a majority vote of the full membership on the recommendation of the Board of Directors. Such action shall be taken by the Board only on the prior recommendation of the Committee on Admissions and Standards (see Section E), which shall be responsible for determining that the applying press satisfies the minimum requirements for membership.

A university press, by its very nature, must be devoted to scholarly and educational ends; the failure of a press to pursue such ends as its fundamental business shall constitute grounds for canceling its membership in the Association. Cancellation of membership shall be effected by a two-thirds vote of the membership on the recommendation of the Board of Directors.

At the invitation of the Board of Directors, international membership may be applied for by (a) university-affiliated scholarly book publishers in parts of the world not embraced by the Americas and (b) such presses within the Americas that publish primarily in languages other than English. To qualify for membership in the Association, a publisher in either class must submit a formal application and provide such materials as requested by the Admissions and Standards Committee, making evident its scholarly publishing program.

Admission to international membership shall be by a majority vote of the membership at an Annual or Special Meeting, a quorum being present, on the prior recommendation of the Committee on Admissions and Standards and the Board of Directors. International membership may be canceled by a two-thirds vote of the Board of Directors, a quorum being present. International members shall enjoy all rights and privileges of membership except the right to vote in any business conducted by the Association. Any reference elsewhere in the By-Laws to a voting right, therefore, shall be so read as to exclude international members. Uniform dues for international members shall be set from time to time by the Board.

At the invitation of the Board of Directors, university presses within the Americas may apply for affiliate status provided that they satisfy all requirements set forth in Section C of these Guidelines except for the number of books published and in regard to staffing. Admission to affiliate status shall be by a majority vote of the membership, a quorum being present, on the prior recommendation of the Committee on Admissions and Standards which shall be responsible for determining that the applying press satisfies the minimum requirements for affiliation. Affiliate status may be canceled by a two-thirds vote of the membership, a quorum being present. Affiliates shall enjoy such rights and privileges as determined by the Board of Directors, but in no event shall their rights and privileges extend to service on the Board of Directors or on the Standing Committees of the Association or voting in any business conducted by it. Any reference elsewhere in the By-Laws to a voting right, therefore, shall be so read as to exclude affiliates. Uniform annual fees shall be set from time to time by the Board.

At the invitation of the Board of Directors, presses of non-degree-granting scholarly institutions and associations may apply for associate membership, providing those institutions are incorporated as not-for-profit and that the presses satisfy the requirements for affiliate membership, except that the auspices and structures of the parent organizations of such presses will in all instances be those of non-degree-granting institutions or scholarly associations rather than those of universities. In the absence of an editorial committee or board, an applicant for associate membership shall observe commonly accepted standards of editorial review.

Admission to associate status shall be by a majority vote of the membership, a quorum being present, on the prior recommendation of the Committee on Admissions and Standards and the AAUP Board of Directors. Associate members shall enjoy such rights and privileges as determined by the Board of Directors, but in no event shall their rights and privileges extend to service on the Board of Directors or on the Standing Committees of the Association or to voting in any business conducted by it. Any reference elsewhere in the By-Laws to a voting right, therefore, shall be so read as to exclude associate members. Associate members shall not be eligible to participate in the Association's statistical programs. Uniform annual fees for associate members shall be set from time to time by the Board, and associate members may number no more than thirty percent of the full members of the Association. An associate membership may be canceled at any time by a two-thirds vote of the membership, a quorum being present.

C. Desiderata for an Applying Press

In elaboration of the general considerations set forth in the preceding section, the following guidelines have been formally adopted by the Association:

1. A committee or board of the faculty of the parent institution or institutions shall be charged with certifying the scholarly quality of the books and journals that bear the institutional imprint, and publication of five or more scholarly books each year for a period of not fewer than twenty-four months preceding the date of application shall be required for admission to membership. The word "scholarly" is used here in the sense of original research of a character usually associated with the scholarly interests of a university or college of the first class. (Textbooks, manuals of a synthetic

character or intended for class use, and serial publications sponsored by, or under the control of, other departments or divisions of the university or college are not to be included in the aforementioned minimum scholarly publishing requirement.) A scholarly journals program (one or more journals) may be substituted for one book to satisfy this requirement.

2. An acceptable scholarly publishing program shall have the benefit of the service of not fewer than three full-time employees, of whom one shall have the rank and functions of Director. This official shall report, organizationally, to the President of the university or college, or to an officer at the vice-presidential or decanal level having both academic and fiscal authority, or to the designated representative of a group of such institutions who shall have both kinds of authority.

3. The formal application and supporting data from a press seeking membership in the Association shall be accompanied by a statement from the head of the parent institution, or the designated representative of a group of institutions, outlining the immediate and long-term intentions and financial expectations of the institution or group of institutions for its press, and reflecting a realistic appreciation of the cost of supporting a serious program of scholarly publication.

D. Admission

Admission of a new member to the Association shall take effect immediately following an affirmative vote of a majority of the Association's full membership at the Annual Meeting or a Special Meeting.

E. The Committee on Admissions and Standards

The official agency for the administration of these guidelines shall be the Committee on Admissions and Standards, which shall operate under authority delegated by the Board of Directors, and which shall consist of six members, two of whom shall be appointed for terms of three years each by the incumbent President in each successive year, and three of whom, at least, shall be the director, the editor, and the controller, accountant, or business manager of a member press. In making appointments, the President shall ensure that no member of the committee serves two successive terms. The President shall also appoint a successor to complete the unexpired term of any member of the committee who resigns an appointment or is, for any reason, unable to continue in service; and any person who is appointed as a replacement may, if the President so wishes, be reappointed for a full term following expiration of his or her initial term as a replacement. The President shall also each year appoint a chair of the committee from among its six members. The chairs shall each serve a term of one year, and may not succeed themselves in office.

All inquiries from prospective applicants for membership in the Association are to be directed to the chair of the Committee on Admissions and Standards, who shall advise the candidate of the full substance of these Guidelines on Admission to Membership and Maintenance of Membership, and shall require as evidence of satisfactory compliance with them:

1. Submission to each member of the committee of one copy of each of the ten or more scholarly books published by the applicant and certified by its faculty editorial board or committee, at the rate of five per calendar year in the twenty-four months preceding the date on which the application for membership is filed, and full runs of the issues of any journals for the year or years in which they serve in place of one of the five books.

2. Provision to each member of the committee a complete list, by name and title, of the staff of the applicant press, to be prepared in that form in which such information is given for active members in the most recent edition of the *Directory* of the Association of American University Presses, Inc.

3. Submission to the chair in the original form, and to the other members of the committee as photocopies, of statements from the head of the parent institution, in which are made those affirmations required under Section C, paragraphs 2 and 3, above. The Committee on Admissions and Standards may ask of an applicant press in addition that it furnish, as a supplement to those institutional affirmations required under Section C, paragraph 3, above, copies of its financial operating statements for the two most recently completed fiscal years.

Following the filing of a formal application for membership and notification by the chair to the applicant of its acceptance for consideration, the candidate press shall be regarded as having entered a period of probation, which will last for a period of time no longer than one year, at the end of which, if not sooner, its candidacy will be acted upon as prescribed under the By-Laws, and during which it shall enjoy the following privileges of membership: (a) the right to send delegates to the Annual Meeting, and (b) the right to send representatives to all training sessions, workshops, symposiums, and conferences dealing with professional activities of scholarly publishers and enjoying the support of the Association.

Once a university press satisfying the requirements for membership stated herein has been admitted to active status by action of the membership at the Annual Meeting or a Special Meeting, it shall be required to submit each year to the Central Office of the Association, for publication in the annual *Directory* of members, both a roster of its current staff and an indication of the number of books and journals it has published in each of the two calendar years preceding and that have been certified as to scholarship by its editorial board or committee. And it shall be the responsibility of the Committee on Admissions and Standards to review each listing of an active press in each annual edition of the membership *Directory*, and to undertake action as follows when any member is shown to have fallen below the qualifying criteria for membership: (a) to notify the member of its apparent delinquency under the Guidelines and to offer the full assistance and cooperation of the Association in bringing about satisfactory solutions to its problems; (b) to advise the President and the Board that notification of an apparent delinquency has been sent and an offer of assistance made; (c) to inform the President and the Board of any response received from the member press following its notification; and (d) to recommend to the President and the Board any action that the committee deems appropriate.

With respect to the scholarship of published works, the Association will accept the certification of the press's own faculty board or committee, and will not pass on the scholarship of any individual work. However, the Committee on Admissions and Standards will take into account the observance by the press of commonly accepted standards of editorial review, ordinarily including at least one positive evaluation by a qualified scholar not affiliated with the author's own institution.

When the delinquent press fails to resolve its difficulties within one year of the chair's notice, the Committee on Admissions and Standards shall submit to the Board of Directors a full report of the situation, and recommend, for endorsement by the Board and transmission to the membership for ratification, that the membership of the delinquent press be terminated. Two years from the date of its expulsion, a press shall be entitled to apply for readmission through initiation of the procedures herein prescribed.

Personnel Index

A-Srinivasan, Seetha	95
Abascal, Juan L.	130
Abel, Marilyn	43,90
Abel, Richard M.	95
Abiad, Ray	137
Abrams, Susan E.	43
Acker, Fay	67
Ackerman, John G.	51
Ackermann, William C.	69
Acuña Guzmán, Juan	161
Adair, Gene	151
Adams, Lee	26
Adams, Paul	64
Adams, Sandy W.	77
Adams, Stephen	47
Addison, Herb	120
Adkins, Lain	118
Adkinson, Judy	77
Agree, Peter	51
Akenson, Donald H.	85
Akl, Nabila	26,27
Albers, Susie	80
Albert, Pam	71
Alberti, Janet	38
Alderfer, Joseph	44
Alexander, James	38
Alexander, Jo	119
Alexander, Roy	110
Alldén, Lars	137
Allen, Judith Wesley	27
Allen, Virginia	43
Allende Morales, Francisco	160
Alley, John R. Jr.	163
Almaguer, Carlos	49
Alter, Judy	155
Althoff, Victoria	117
Altreuter, Judith	98
Alvarez Ortíz, Victor	161
Alwood, Lisa	117
Ambrose, Natalie	99
Ames, Michael	150
Anders, Gerry	83
Anderson, Alison	123
Anderson, Ann-Marie	150
Anderson, Cheryl	139
Anderson, Dorothea	80
Anderson, Elaine	38
Anderson, Janet	165
Anderson, Marc	38
Anderson, Mary	167
Anderson, Nana L.	163
Ankrom, Jeff	71
Anstey, Donna	175
Anthony, Alta	78
Anthony, Dorothy	167
Antony, Peter	90
Antwine, Ray	60
Aono, Lucille	66
Apostolik, Charles J.	59,60
Arava, Douglas	35
Armato, Douglas	76,77
Armbruster, Doreen	170
Armstead, Stacey L.	77
Arnold, Sharon	116
Aronson, Michael	63
Arrigo, Jan	121
Artigiani, Susan	101
Asbury, Dana	107
Asbury, Robin Sumner	141
Asmussen, Gretchen	94
Aspinwall, Margaret	90
Atto, Donna	119
Atwood, Joyce	146
Ault, Charles H.E.	150
Austin, Jon	52
Austin, Will	118
Ayr, Laura	30
Babbitt, Donald G.	23
Bacher, Arlene	136
Bachman, Margie K.	126
Backus, Charles	164
Baehrecke, Astrid	88
Bahcall, Jill	112
Baker, Victoria	30
Bakhle, Janaki	94
Bakken, Melody	172
Bakken, Per	137
Baldini, J. Randall	101
Baldock, Robert	175
Ball, Larry Durwood	107
Banuazizi, Atissa	30
Barbasa, Santos	66
Barber, James A. Jr.	100
Bardes, Richard E.	26
Barling, Richard	37
Barnard, Michele	43
Barnett, Stephen	102
Barr, Pamela	90
Barrett, Nancy	69
Barrett, Sheila	64
Barrie, Ellen	122
Barry, Edith	121
Barry, Edward W.	120
Barry, Elizabeth	121
Bartlett, David M.	150
Bartlett, Timothy	108
Barton, Bruce	44
Barton, Joan	33
Basmajian, Nancy	116
Batchelor, Howard	62
Bateman, Lewis	110
Bates, Marcie	115
Batt, Brenda	66
Bauer, George W.	118
Bauer, Margaret	100
Bauer, Randi	137

Smith, Dianne	141	Strickland, Georgiana	82
Smith, Ellen F.	145	Strickland, Sherri	105
Smith, Frank	37	Stringer, Clarence	96
Smith, J. Reynolds	53	Stritch, Jim	175
Smith, James	67	Strong, Thomas	175
Smith, Joyce C.	154	Strothman, Wendy J.	30
Smith, Patricia	123	Styles, Deborah M.	32
Smith, Robin	38	Sullivan, Arlene W.	76
Smith, Stephanie	69	Sunley, Madeline	88
Smith, Stephen W.	143	Sussman, Gerald	122
Smyth, Frances P.	99	Sutherland, Cameron R.	104
Snodderly, Dan	162	Sutton, Laura	59
Snodgrass, Jennifer	64	Swain, Beth	28
Sochi, Ann	87	Sweeney, Kathe	108
Soden, Patrick	167	Swierzowski, Terry	146
Solomon, Sherry	152	Syrotiak, Cele	175
Sorenson, Nicole	56	Szidon, Tom	114
Sorlie, Terje	137	Szittya, Brenda	32
Speth, Linda	74	Szuter, Christine R.	27
Spevack, Judy	146	Talbot, Bruce	140
Spiegel, Ruth W.	139	Talley-Jones, Kathy	62
Spooner, Michael	163	Tamminen, Suzanna	105
Spottiswood, John	44	Tani, Irma	41
Stafford, Mary Ann	121	Tarbet, Cathy	164
Stanford, Don	88	Tartar, Helen	144
Stanforth, Christi	110	Tarver, Julidta C.	167
Stanley, Margaret F.	61	Taylor, Jean	168
Stanton, Alice K.	118	Taylor, Rubye F.	19
Stanton, Angela	154	Tegarden, Deborah	128
Stanton, Elizabeth	87	Tenenbaum, Rona	136
Stanton, Henry	87	Tenorio, JoAnn	66
Starbuck, Margaret	117	Testa, Sam	121
Stascavage, S. Anne	95	Thatcher, Sanford G.	125
Staskevich, Jean	117	Thomas, Alan	43
Stearn, Estelle	44	Thomas, Gloria	97
Stebbins, Katherine	49	Thomas, Hargis	121
Steele, Diane	115	Thomas, Patricia S.	54
Stein, Kathy N.	99	Thompson, George F.	77
Steinberg, Elizabeth A.	172	Thompson, Jan	27
Steinborn, Marilyn M.	156	Thompson, Molly	59
Stempin, Carl	145	Thompson, Patricia	153
Stern, Janet	128	Thornton, Jackie	154
Stetson, Dave	54	Tifft, Douglas	105
Stetter, John F.	142	Tilson, Charlotte	28
Stevens, Brooke	88	Timko, Kathleen Pike	167
Stevens, Fiona	88	Tingle, Leslie	152
Stevens, Gioia	121	Tinsley, Jane C.	164
Stewart, Lynn	145	Titus, Peter	121
Stewart, Rachel	71	Todd, Beverly	118
Stewart, Shirley	153	Toff, Nancy	120
Stiles, T.J.	121	Tollefson, Carla	74
Stillman, Neil	148	Tom, Henry Y. K.	77
Stinchcomb, Rick	118	Tom, Linda	167
Stobaugh, Debbie	96	Tomas, Cindy	55
Stong, Colby	121	Tomé, Jesús	130
Stowe, Julie	165	Toor, Rachel	53
Strauss, Dave	148	Topkis, Gladys	175
Strickland, Edward A.	42	Torres, Nancy	130